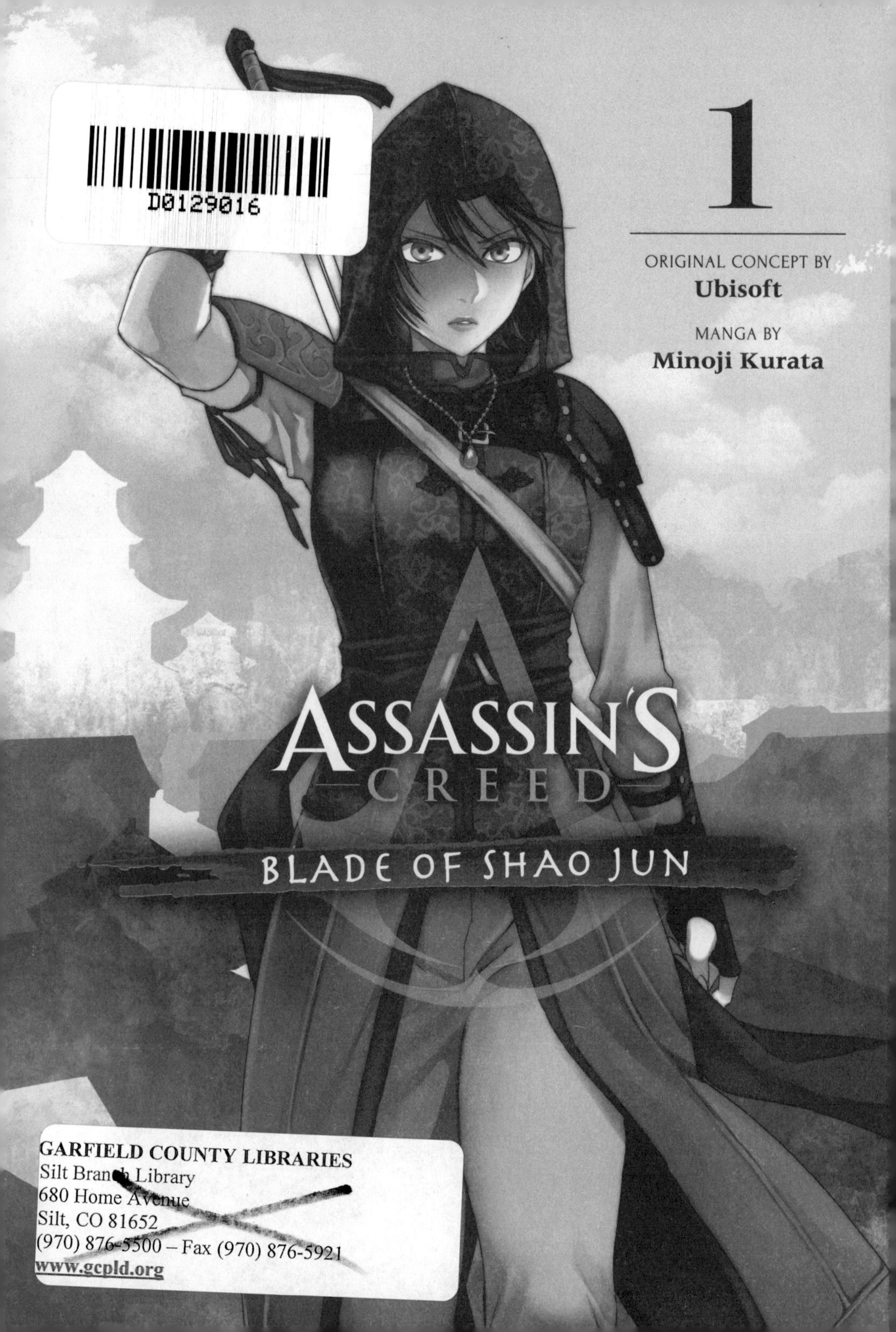

1

ORIGINAL CONCEPT BY
Ubisoft

MANGA BY
Minoji Kurata

ASSASSIN'S CREED

BLADE OF SHAO JUN

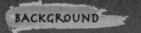

The year is 1526 AD, and the Ming Dynasty rules in China.

Though the dynasty has experienced untold prosperity, a great political purge by the current emperor is leading to devastating turmoil. China's last Assassin is Shao Jun. Her allies were all killed two years prior, but she now returns to her motherland seeking revenge.

However, there is an unthinkable secret at the core of this Assassin's very life...

THE EIGHT TIGERS

A gang of tyrannical eunuchs backed by the emperor's patronage. But who are they really...?

WANG YANGMING

A renowned scholar and general known as the founder of the Yangmingism school of neo-Confucianism.

SHAO JUN

China's last Assassin.

CONTENTS

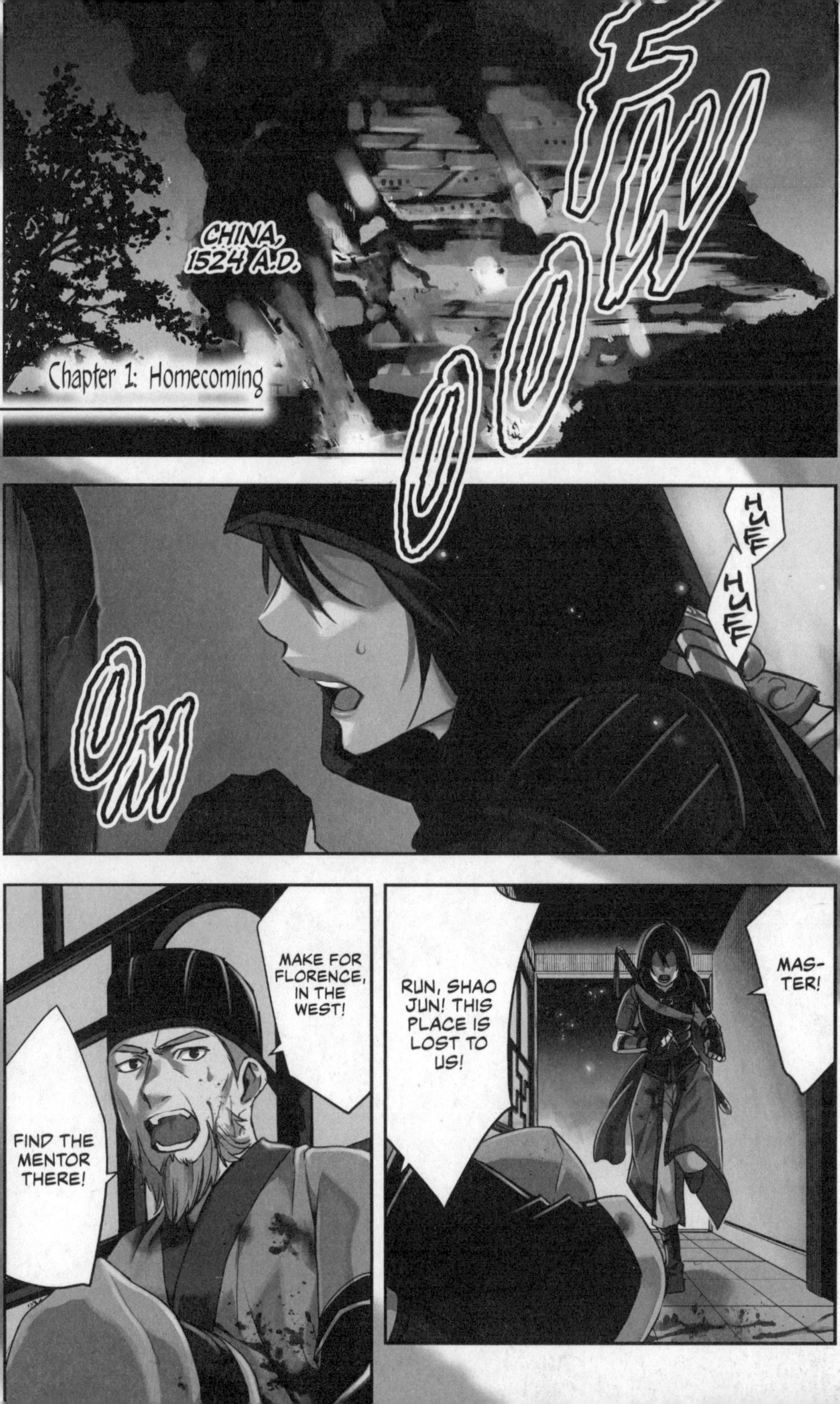
CHINA, 1524 A.D.
Chapter 1: Homecoming
HUFF HUFF
MAS-TER!
RUN, SHAO JUN! THIS PLACE IS LOST TO US!
MAKE FOR FLORENCE, IN THE WEST!
FIND THE MENTOR THERE!

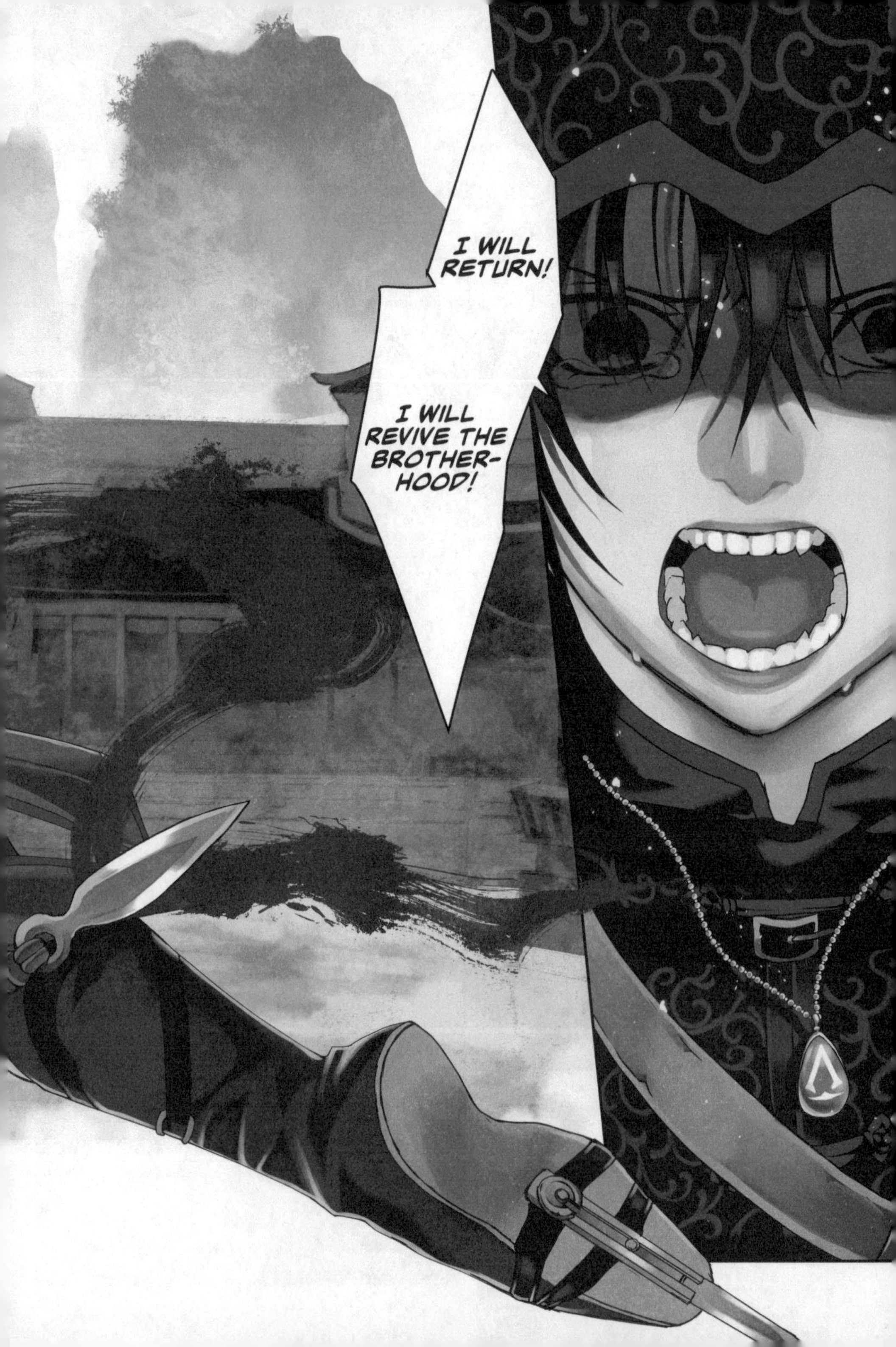
I WILL RETURN!
I WILL REVIVE THE BROTHER-HOOD!

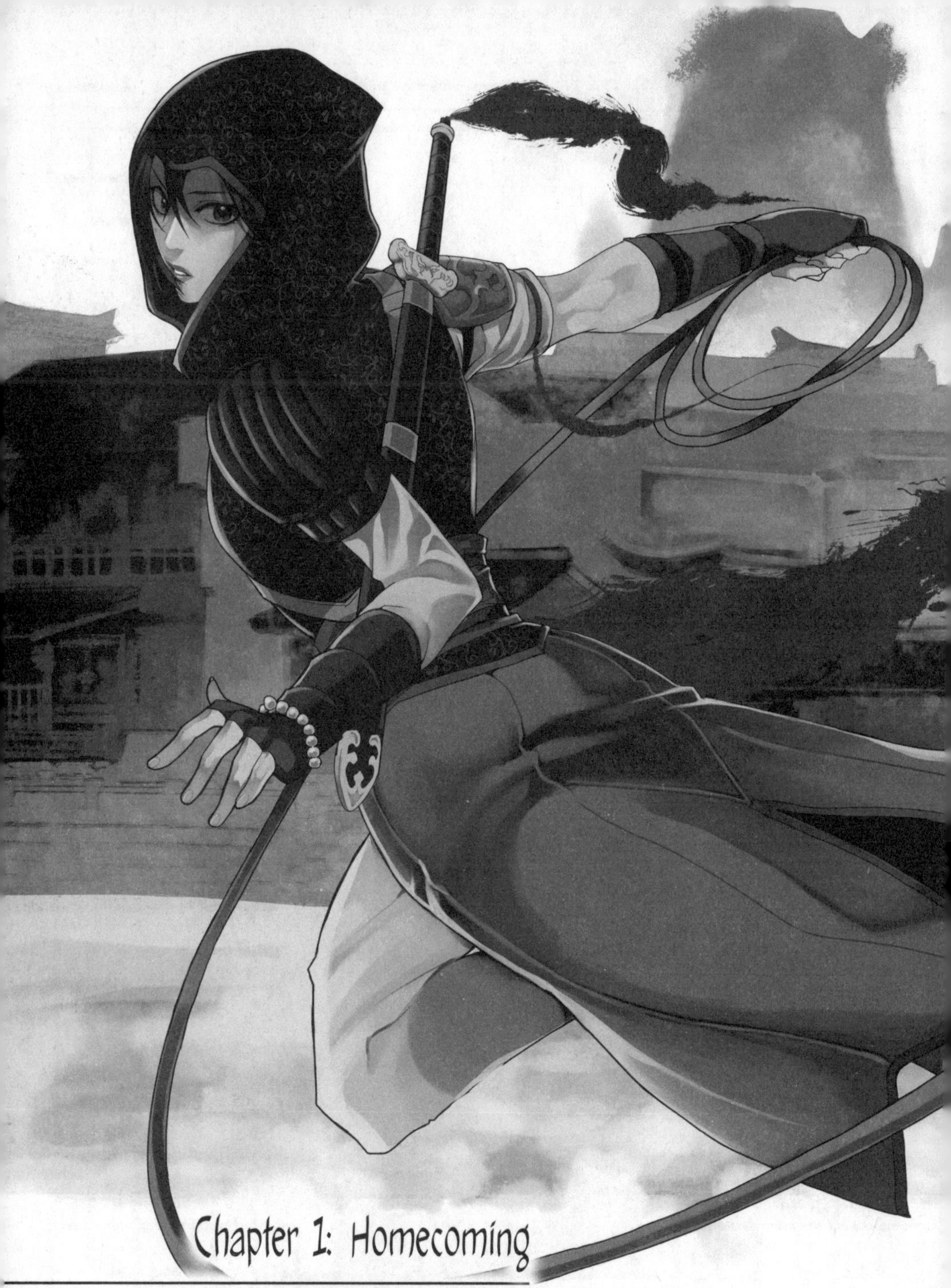

Chapter 1: Homecoming

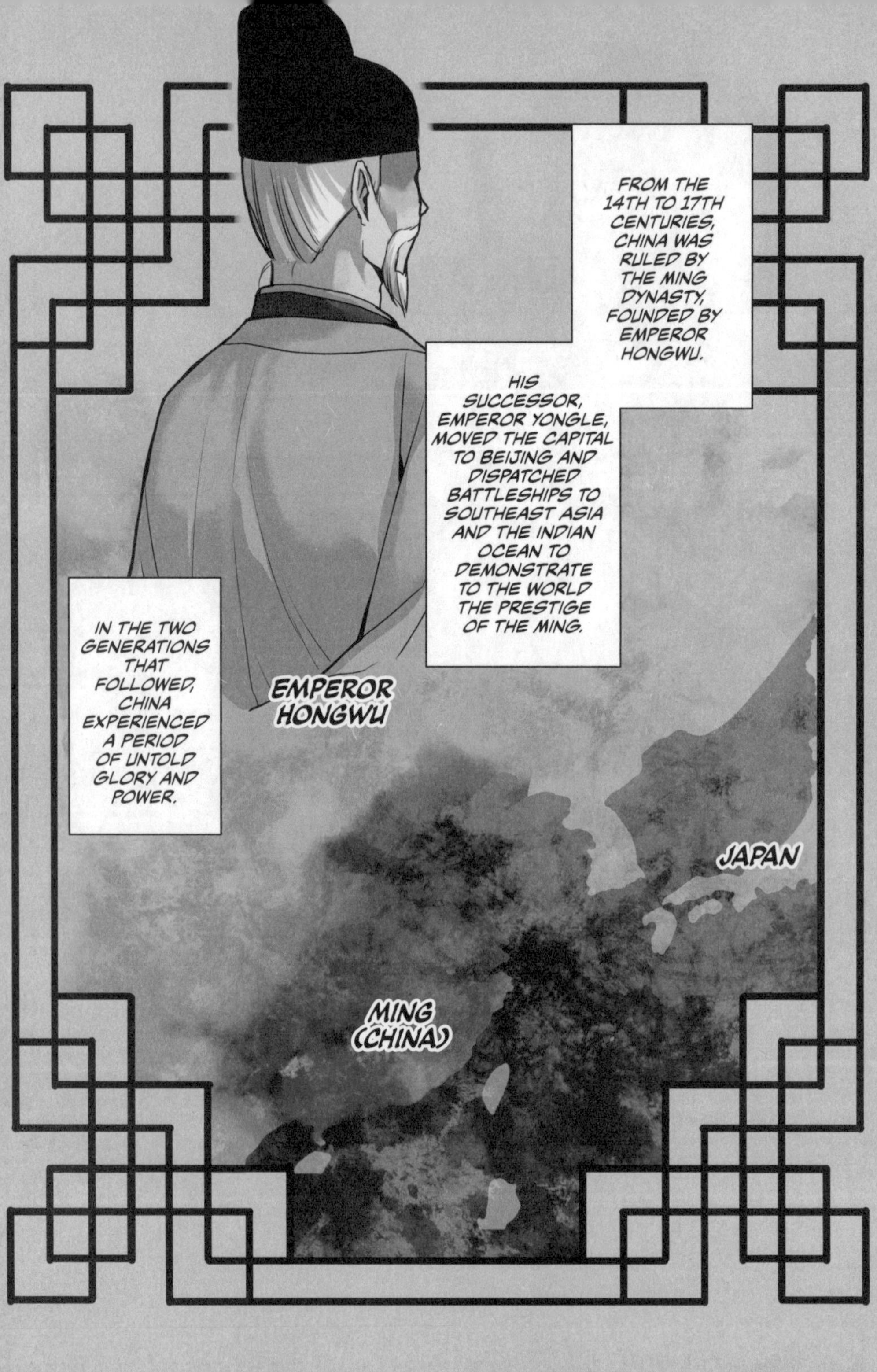
FROM THE 14TH TO 17TH CENTURIES, CHINA WAS RULED BY THE MING DYNASTY, FOUNDED BY EMPEROR HONGWU.
HIS SUCCESSOR, EMPEROR YONGLE, MOVED THE CAPITAL TO BEIJING AND DISPATCHED BATTLESHIPS TO SOUTHEAST ASIA AND THE INDIAN OCEAN TO DEMONSTRATE TO THE WORLD THE PRESTIGE OF THE MING.
EMPEROR HONGWU
IN THE TWO GENERATIONS THAT FOLLOWED, CHINA EXPERIENCED A PERIOD OF UNTOLD GLORY AND POWER.
JAPAN
MING (CHINA)

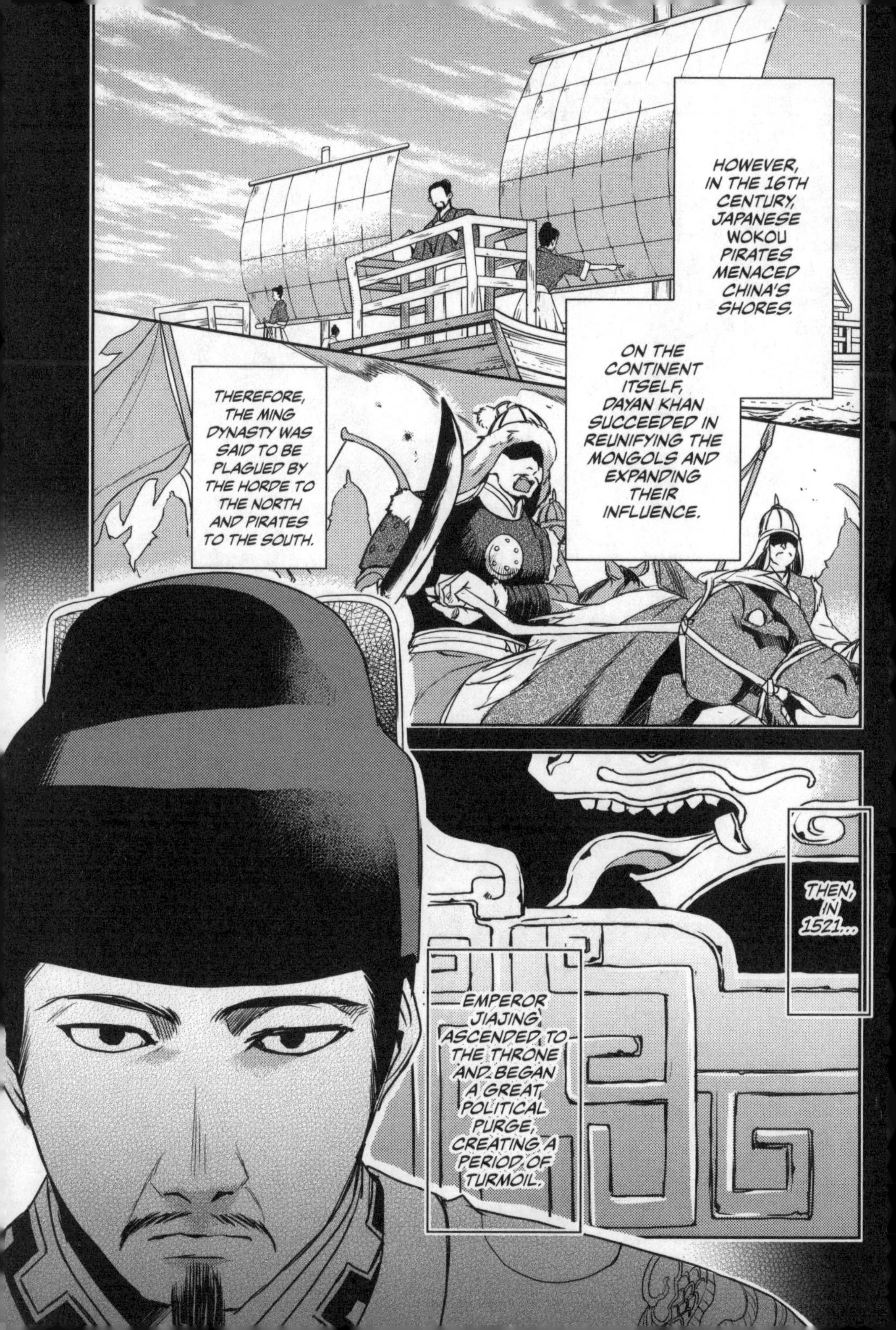
HOWEVER, IN THE 16TH CENTURY, JAPANESE WOKOU PIRATES MENACED CHINA'S SHORES.
ON THE CONTINENT ITSELF, DAYAN KHAN SUCCEEDED IN REUNIFYING THE MONGOLS AND EXPANDING THEIR INFLUENCE.
THEREFORE, THE MING DYNASTY WAS SAID TO BE PLAGUED BY THE HORDE TO THE NORTH AND PIRATES TO THE SOUTH.
THEN, IN 1521...
EMPEROR JIAJING ASCENDED TO THE THRONE AND BEGAN A GREAT POLITICAL PURGE, CREATING A PERIOD OF TURMOIL.

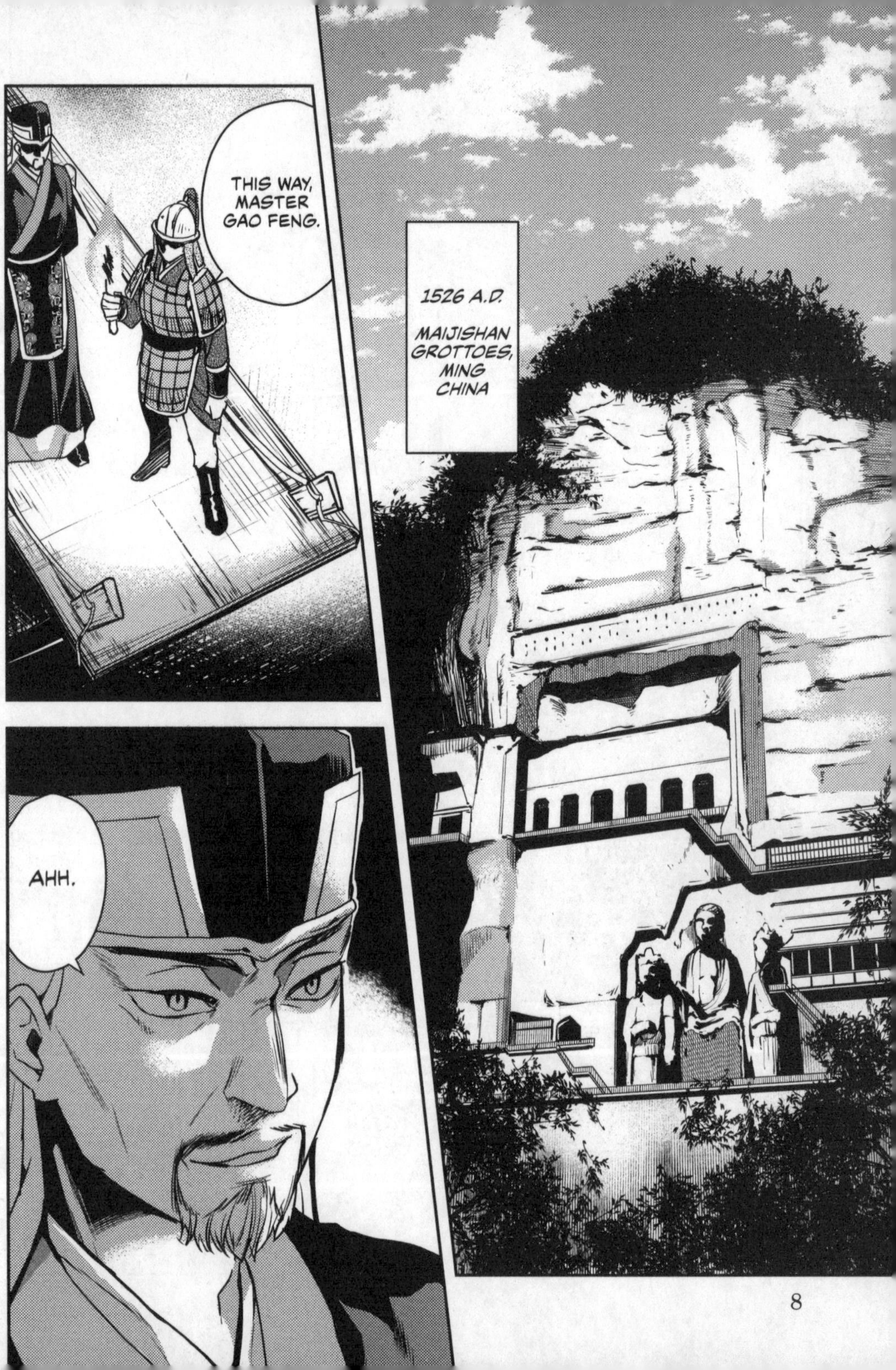
1526 A.D.
MAIJISHAN GROTTOES, MING CHINA
THIS WAY, MASTER GAO FENG.
AHH.

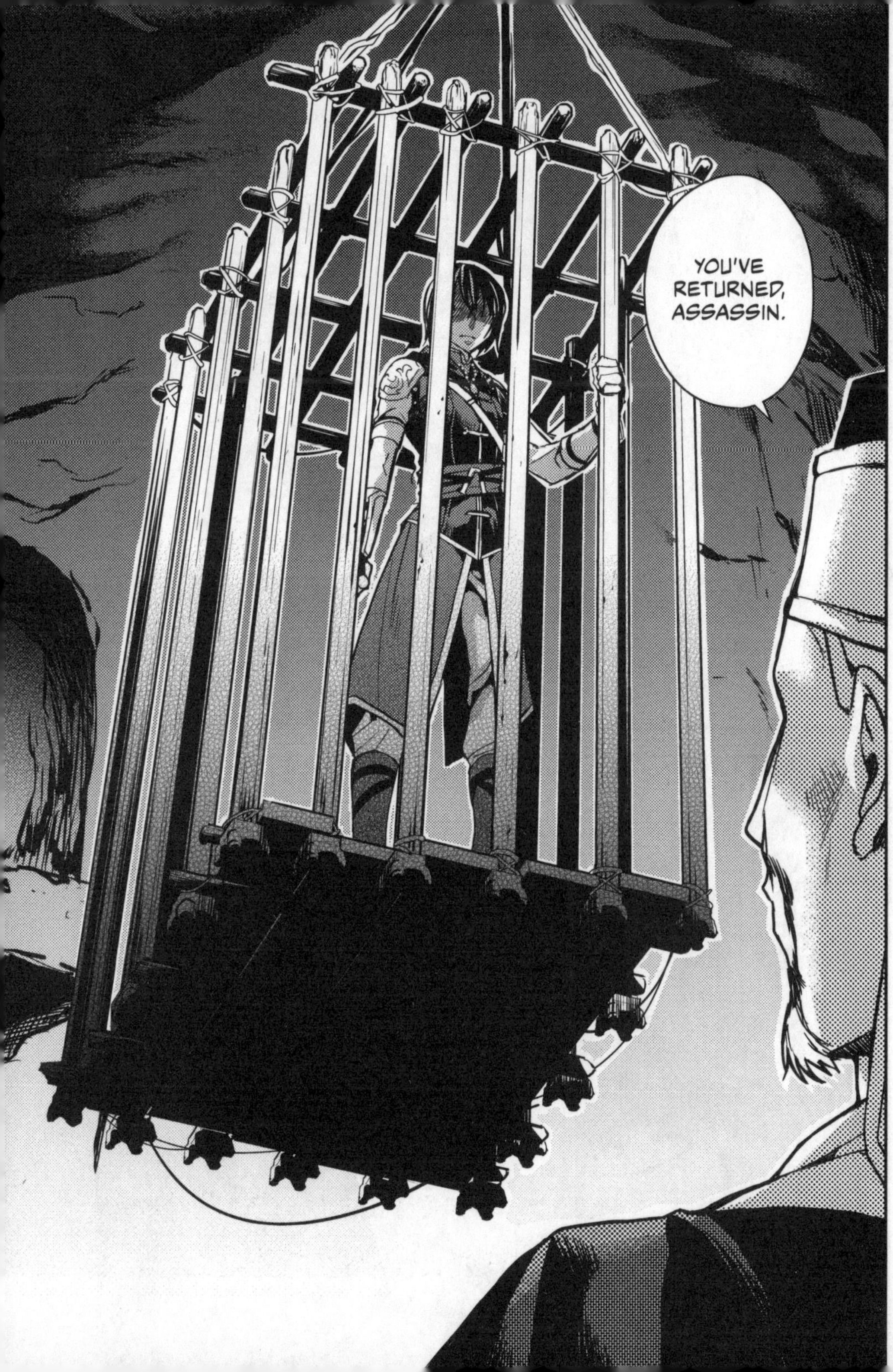
YOU'VE RETURNED, ASSASSIN.

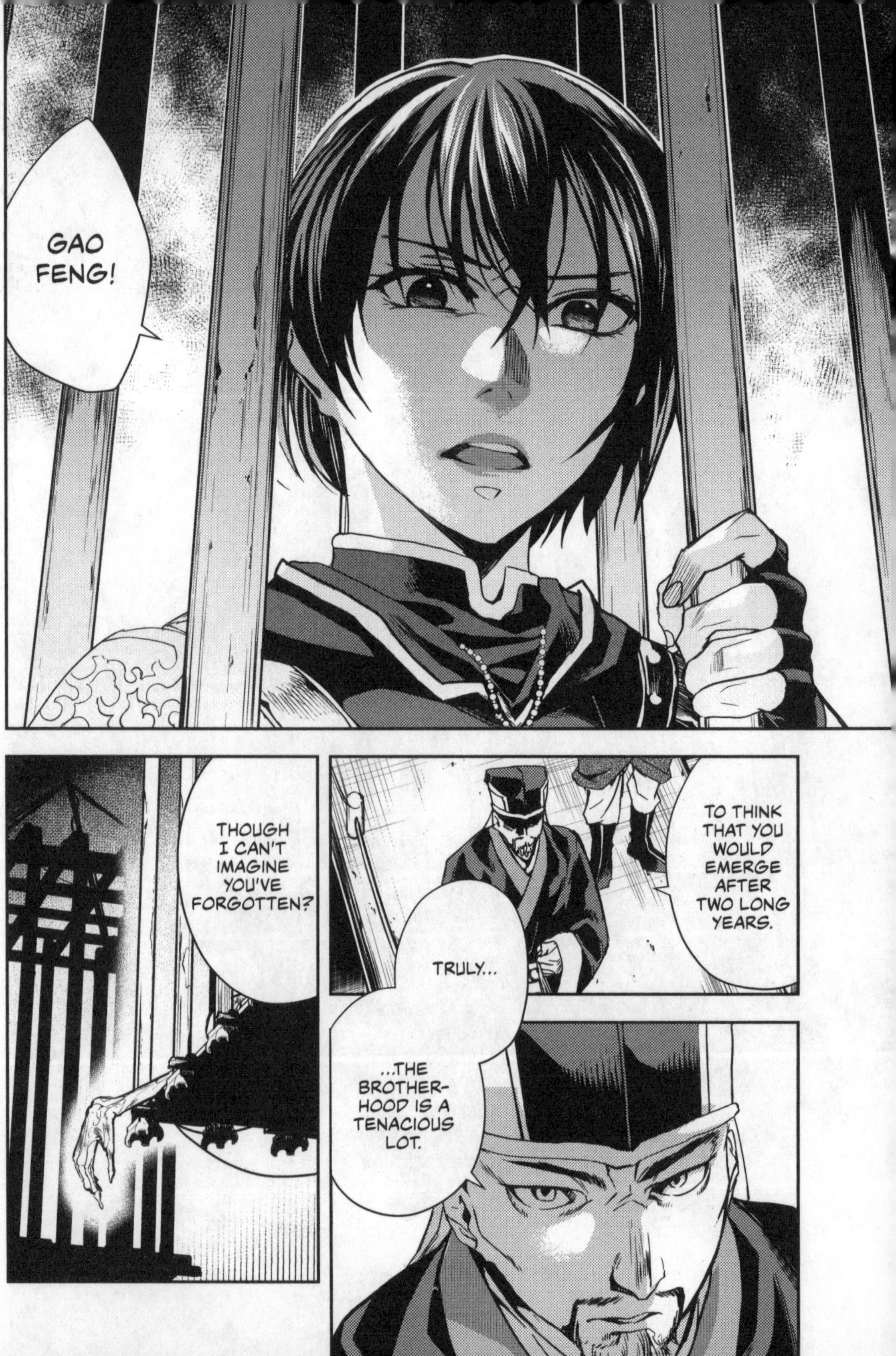
GAO FENG!
TO THINK THAT YOU WOULD EMERGE AFTER TWO LONG YEARS.
TRULY...
...THE BROTHER-HOOD IS A TENACIOUS LOT.
THOUGH I CAN'T IMAGINE YOU'VE FORGOTTEN?

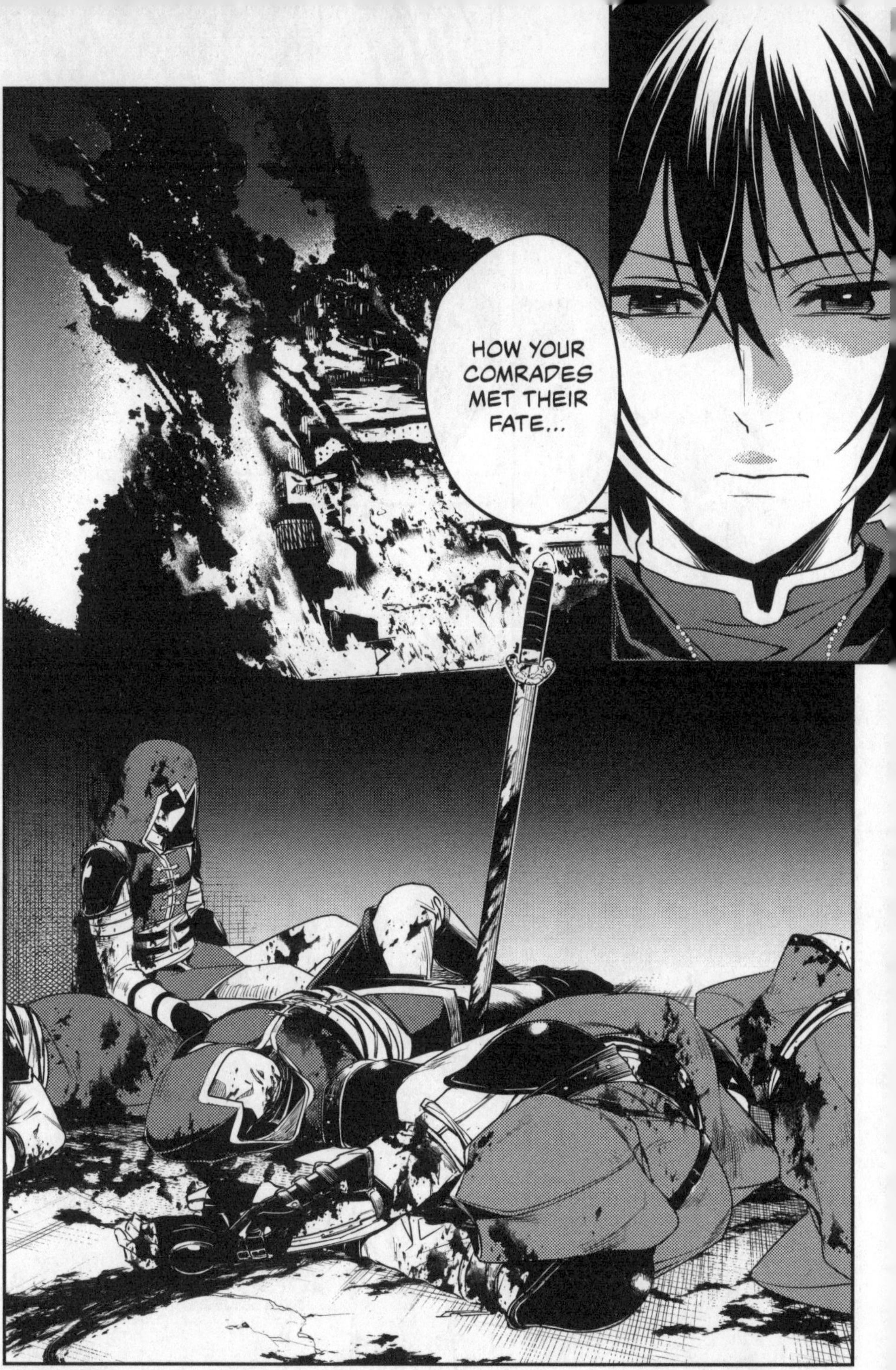
HOW YOUR COMRADES MET THEIR FATE...

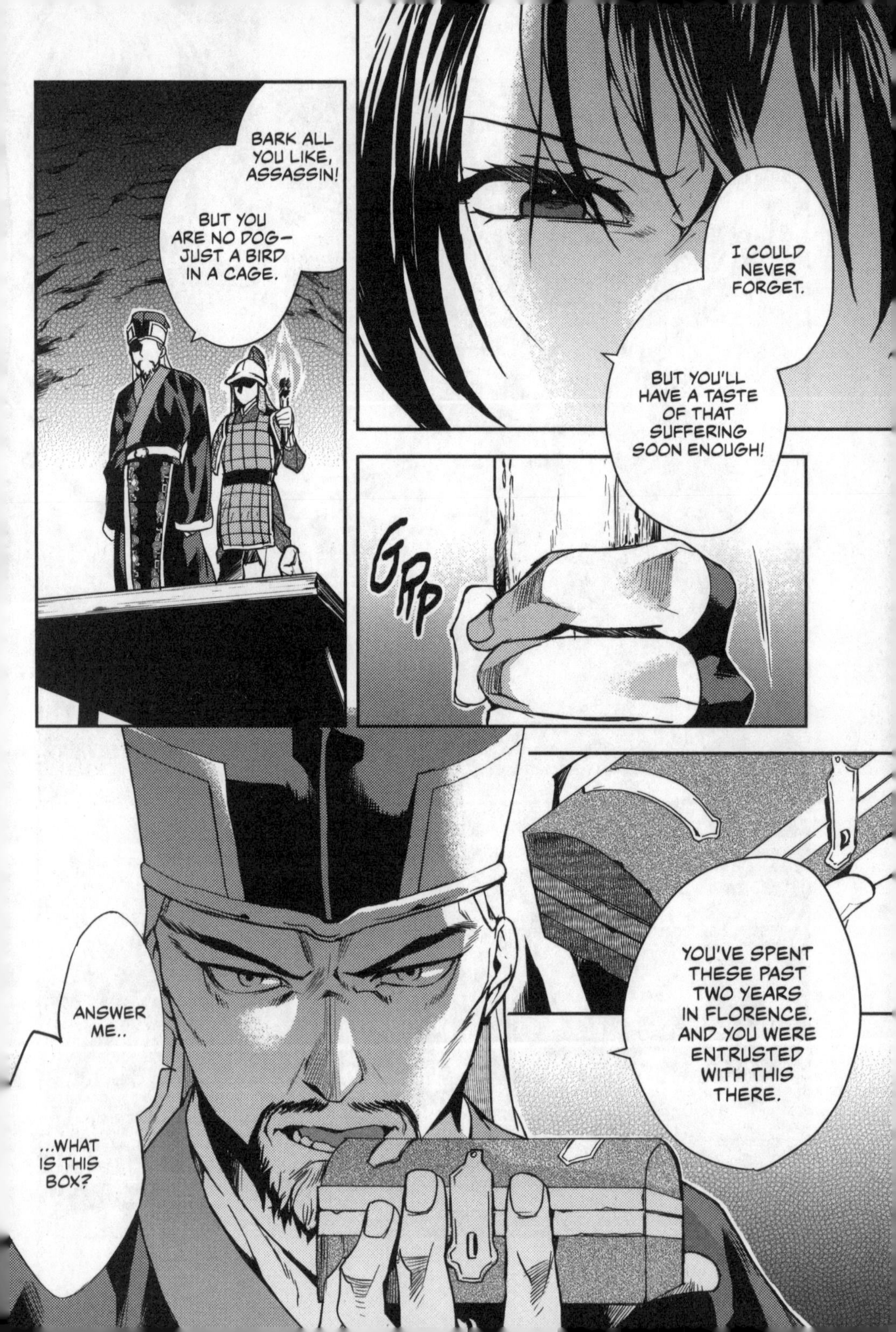
I COULD NEVER FORGET.
BUT YOU'LL HAVE A TASTE OF THAT SUFFERING SOON ENOUGH!
GRP
BARK ALL YOU LIKE, ASSASSIN!
BUT YOU ARE NO DOG—JUST A BIRD IN A CAGE.
YOU'VE SPENT THESE PAST TWO YEARS IN FLORENCE. AND YOU WERE ENTRUSTED WITH THIS THERE.
ANSWER ME..
...WHAT IS THIS BOX?

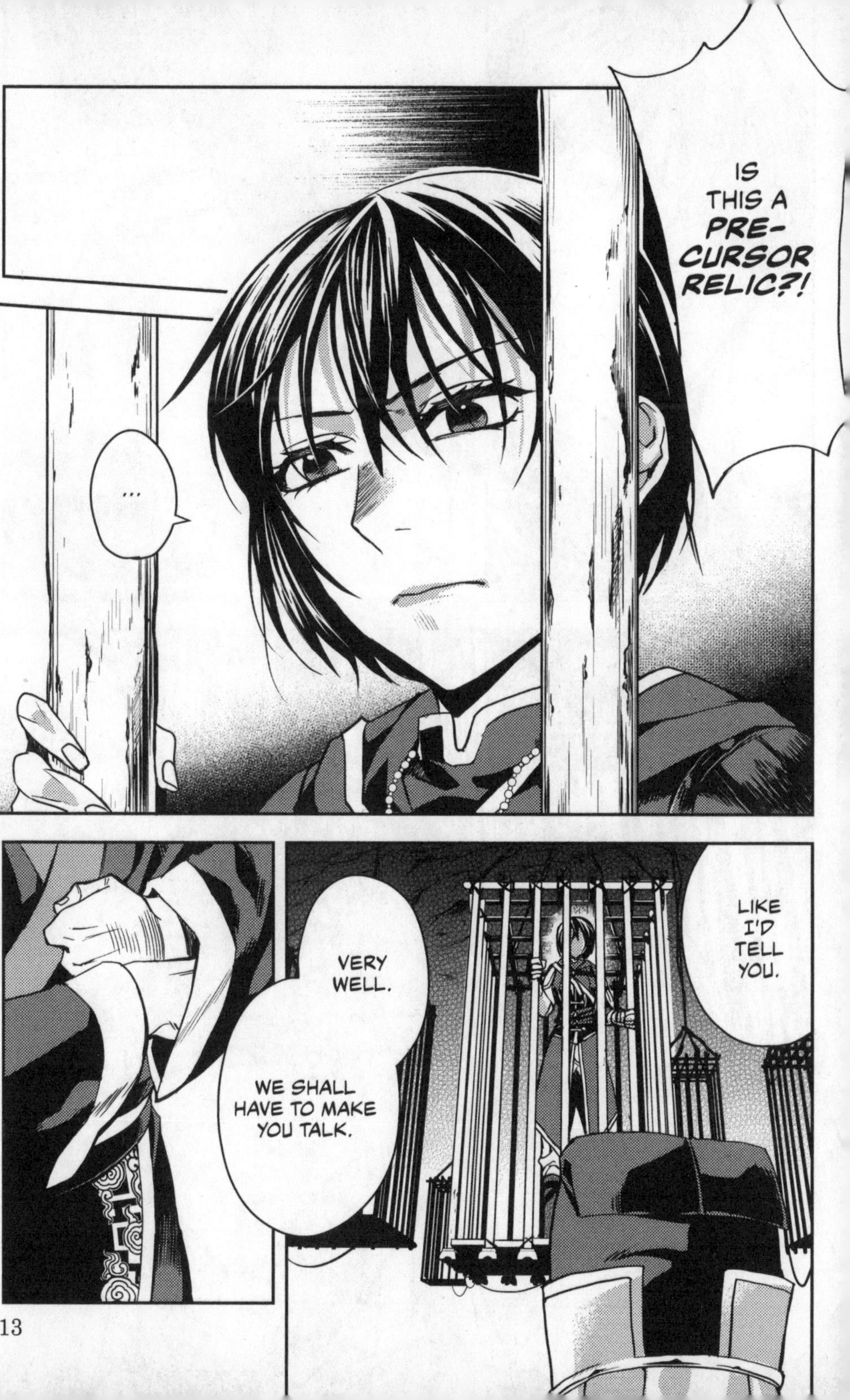
IS THIS A PRE-CURSOR RELIC?!
...
LIKE I'D TELL YOU.
VERY WELL.
WE SHALL HAVE TO MAKE YOU TALK.

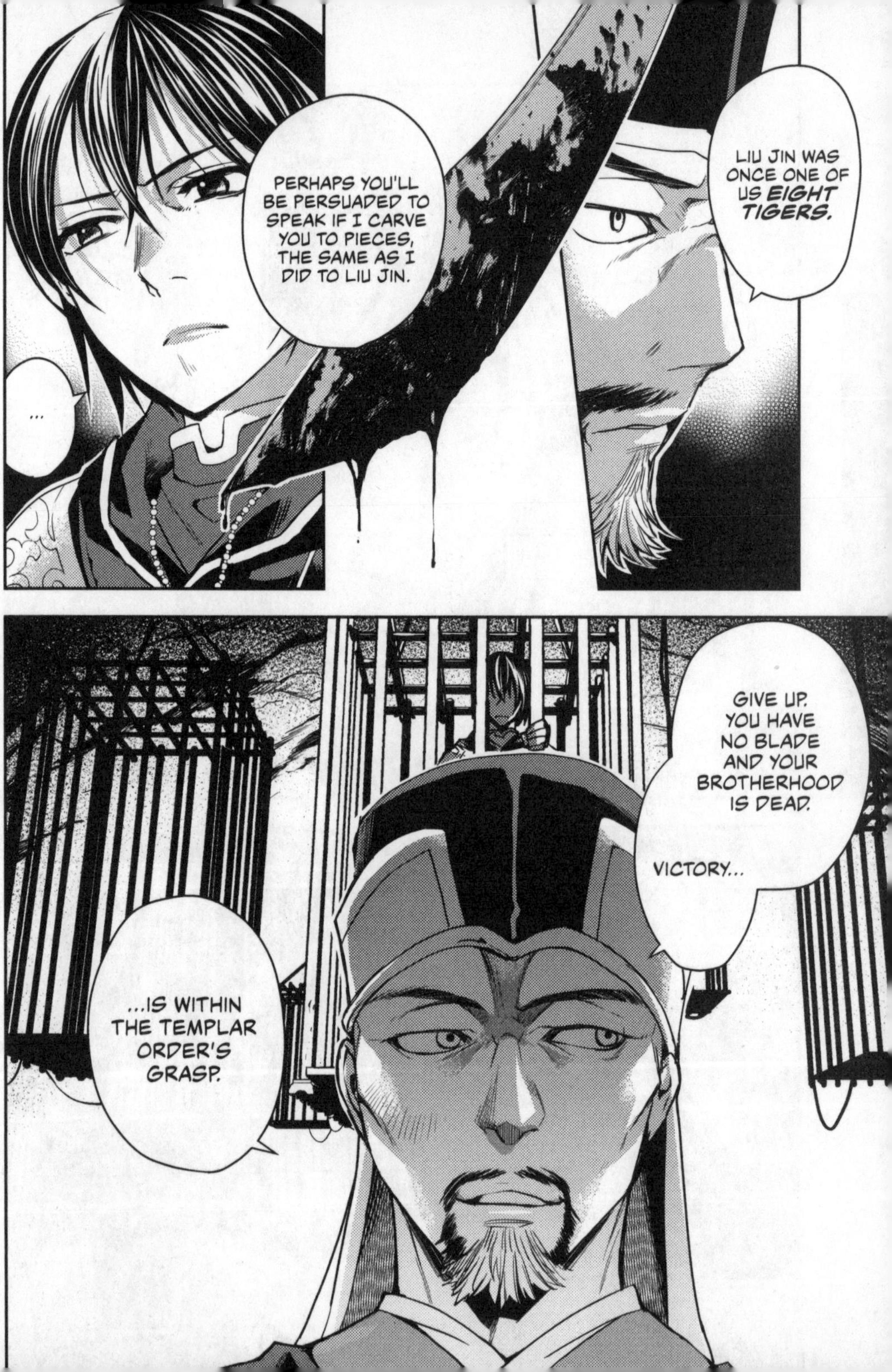
LIU JIN WAS ONCE ONE OF US EIGHT TIGERS.
PERHAPS YOU'LL BE PERSUADED TO SPEAK IF I CARVE YOU TO PIECES, THE SAME AS I DID TO LIU JIN.
...
GIVE UP. YOU HAVE NO BLADE AND YOUR BROTHERHOOD IS DEAD.
VICTORY...
...IS WITHIN THE TEMPLAR ORDER'S GRASP.

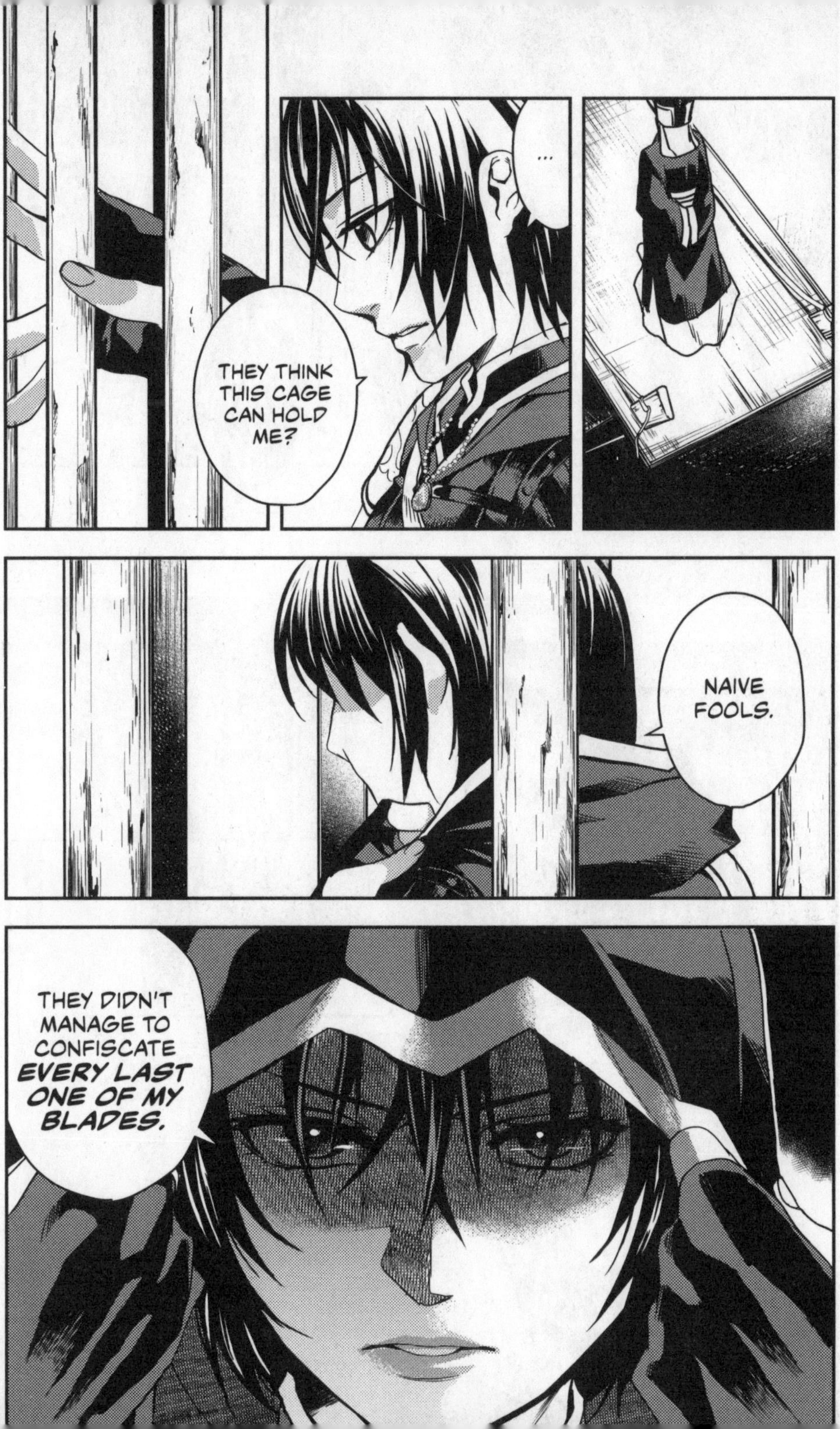
...
THEY THINK THIS CAGE CAN HOLD ME?
NAIVE FOOLS.
THEY DIDN'T MANAGE TO CONFISCATE ***EVERY LAST ONE OF MY BLADES.***

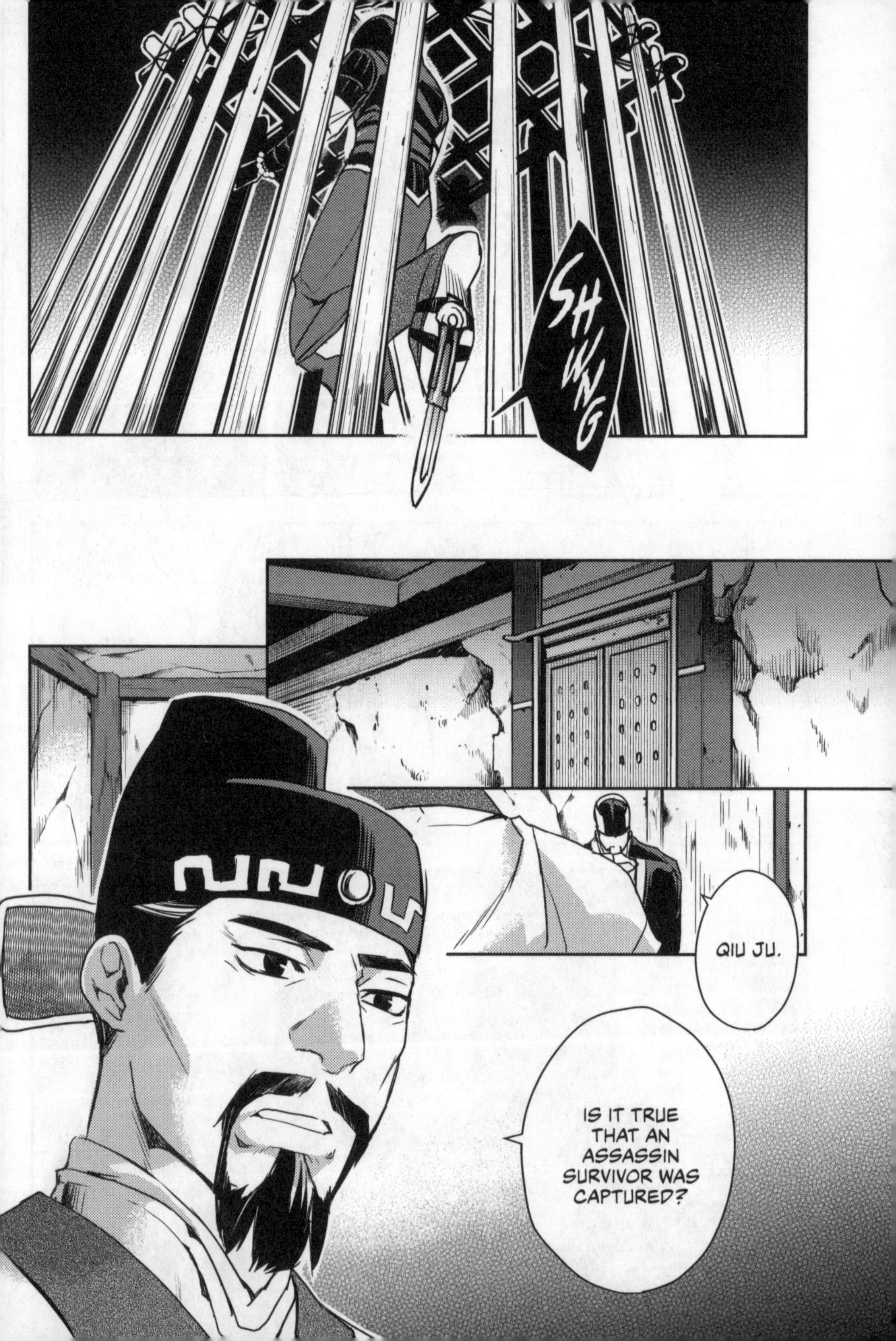
SHWNG
QIU JU.
IS IT TRUE THAT AN ASSASSIN SURVIVOR WAS CAPTURED?

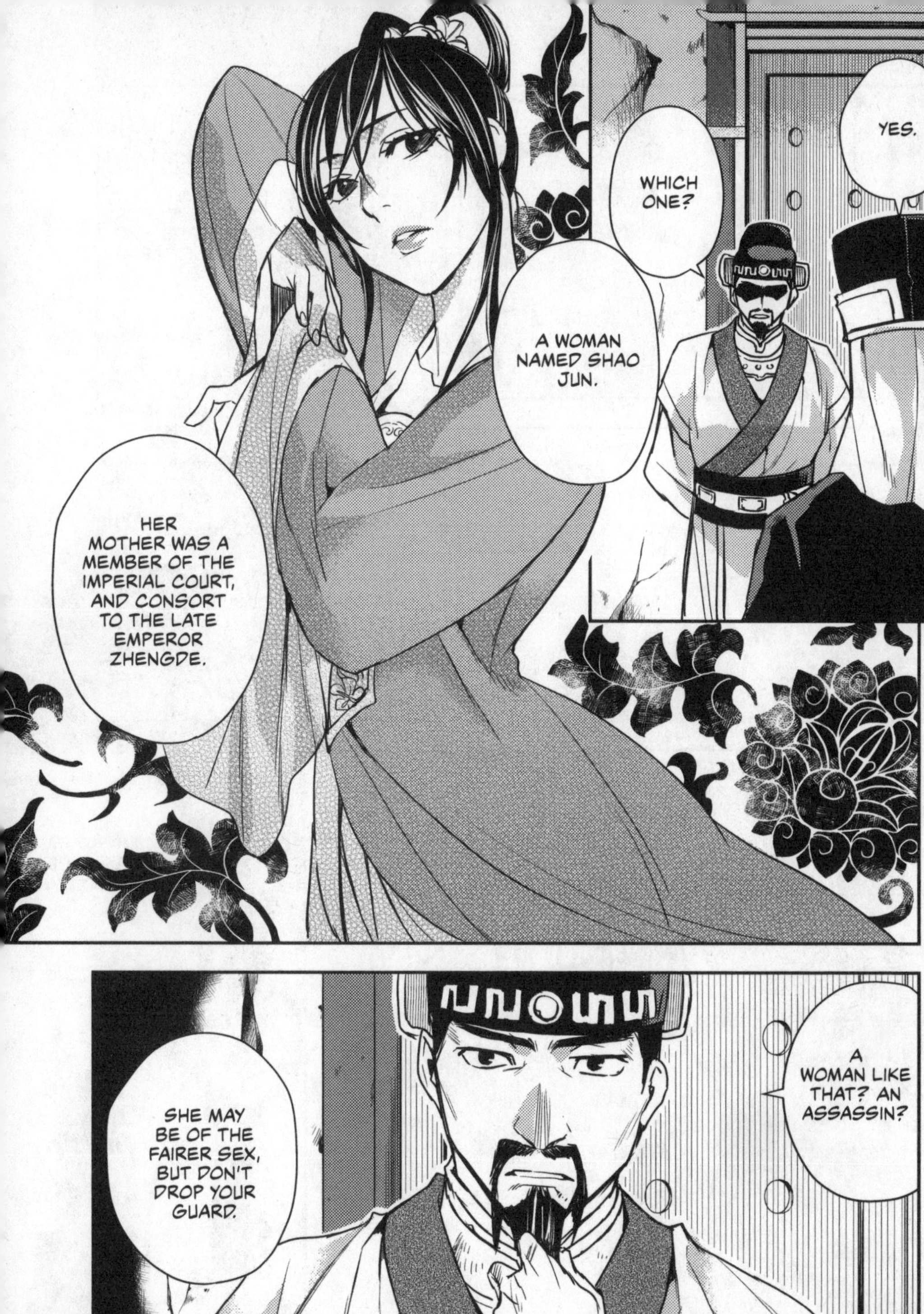
YES.
WHICH ONE?
A WOMAN NAMED SHAO JUN.
HER MOTHER WAS A MEMBER OF THE IMPERIAL COURT, AND CONSORT TO THE LATE EMPEROR ZHENGDE.
A WOMAN LIKE THAT? AN ASSASSIN?
SHE MAY BE OF THE FAIRER SEX, BUT DON'T DROP YOUR GUARD.

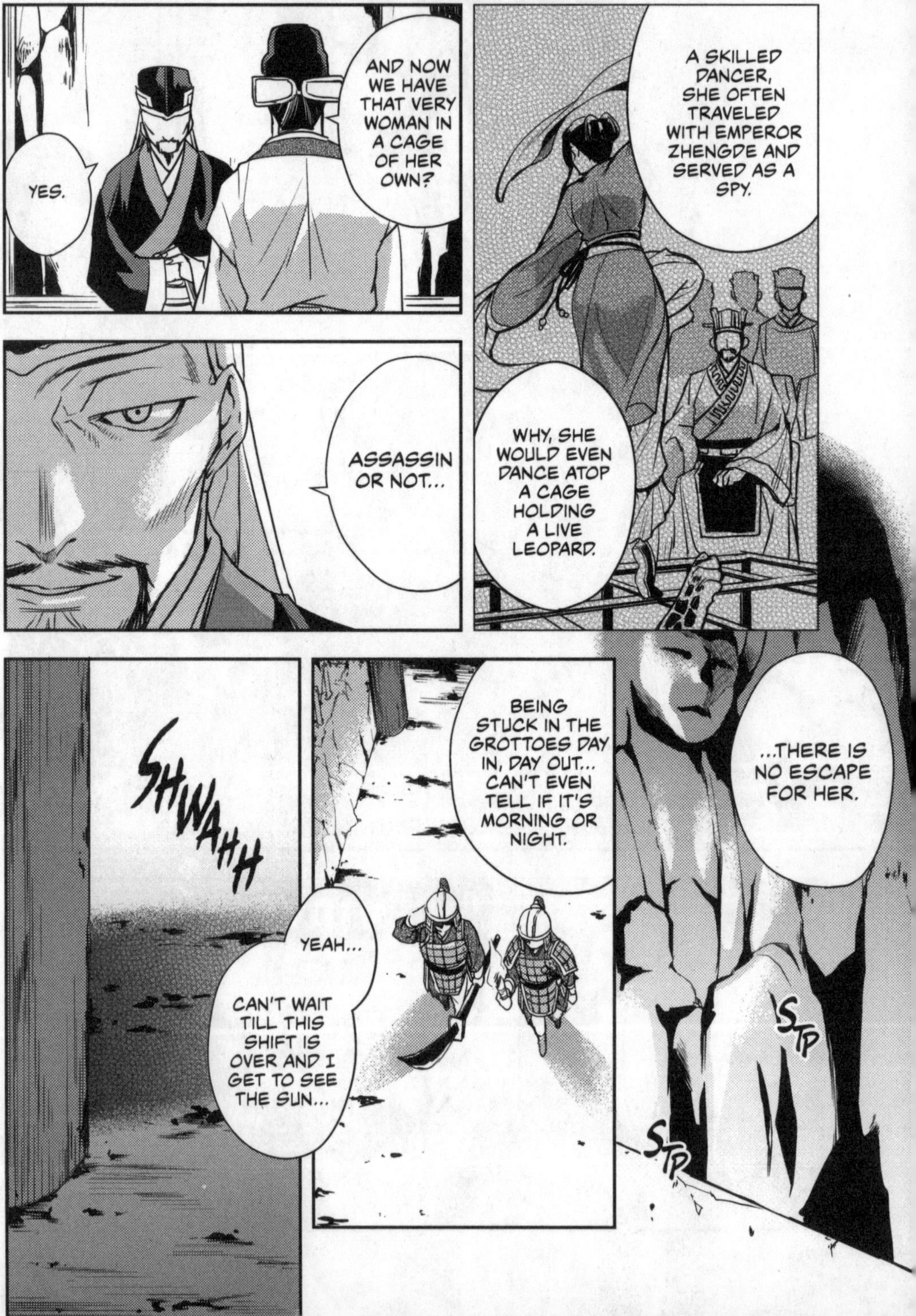
A SKILLED DANCER, SHE OFTEN TRAVELED WITH EMPEROR ZHENGDE AND SERVED AS A SPY.
WHY, SHE WOULD EVEN DANCE ATOP A CAGE HOLDING A LIVE LEOPARD.
AND NOW WE HAVE THAT VERY WOMAN IN A CAGE OF HER OWN?
YES.
ASSASSIN OR NOT...
...THERE IS NO ESCAPE FOR HER.
STP
STP
BEING STUCK IN THE GROTTOES DAY IN, DAY OUT... CAN'T EVEN TELL IF IT'S MORNING OR NIGHT.
YEAH...
CAN'T WAIT TILL THIS SHIFT IS OVER AND I GET TO SEE THE SUN...
SHWAHH

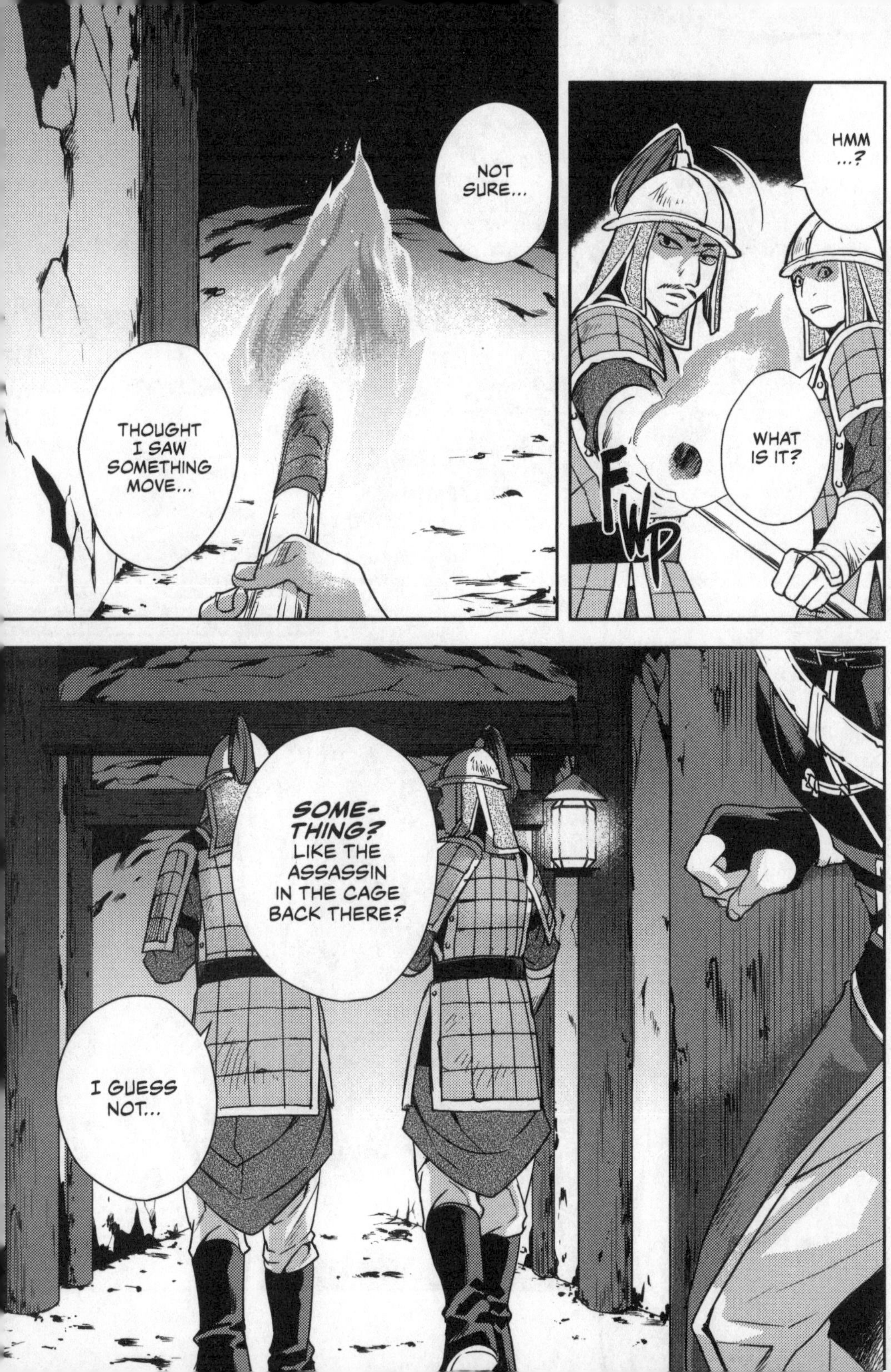
HMM ...?
WHAT IS IT?
FWP
NOT SURE...
THOUGHT I SAW SOMETHING MOVE...
SOMETHING? LIKE THE ASSASSIN IN THE CAGE BACK THERE?
I GUESS NOT...

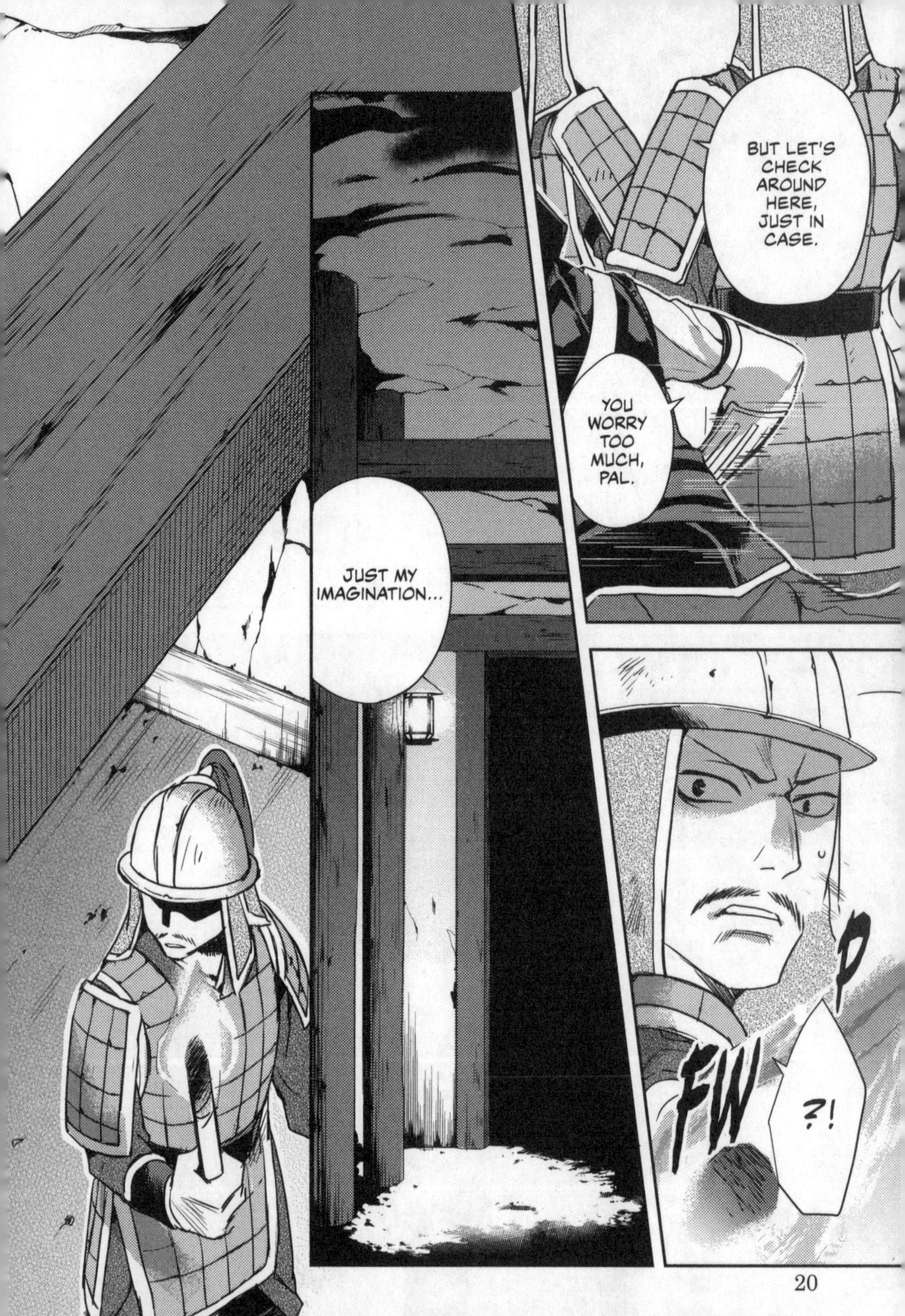
BUT LET'S CHECK AROUND HERE, JUST IN CASE.
YOU WORRY TOO MUCH, PAL.
FWP
?!
JUST MY IMAGINATION...

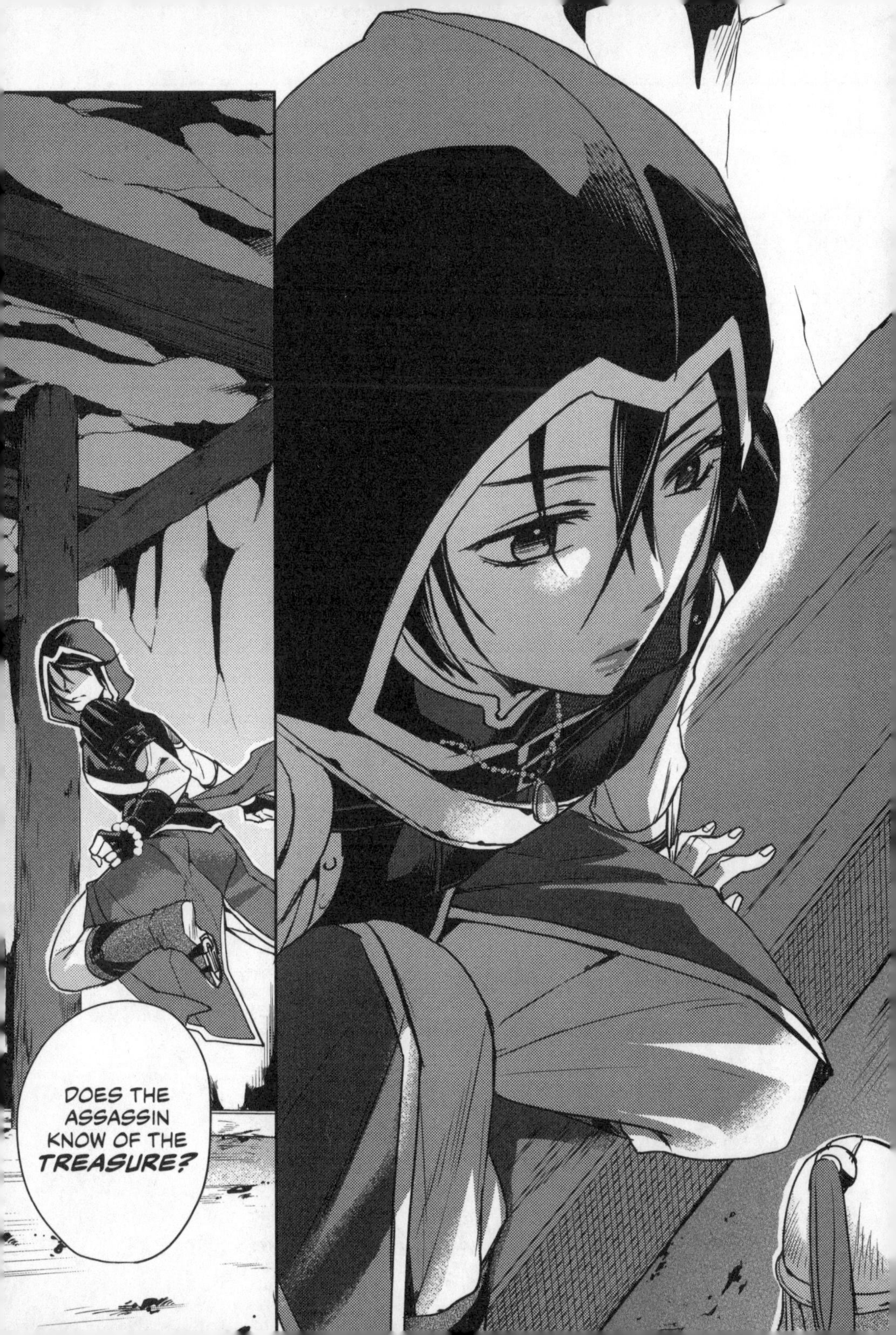
DOES THE ASSASSIN KNOW OF THE *TREASURE?*

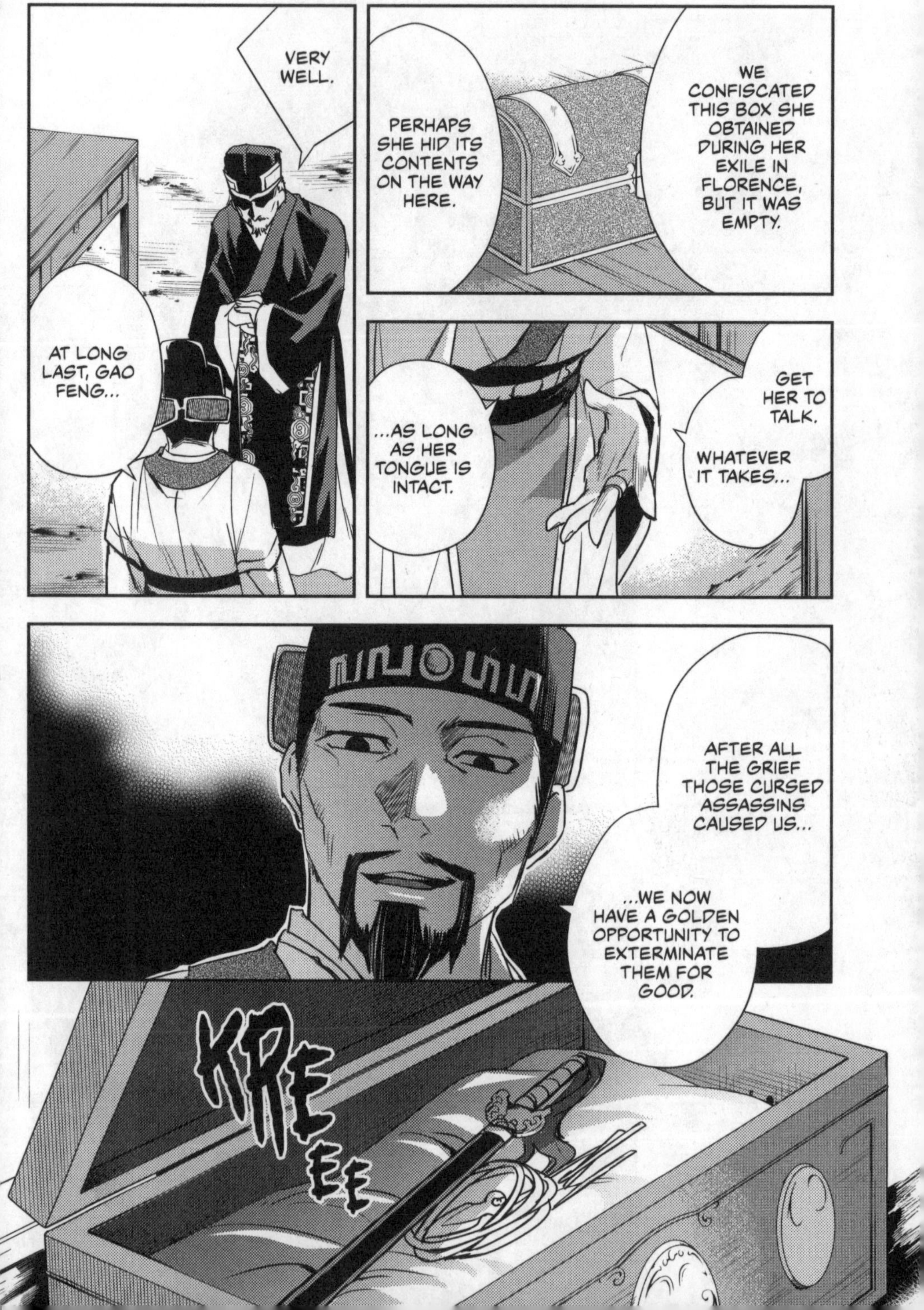
WE CONFISCATED THIS BOX SHE OBTAINED DURING HER EXILE IN FLORENCE, BUT IT WAS EMPTY.
PERHAPS SHE HID ITS CONTENTS ON THE WAY HERE.
GET HER TO TALK.
WHATEVER IT TAKES...
...AS LONG AS HER TONGUE IS INTACT.
VERY WELL.
AT LONG LAST, GAO FENG...
AFTER ALL THE GRIEF THOSE CURSED ASSASSINS CAUSED US...
...WE NOW HAVE A GOLDEN OPPORTUNITY TO EXTERMINATE THEM FOR GOOD.
KREEEE

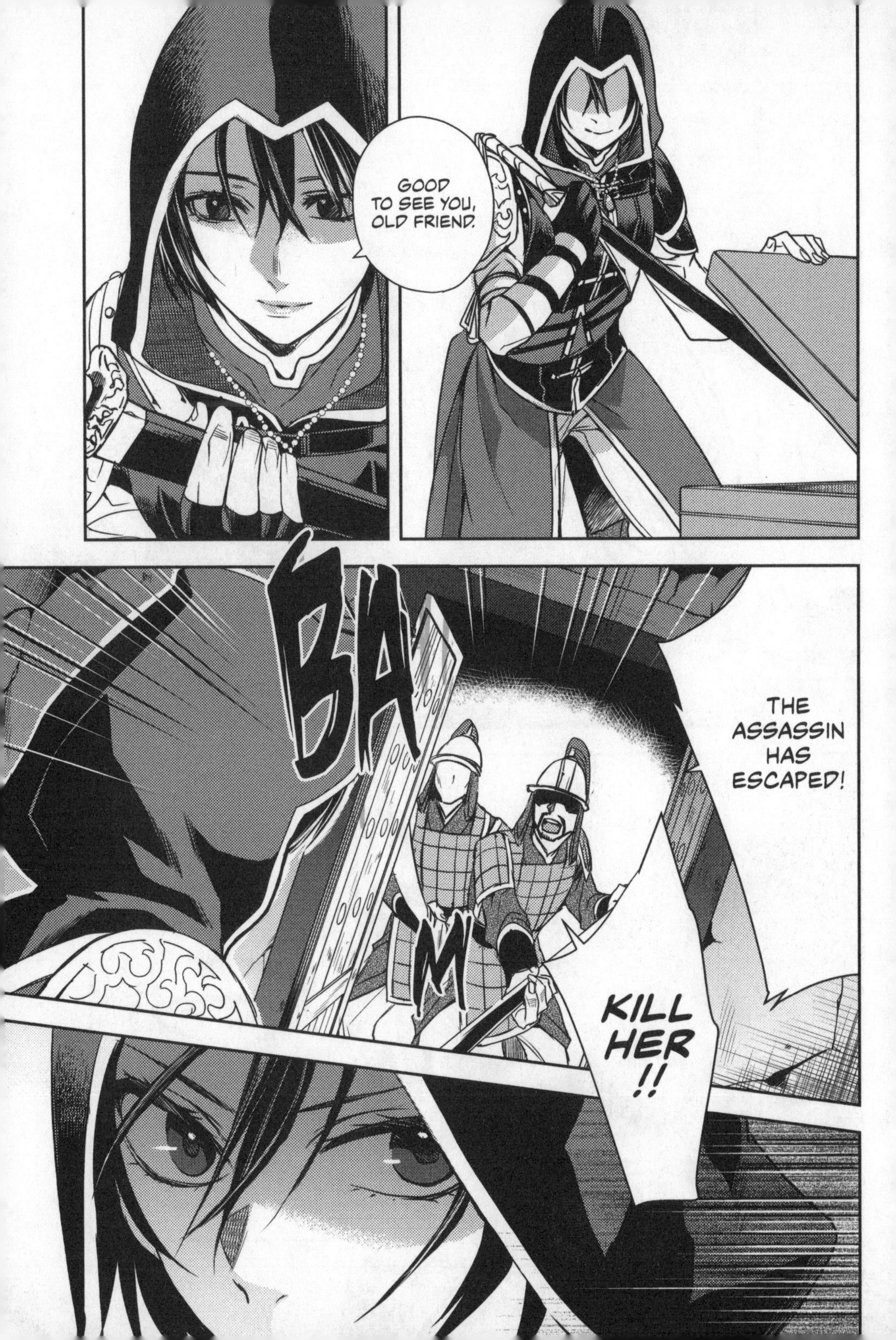
GOOD TO SEE YOU, OLD FRIEND.
THE ASSASSIN HAS ESCAPED!
BAM
KILL HER!!

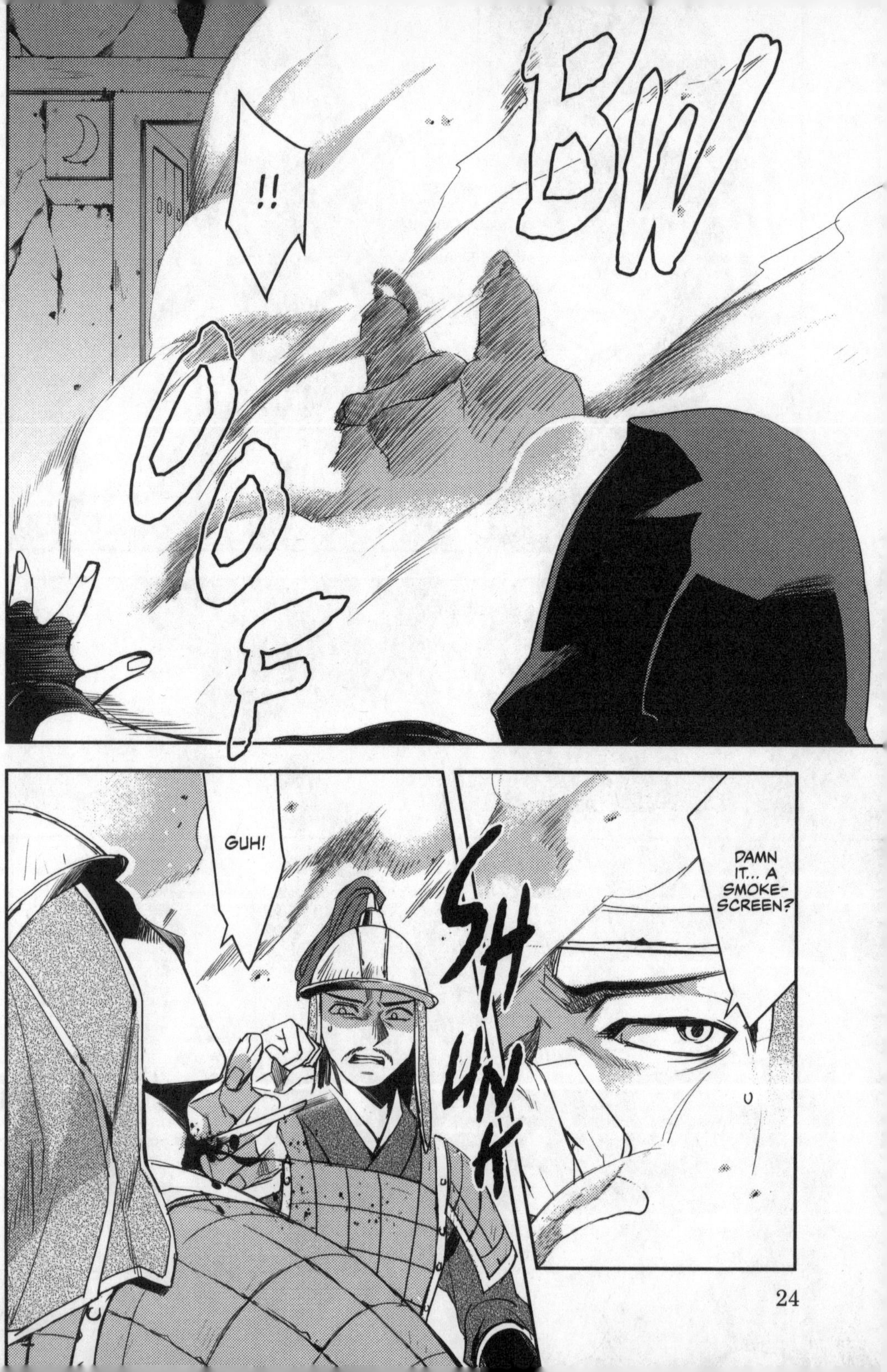

!!
BWOOF
DAMN IT... A SMOKE-SCREEN?
SHUNK
GUH!

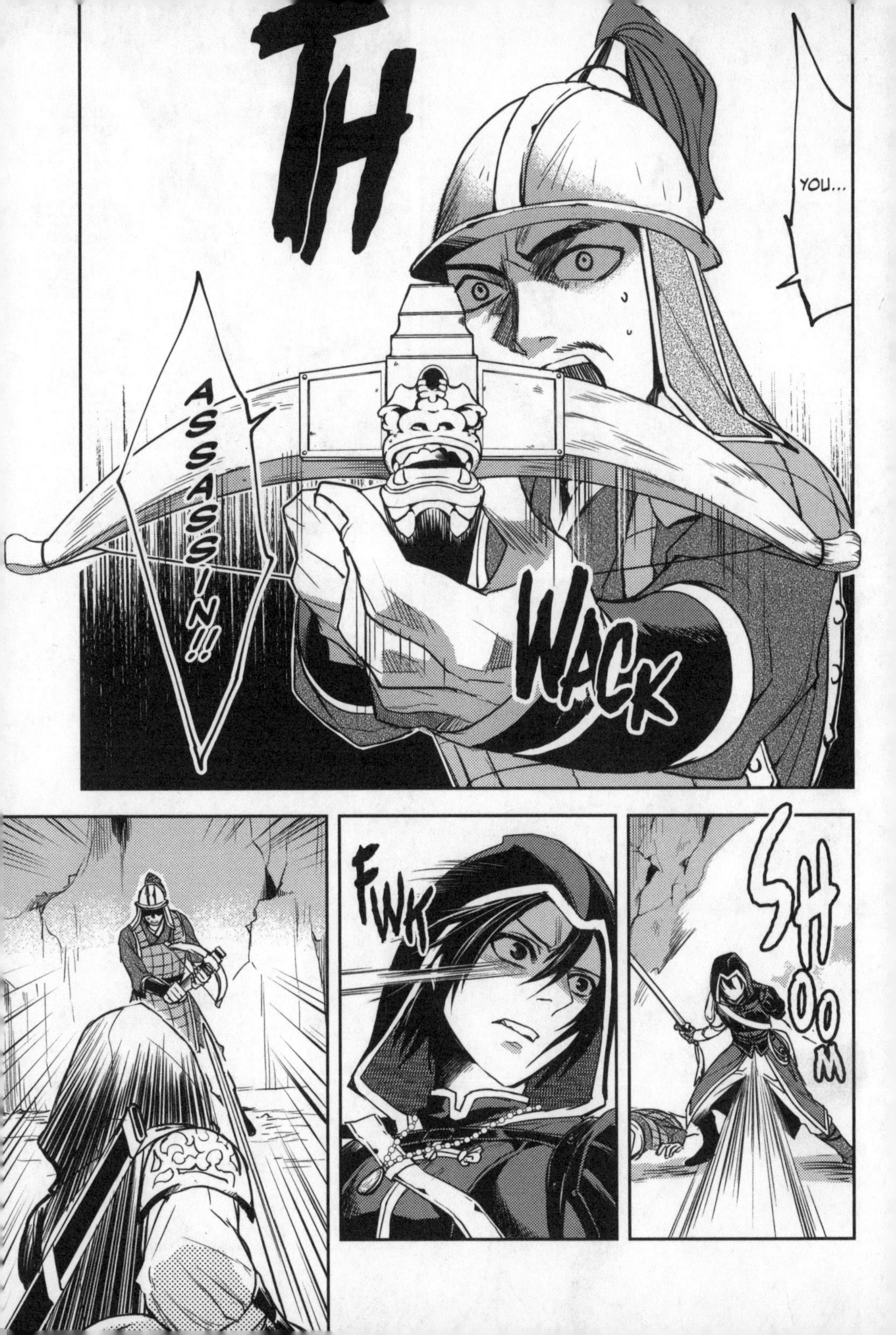
YOU...
TH
WACK
ASSASSIN!!
SHOOOM
FWK

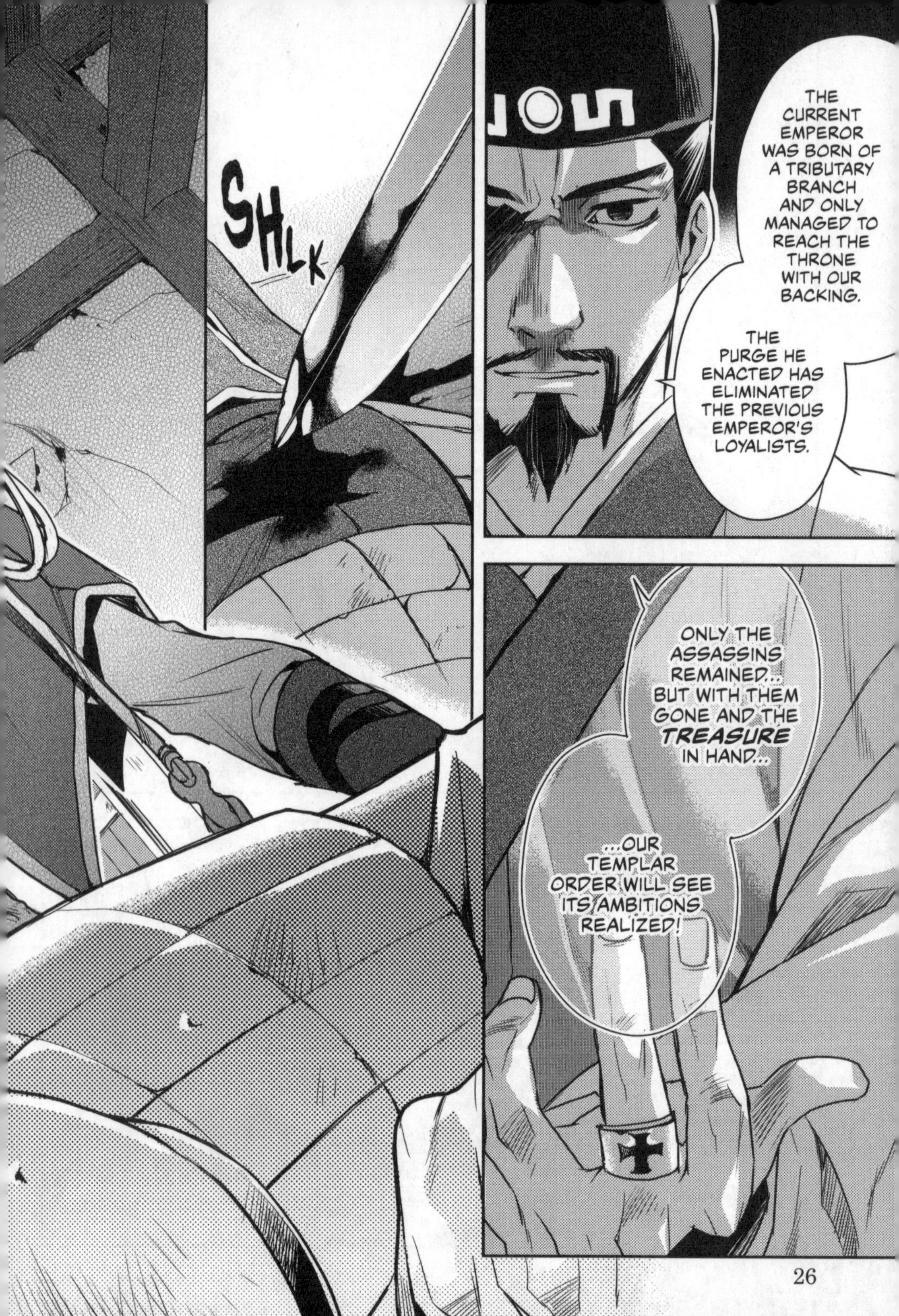
THE CURRENT EMPEROR WAS BORN OF A TRIBUTARY BRANCH AND ONLY MANAGED TO REACH THE THRONE WITH OUR BACKING.
THE PURGE HE ENACTED HAS ELIMINATED THE PREVIOUS EMPEROR'S LOYALISTS.
ONLY THE ASSASSINS REMAINED... BUT WITH THEM GONE AND THE ***TREASURE*** IN HAND...
...OUR TEMPLAR ORDER WILL SEE ITS AMBITIONS REALIZED!
SHLK

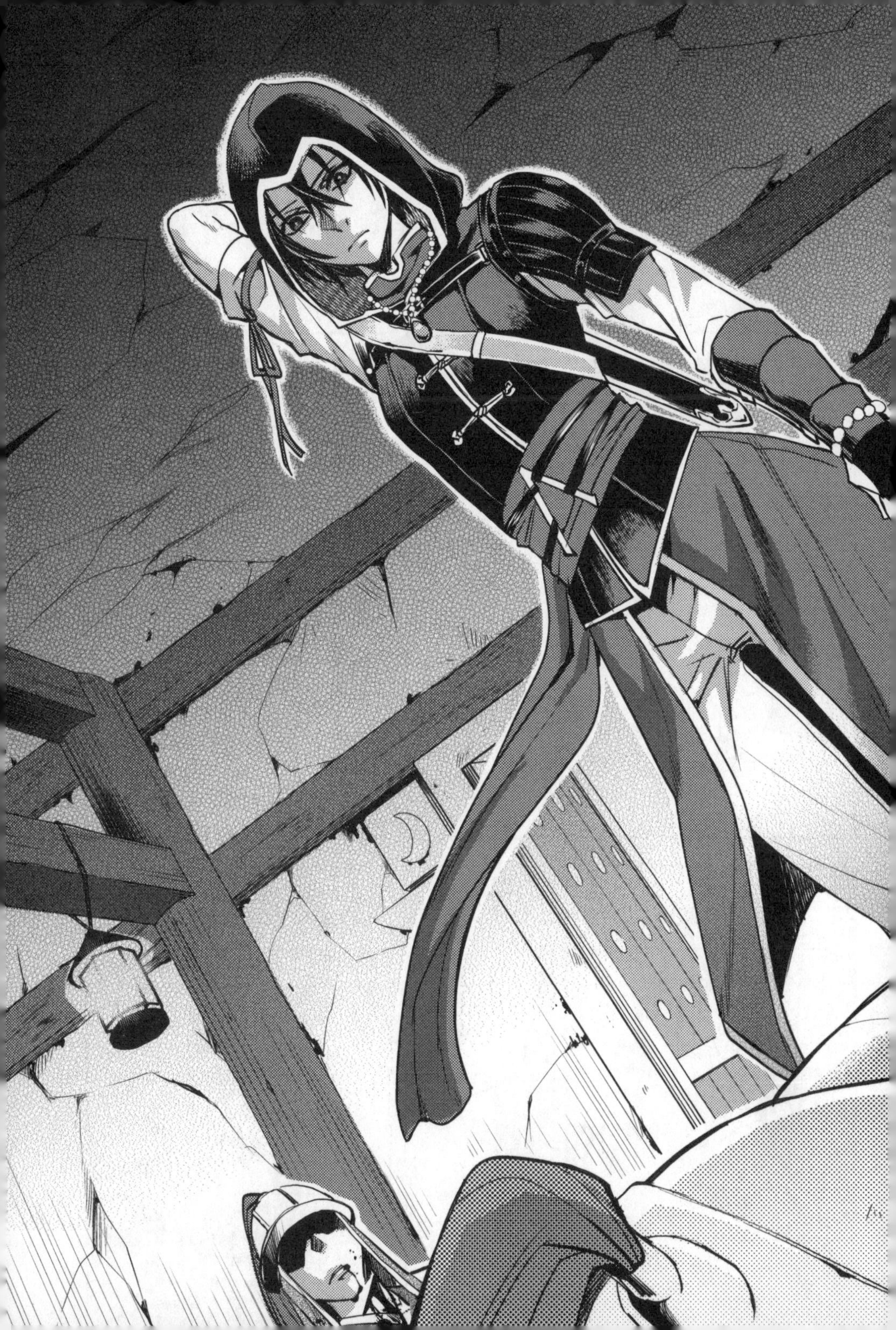

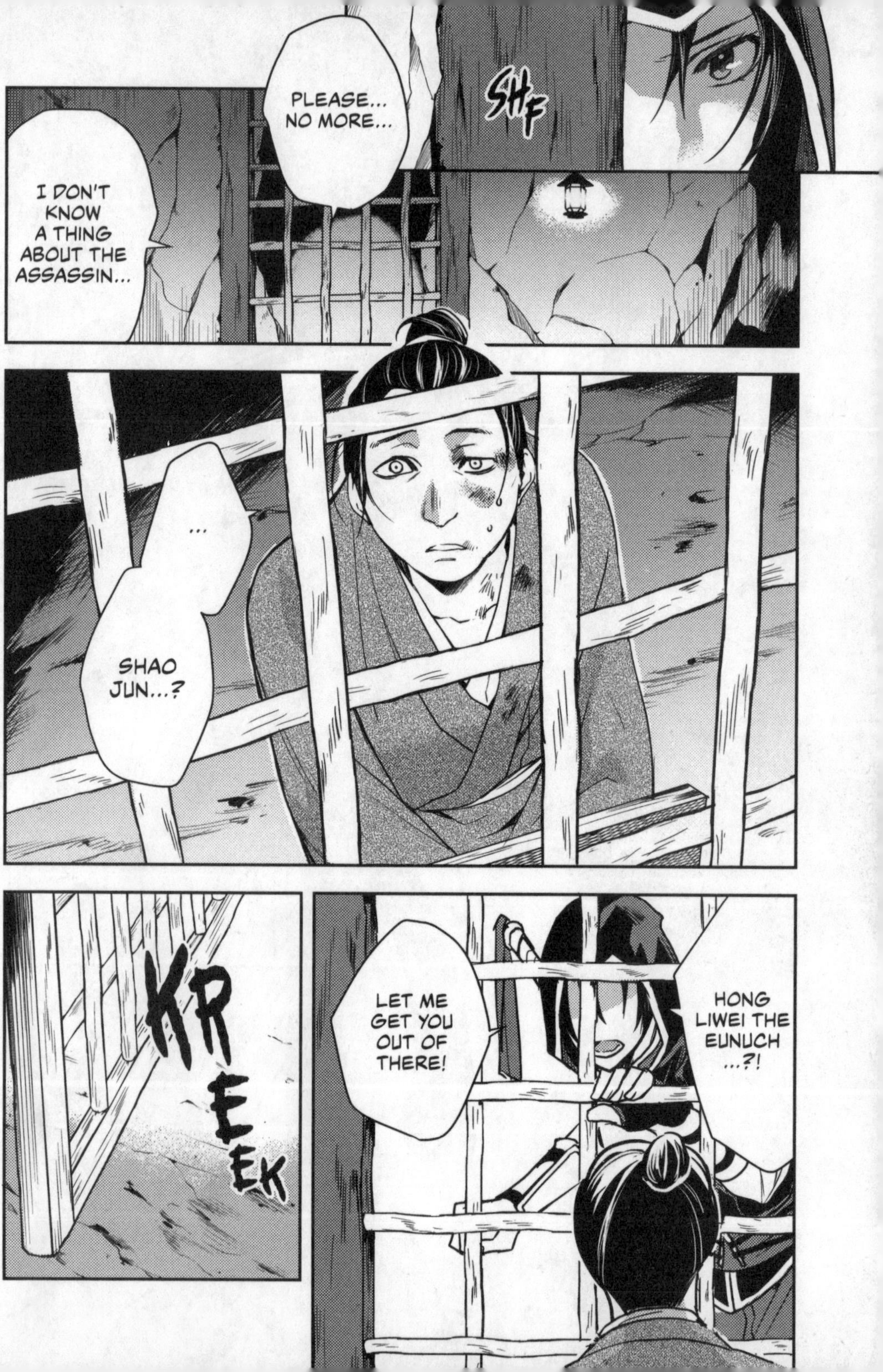
SHF
PLEASE... NO MORE...
I DON'T KNOW A THING ABOUT THE ASSASSIN...
...
SHAO JUN...?
HONG LIWEI THE EUNUCH ...?!
LET ME GET YOU OUT OF THERE!
KREEK

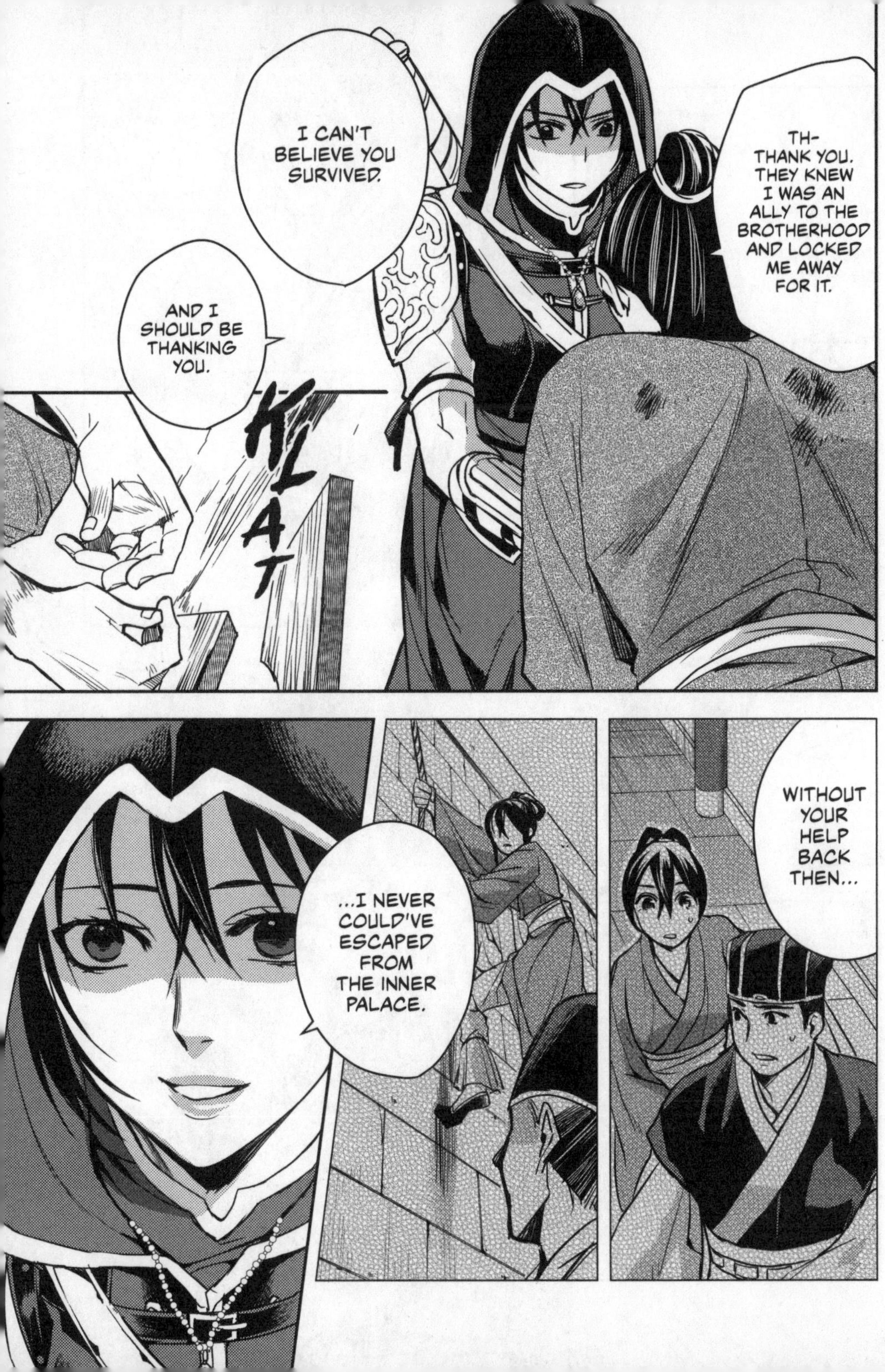
TH- THANK YOU. THEY KNEW I WAS AN ALLY TO THE BROTHERHOOD AND LOCKED ME AWAY FOR IT.
I CAN'T BELIEVE YOU SURVIVED.
AND I SHOULD BE THANKING YOU.
KLAT
WITHOUT YOUR HELP BACK THEN...
...I NEVER COULD'VE ESCAPED FROM THE INNER PALACE.

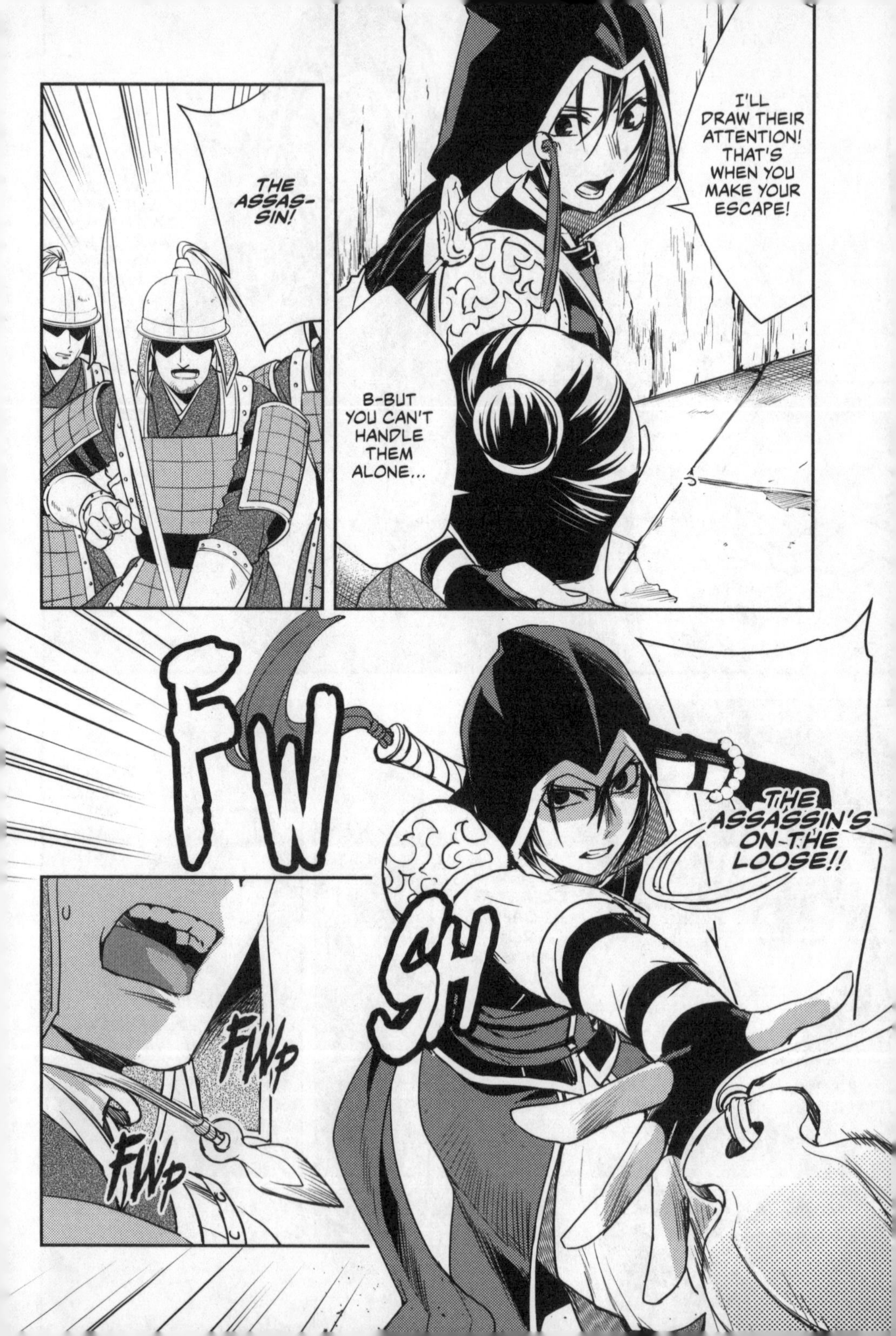
I'LL DRAW THEIR ATTENTION! THAT'S WHEN YOU MAKE YOUR ESCAPE!
B-BUT YOU CAN'T HANDLE THEM ALONE...
THE ASSAS-SIN!
THE ASSASSIN'S ON THE LOOSE!!
FWSH
FWP
FWP

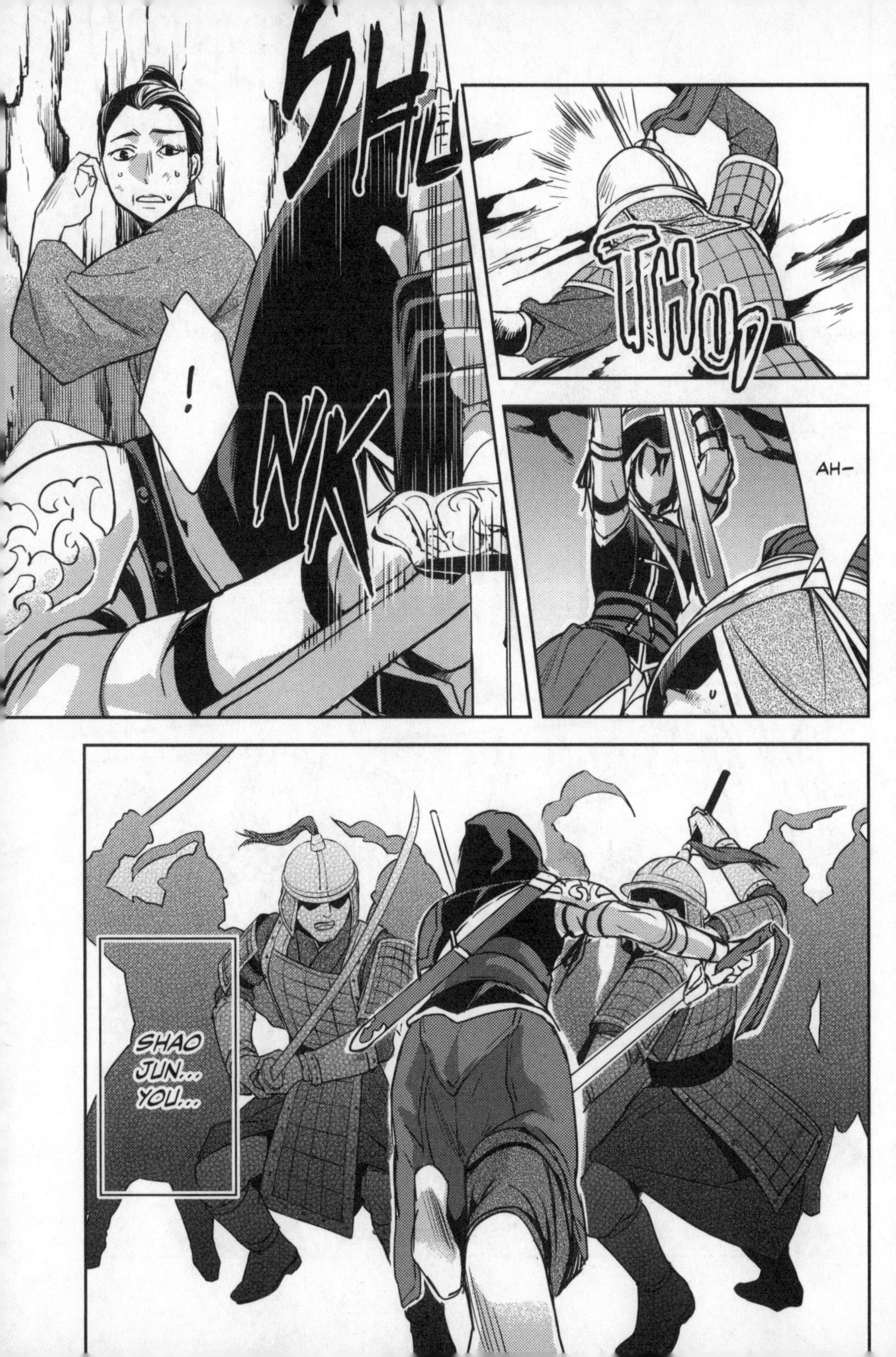
THUD
AH-
SHU
!
NK
SHAO JUN... YOU...

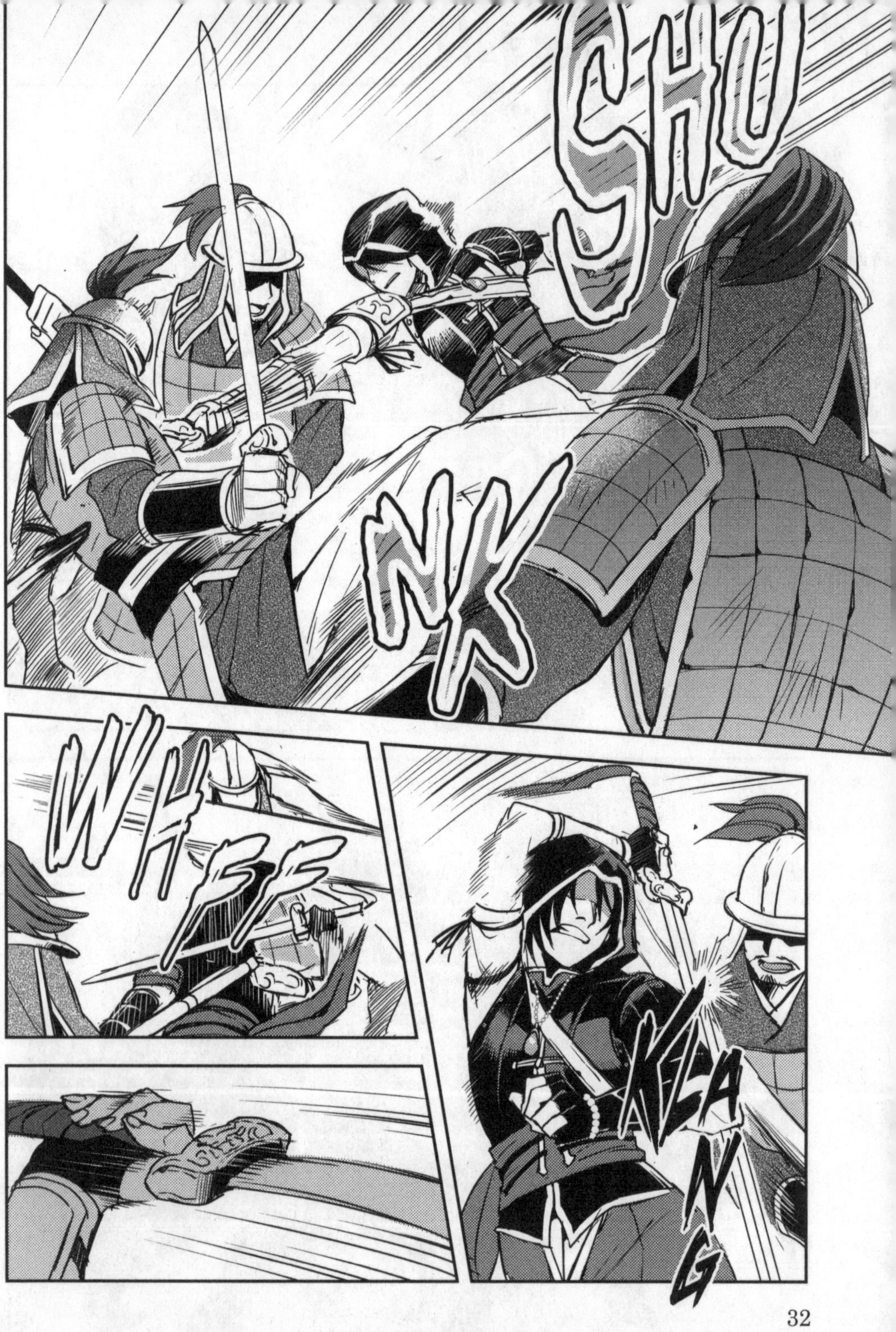
SHU
NK
KLANG
WHFF

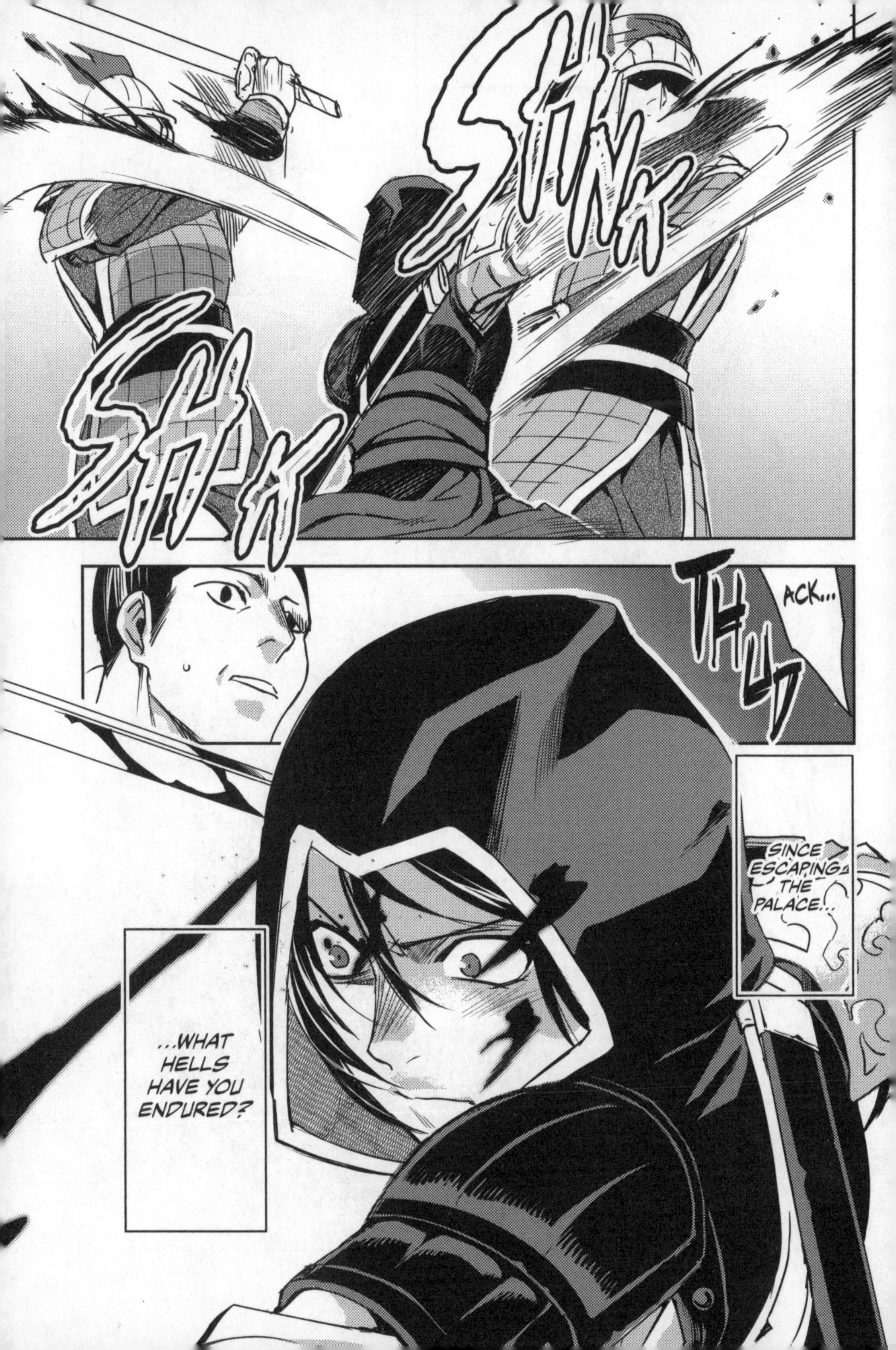
SHNK
SHK
THUD
ACK...
SINCE ESCAPING THE PALACE...
...WHAT HELLS HAVE YOU ENDURED?

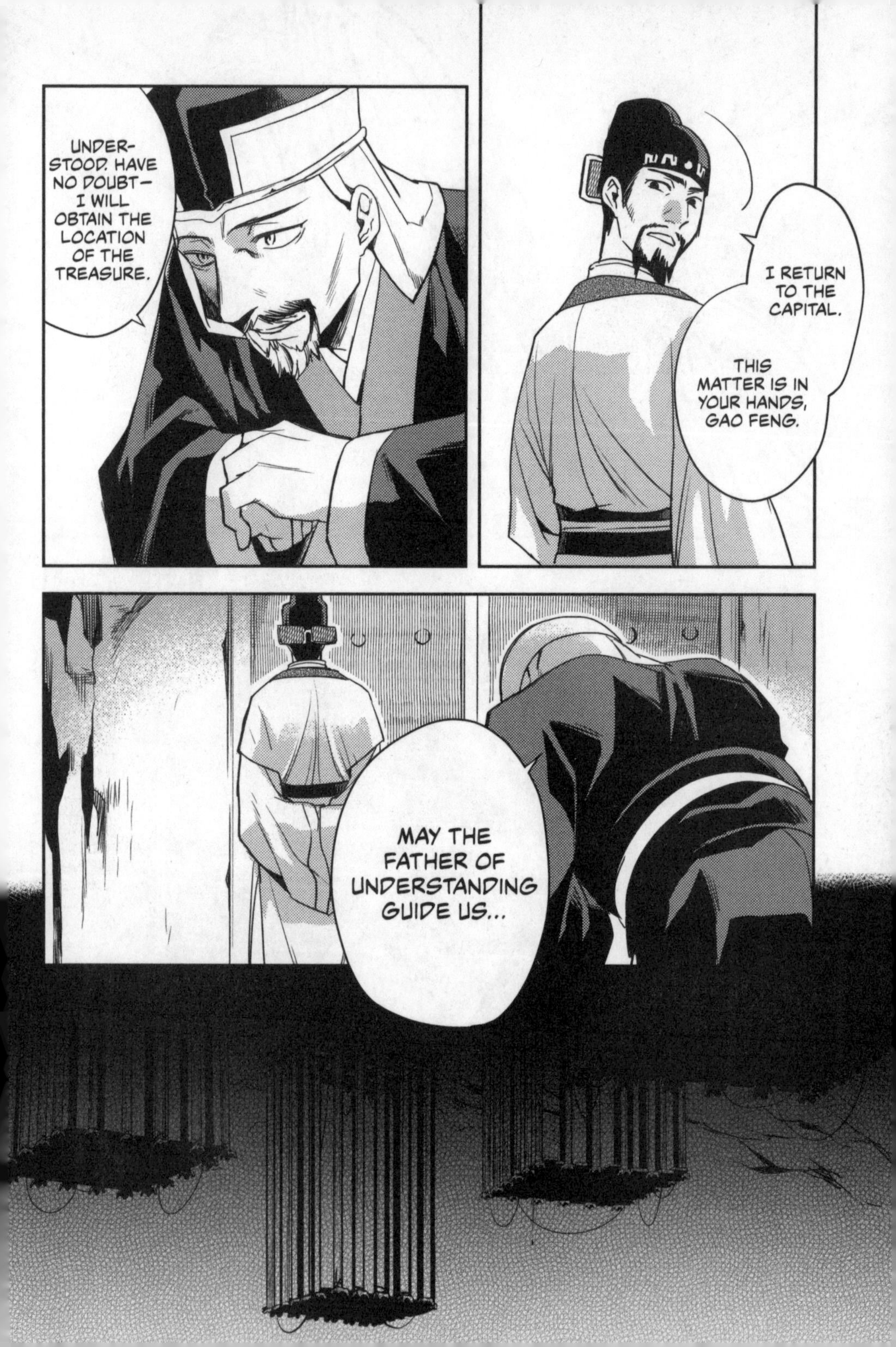
I RETURN TO THE CAPITAL.
THIS MATTER IS IN YOUR HANDS, GAO FENG.
UNDER-STOOD. HAVE NO DOUBT—I WILL OBTAIN THE LOCATION OF THE TREASURE.
MAY THE FATHER OF UNDERSTANDING GUIDE US...

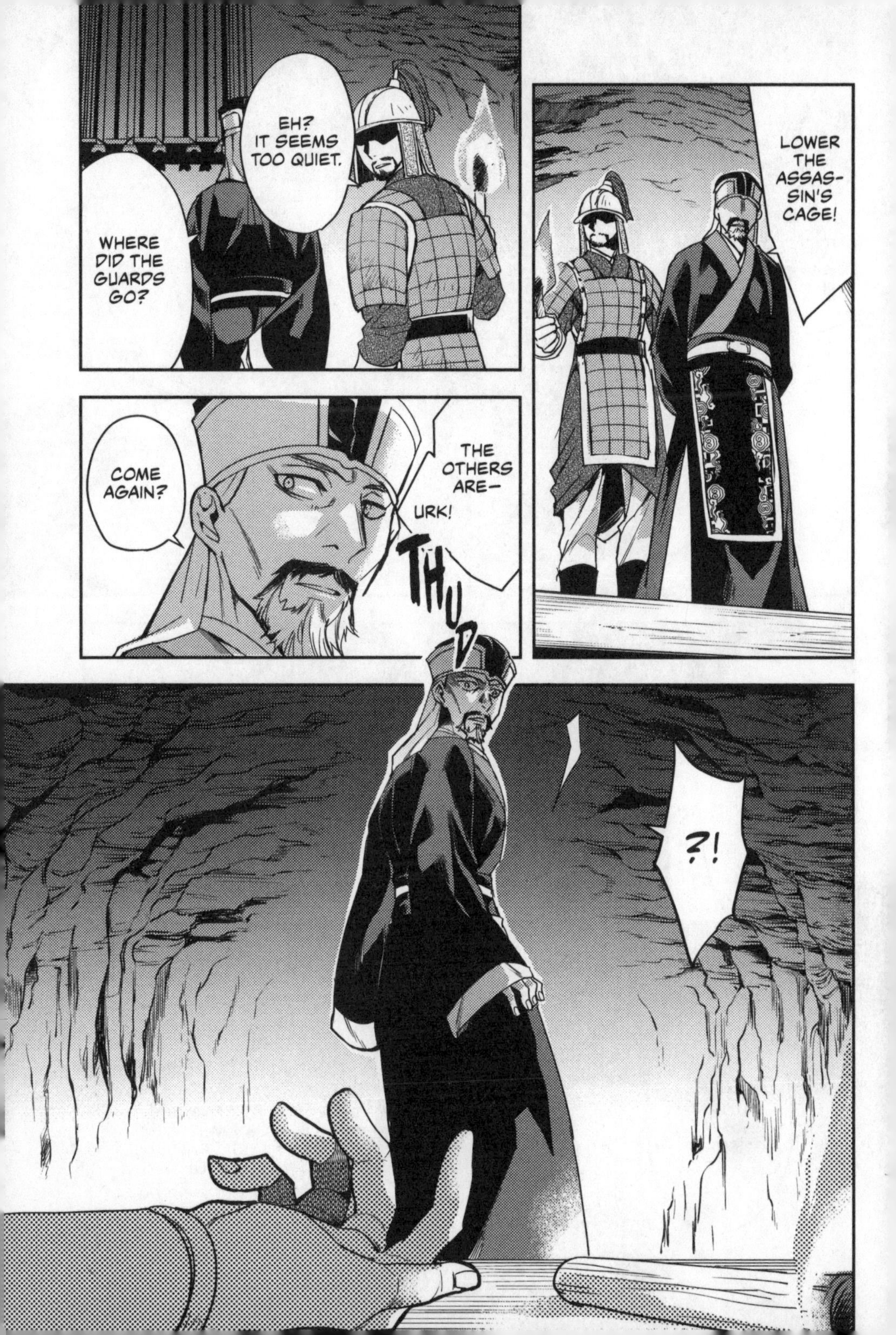
LOWER THE ASSAS-SIN'S CAGE!
EH? IT SEEMS TOO QUIET.
WHERE DID THE GUARDS GO?
COME AGAIN?
THE OTHERS ARE—
URK!
THUD
?!

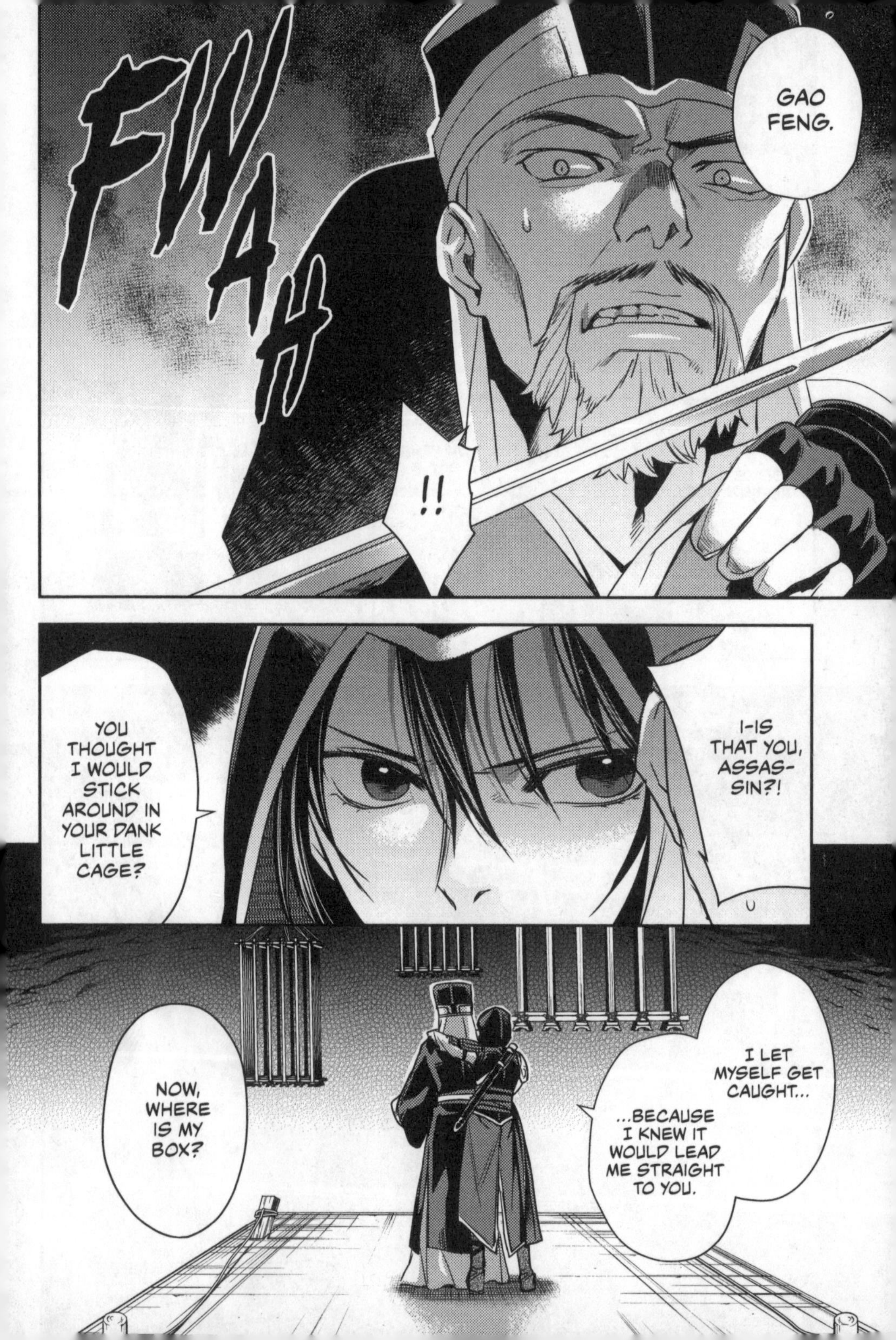
GAO FENG.
FWAH
!!
I-IS THAT YOU, ASSAS-SIN?!
YOU THOUGHT I WOULD STICK AROUND IN YOUR DANK LITTLE CAGE?
I LET MYSELF GET CAUGHT...
...BECAUSE I KNEW IT WOULD LEAD ME STRAIGHT TO YOU.
NOW, WHERE IS MY BOX?

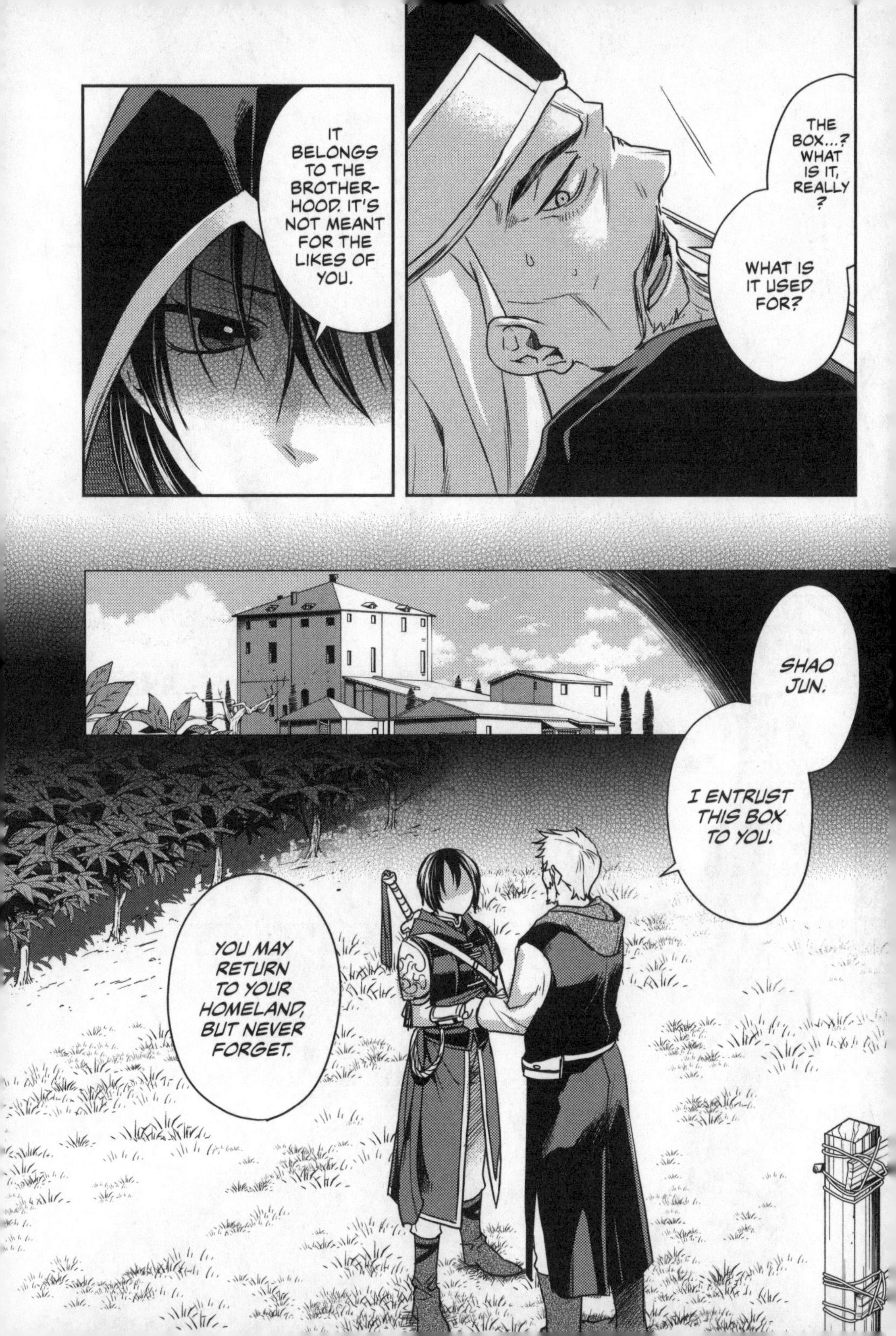
THE BOX...? WHAT IS IT, REALLY?
WHAT IS IT USED FOR?
IT BELONGS TO THE BROTHERHOOD. IT'S NOT MEANT FOR THE LIKES OF YOU.
SHAO JUN.
I ENTRUST THIS BOX TO YOU.
YOU MAY RETURN TO YOUR HOMELAND, BUT NEVER FORGET.

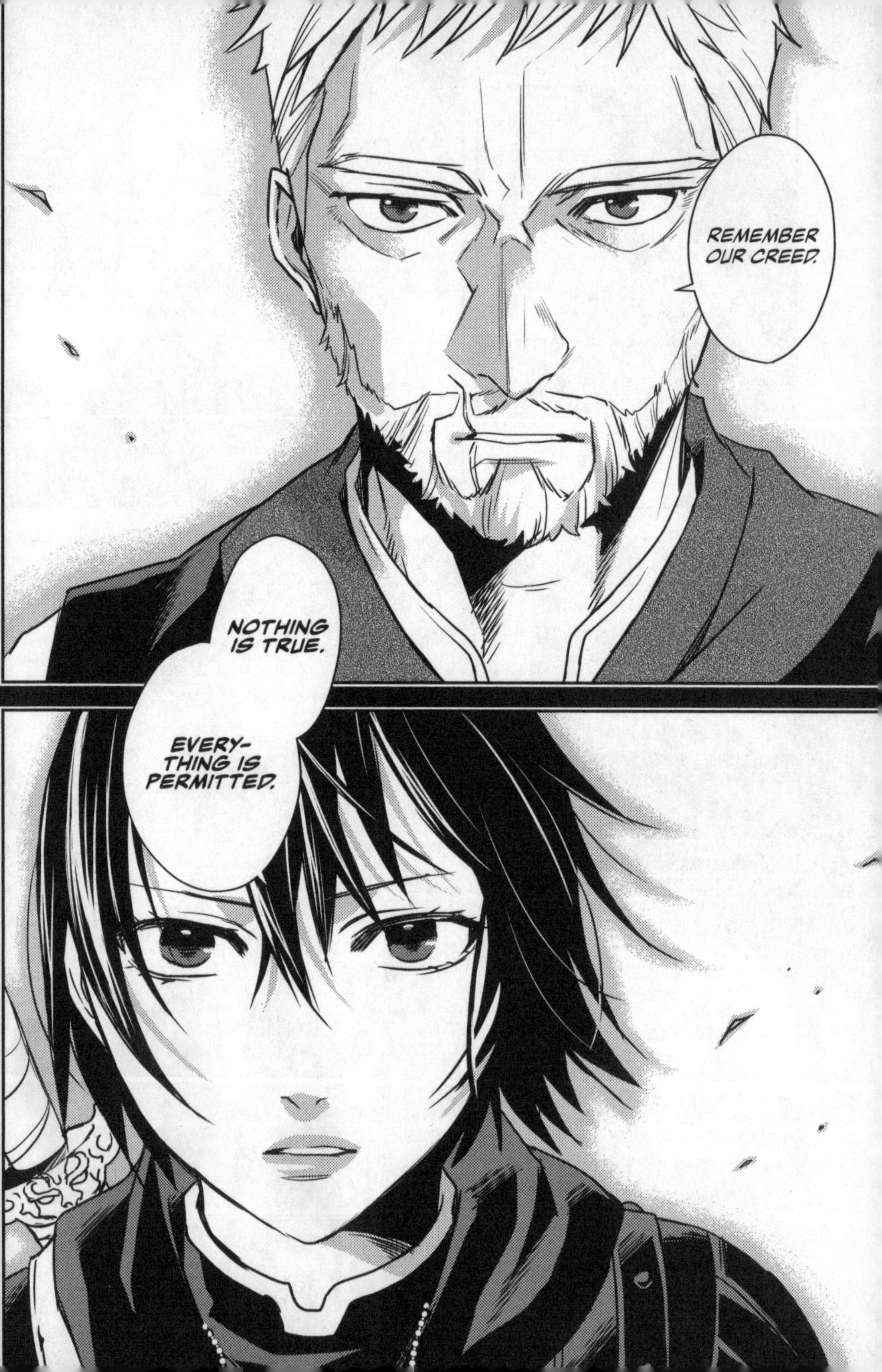
REMEMBER OUR CREED.
NOTHING IS TRUE.
EVERY-THING IS PERMITTED.

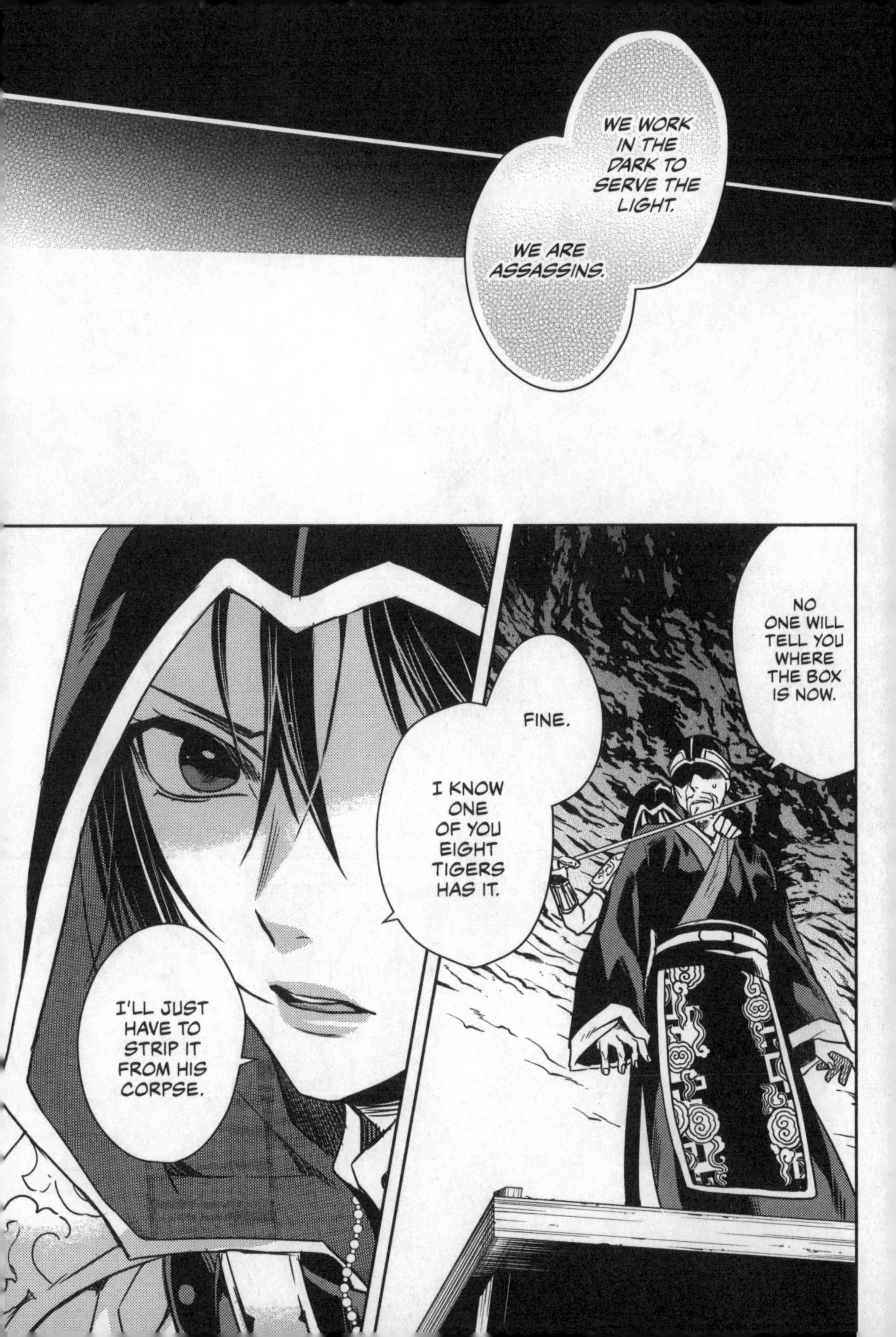
WE WORK IN THE DARK TO SERVE THE LIGHT.
WE ARE ASSASSINS.
NO ONE WILL TELL YOU WHERE THE BOX IS NOW.
FINE.
I KNOW ONE OF YOU EIGHT TIGERS HAS IT.
I'LL JUST HAVE TO STRIP IT FROM HIS CORPSE.

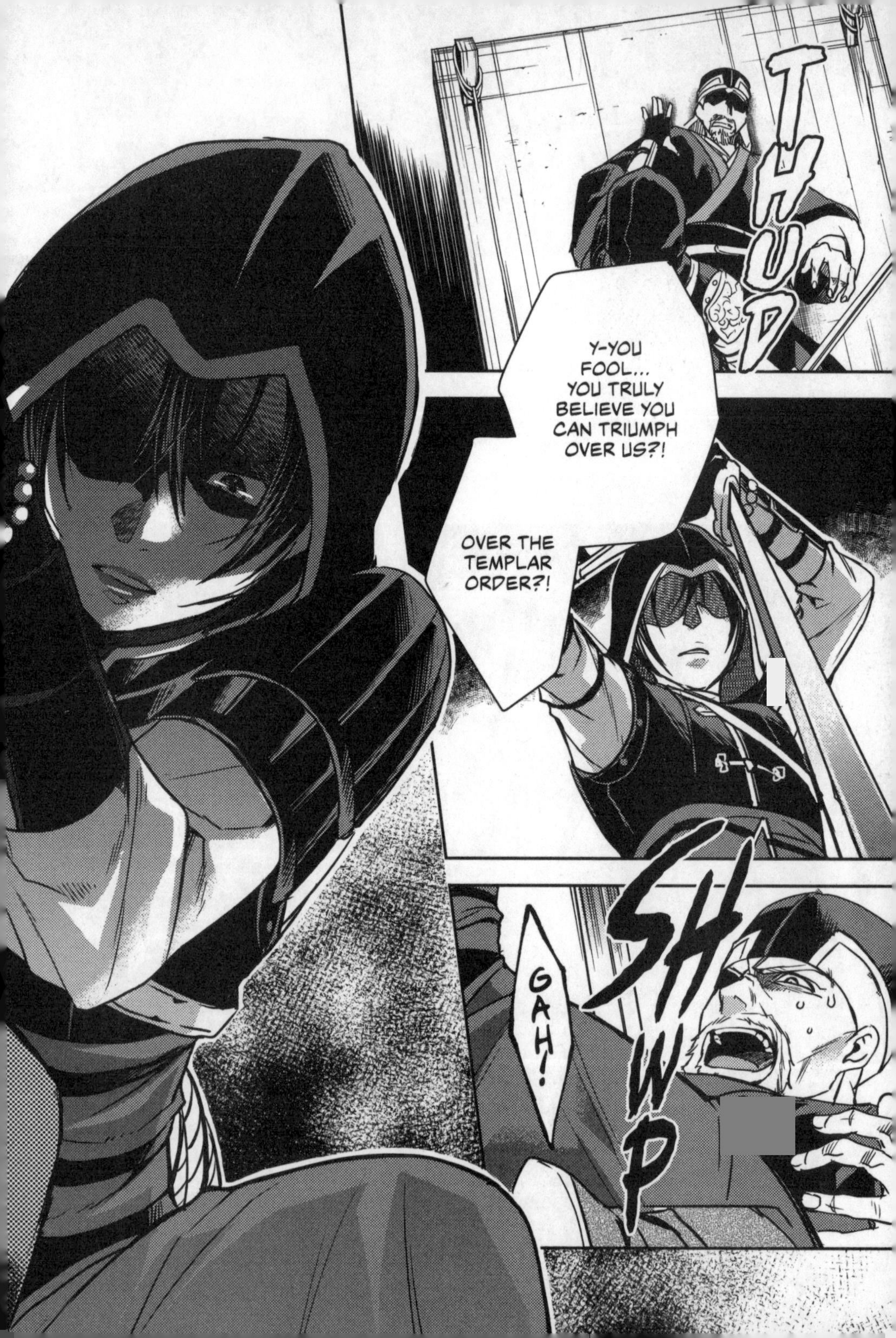
THUD
Y-YOU FOOL... YOU TRULY BELIEVE YOU CAN TRIUMPH OVER US?!
OVER THE TEMPLAR ORDER?!
SHWP
GAH!

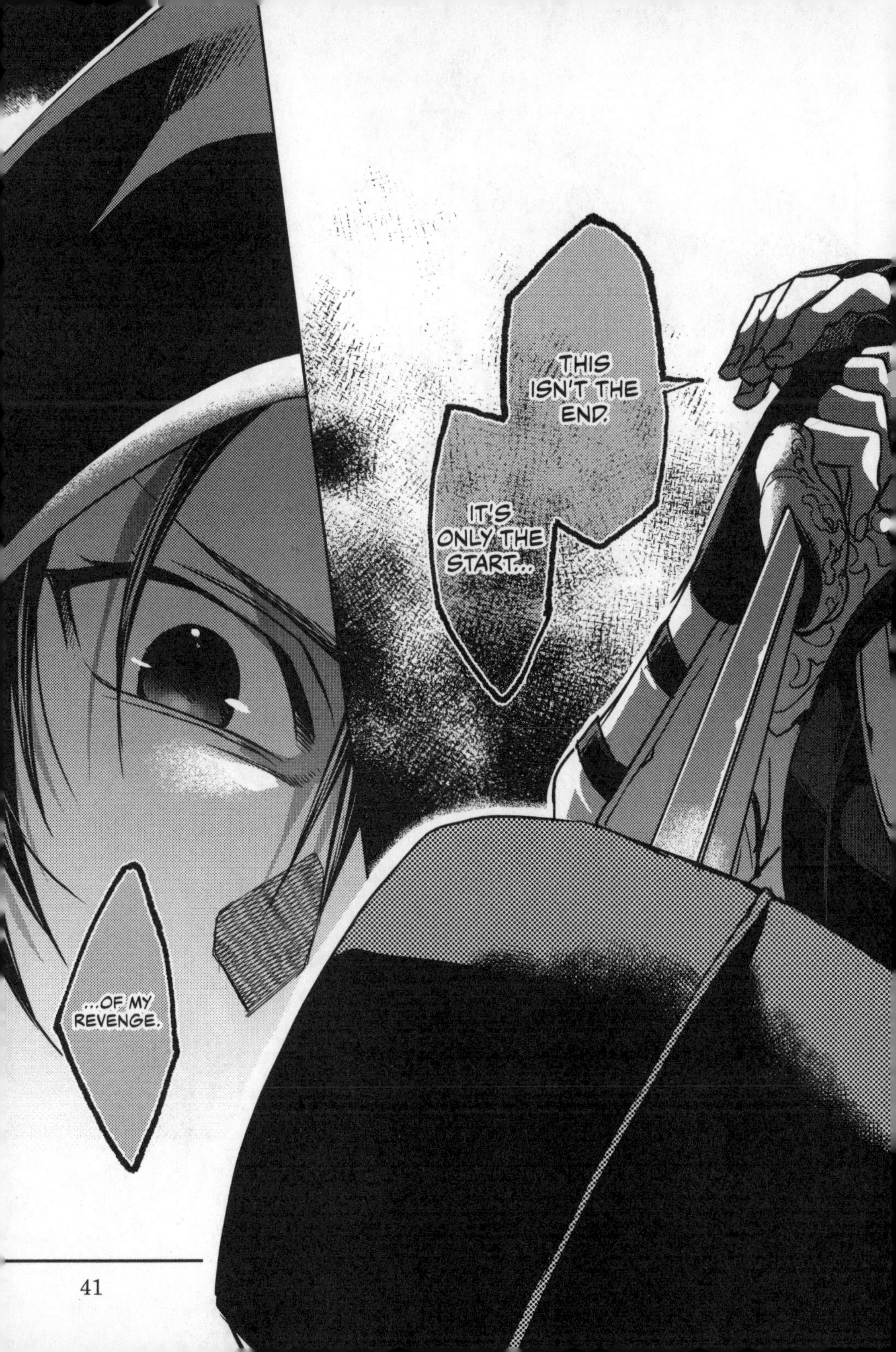
THIS ISN'T THE END.
IT'S ONLY THE START...
...OF MY REVENGE.

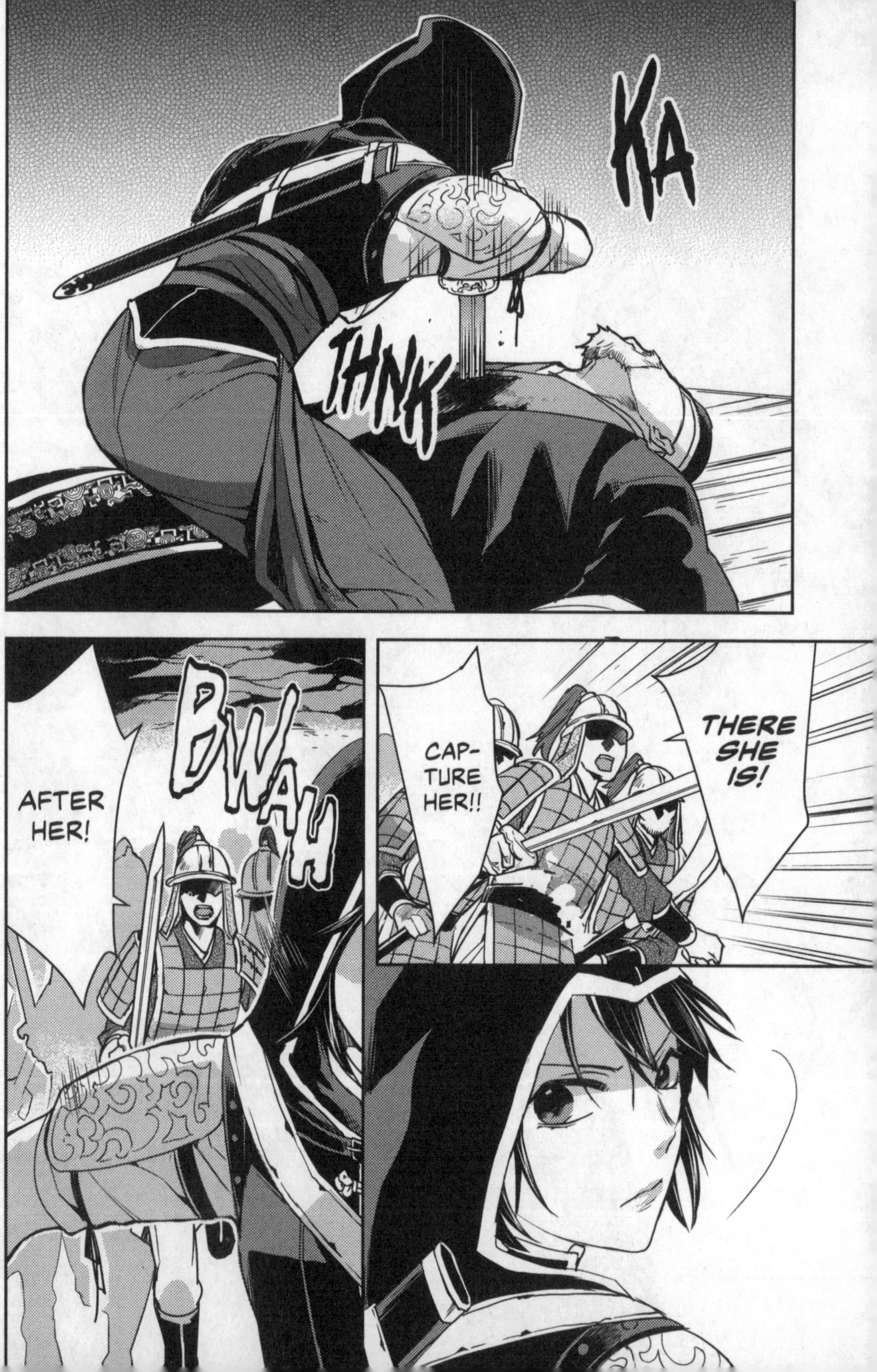
KA
THNK
THERE SHE IS!
CAP-TURE HER!!
BWAH
AFTER HER!

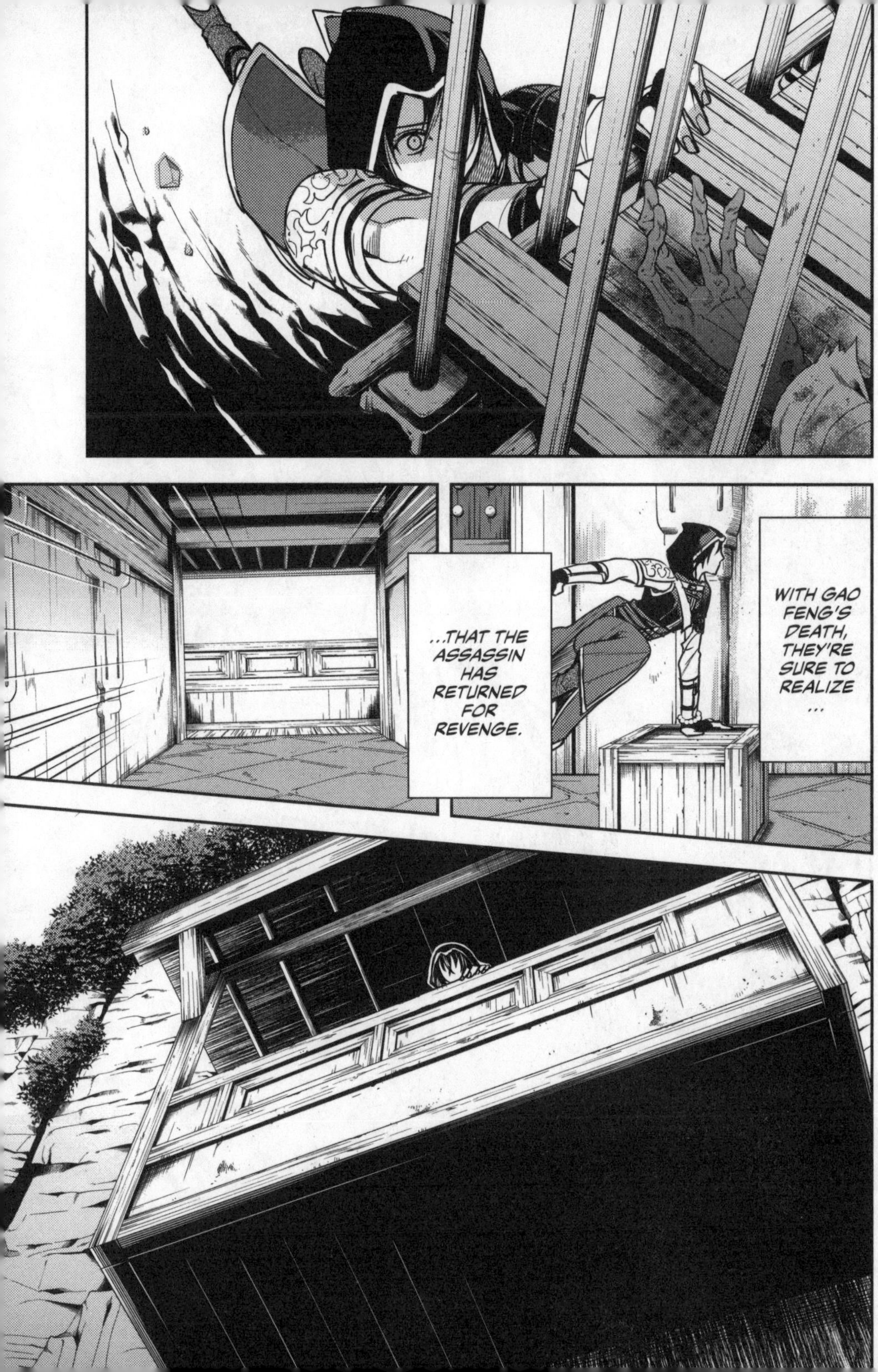
WITH GAO FENG'S DEATH, THEY'RE SURE TO REALIZE ...
...THAT THE ASSASSIN HAS RETURNED FOR REVENGE.

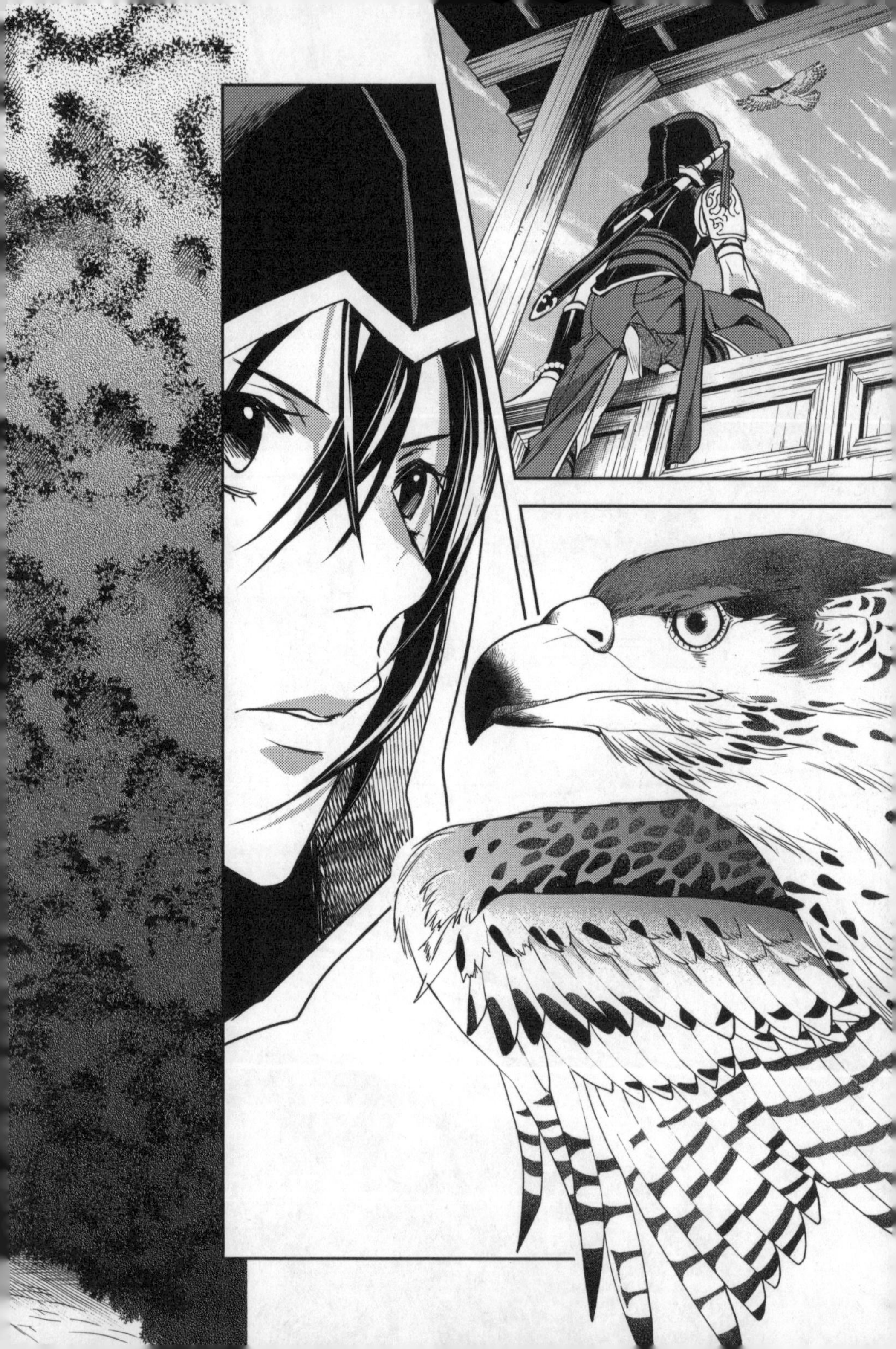

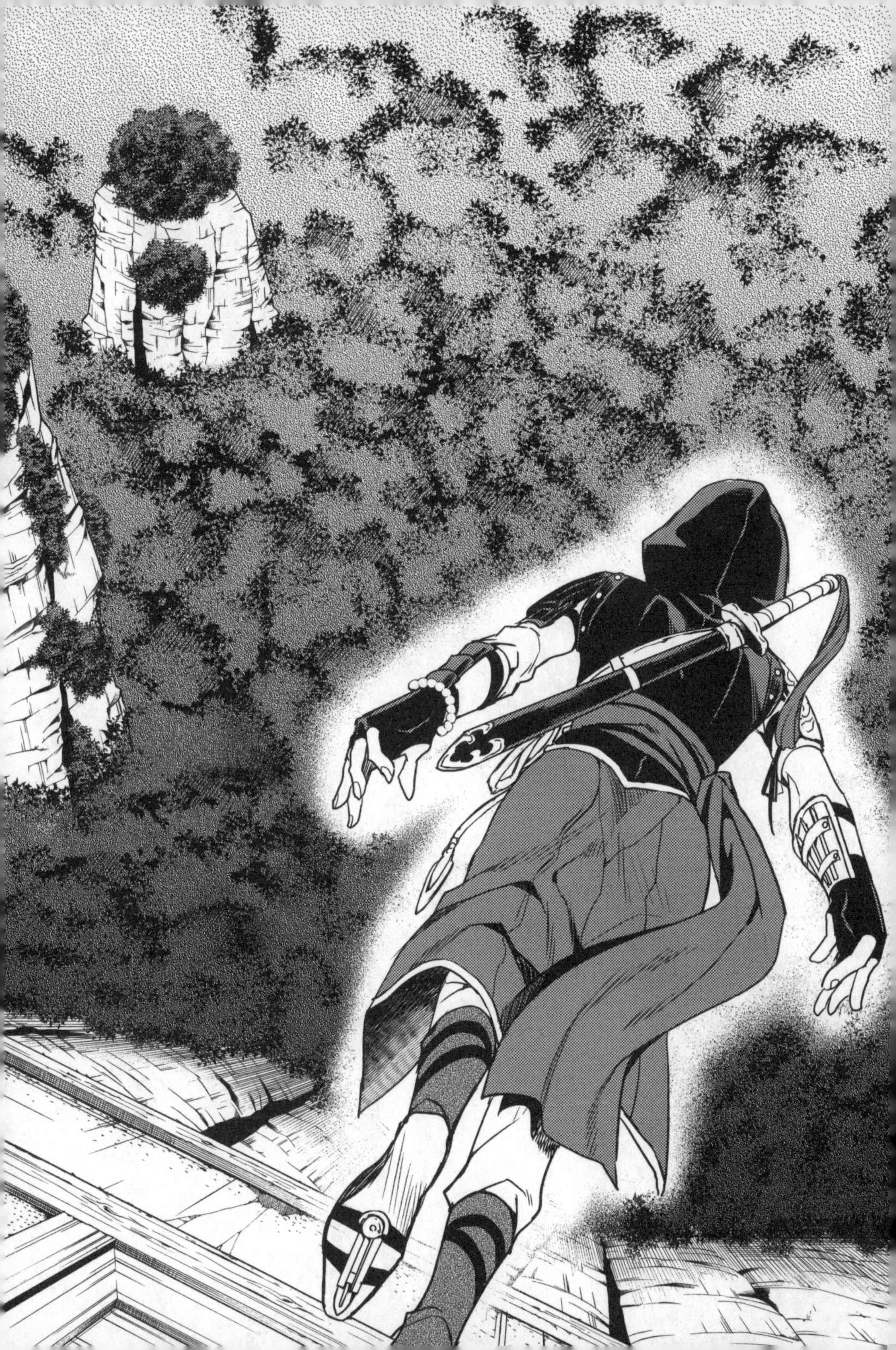

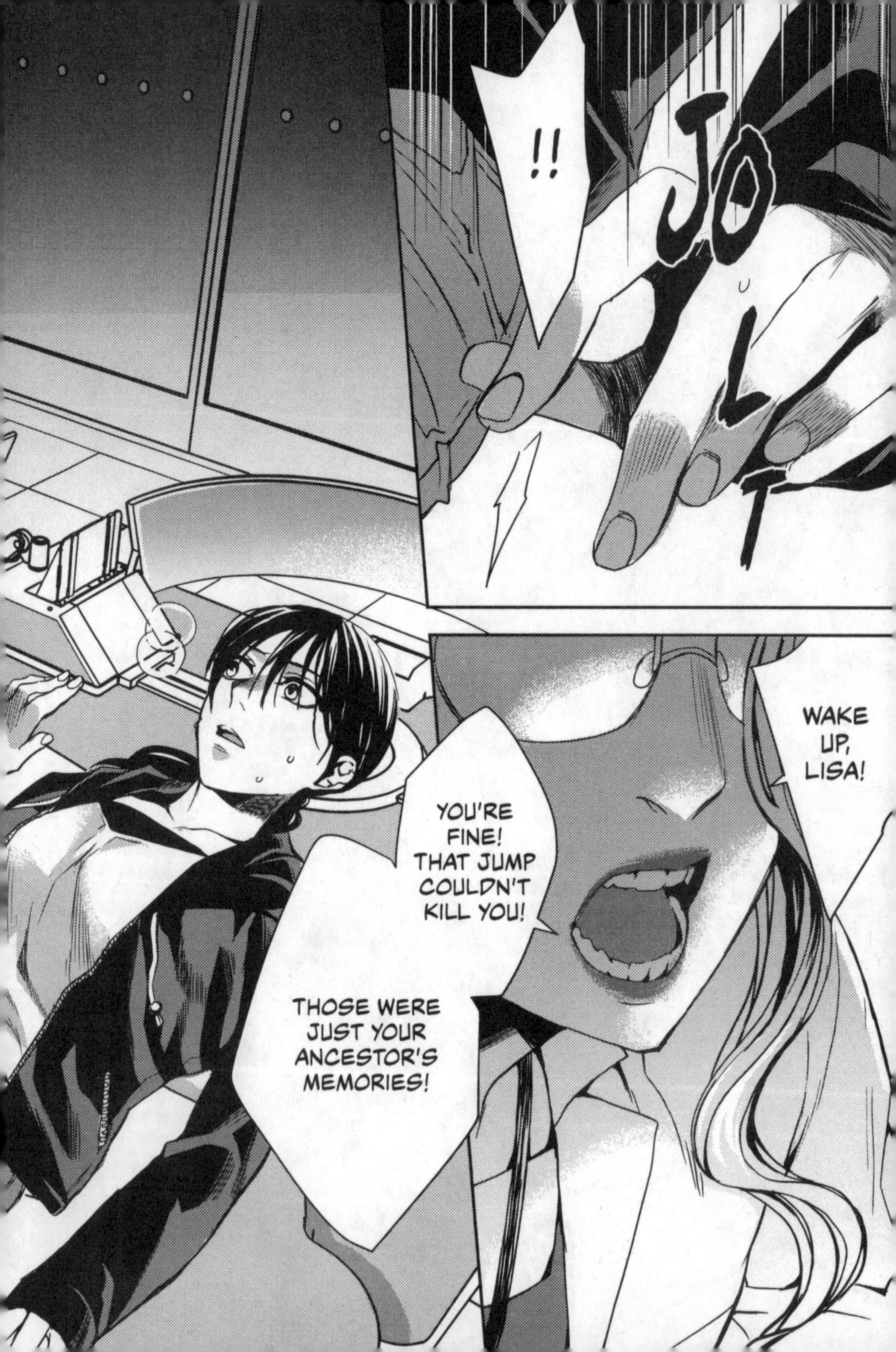
JOLT
!!
WAKE UP, LISA!
YOU'RE FINE! THAT JUMP COULDN'T KILL YOU!
THOSE WERE JUST YOUR ANCESTOR'S MEMORIES!

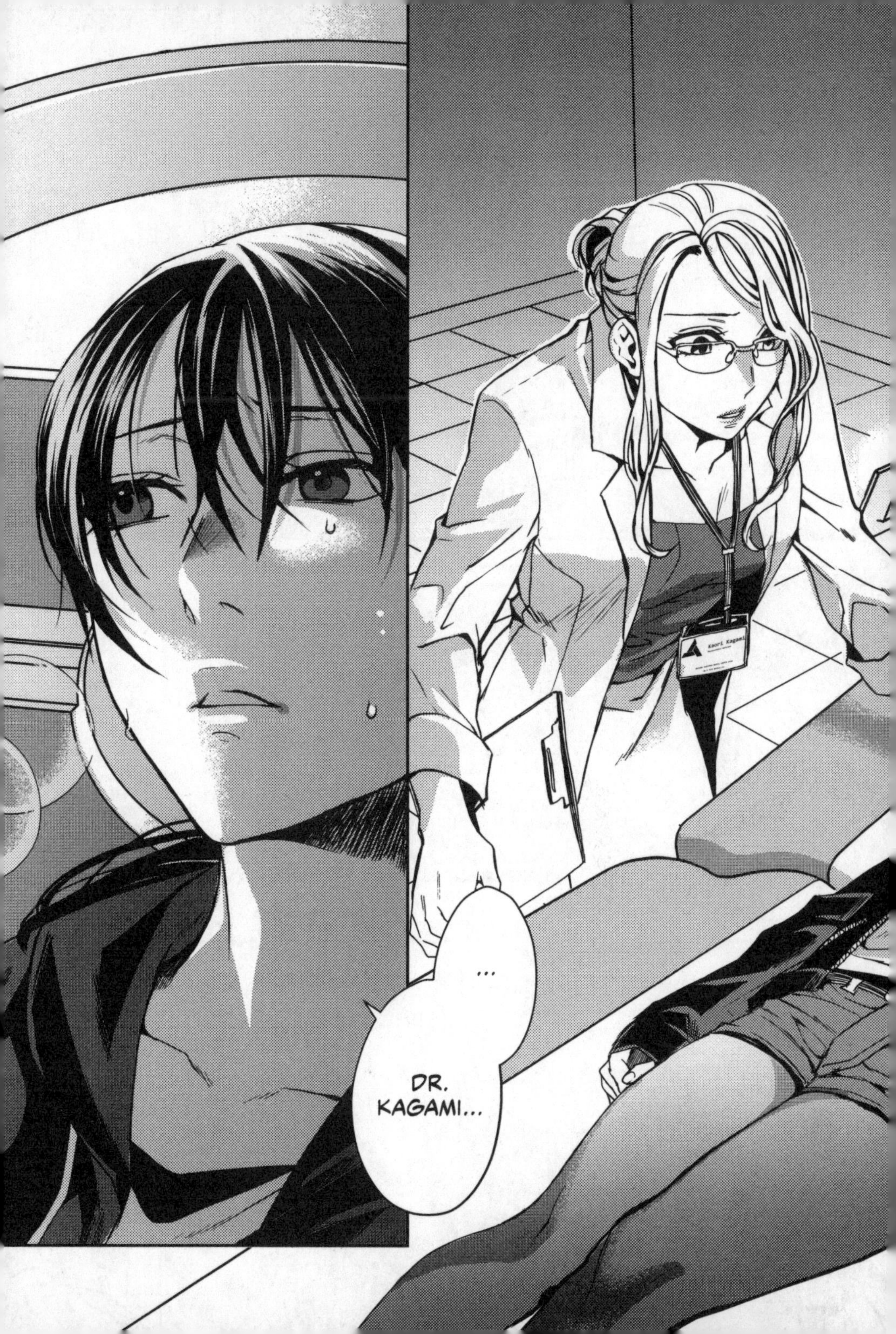
Kaori Kagami
...
DR. KAGAMI...

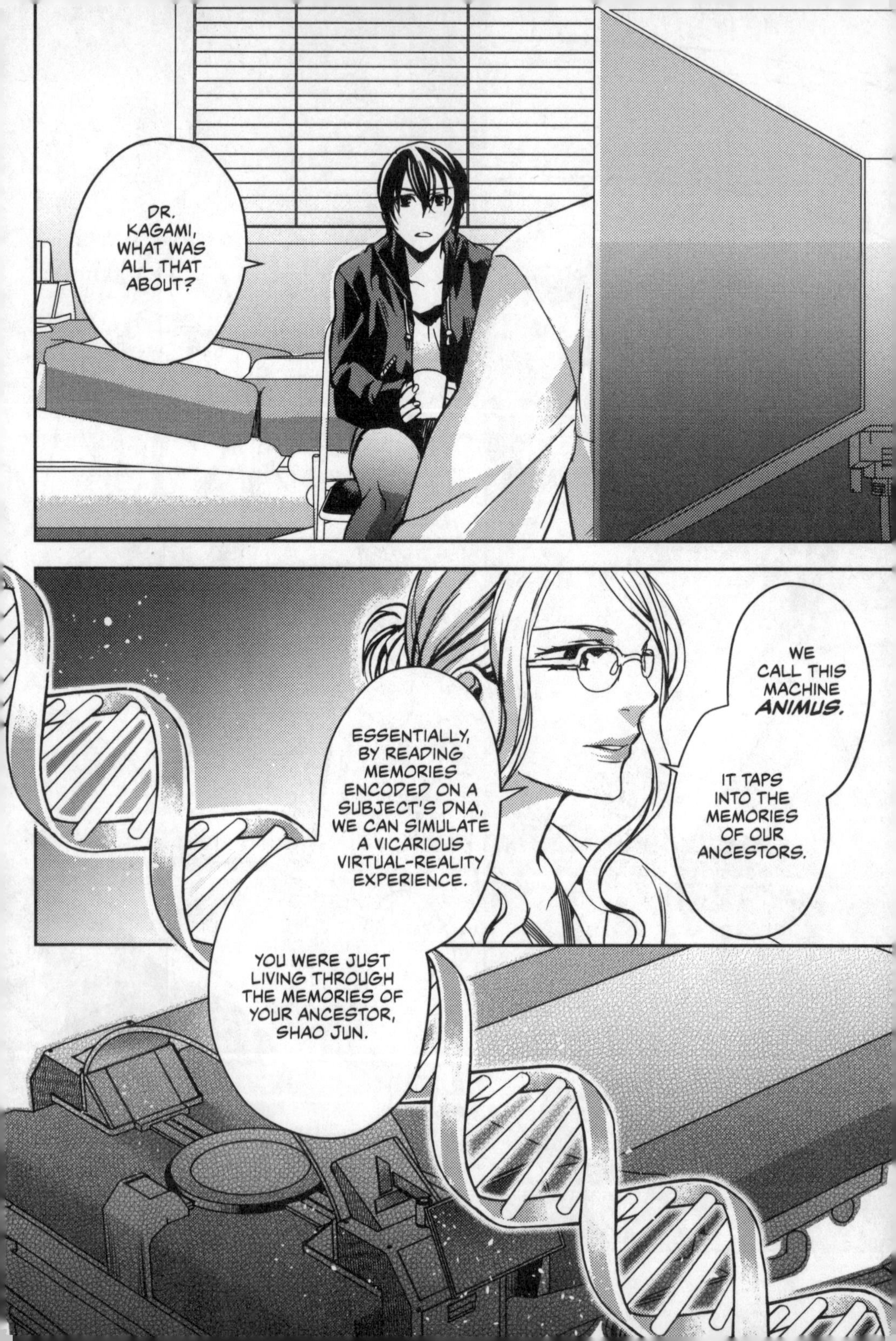
DR. KAGAMI, WHAT WAS ALL THAT ABOUT?
WE CALL THIS MACHINE ***ANIMUS.***
IT TAPS INTO THE MEMORIES OF OUR ANCESTORS.
ESSENTIALLY, BY READING MEMORIES ENCODED ON A SUBJECT'S DNA, WE CAN SIMULATE A VICARIOUS VIRTUAL-REALITY EXPERIENCE.
YOU WERE JUST LIVING THROUGH THE MEMORIES OF YOUR ANCESTOR, SHAO JUN.

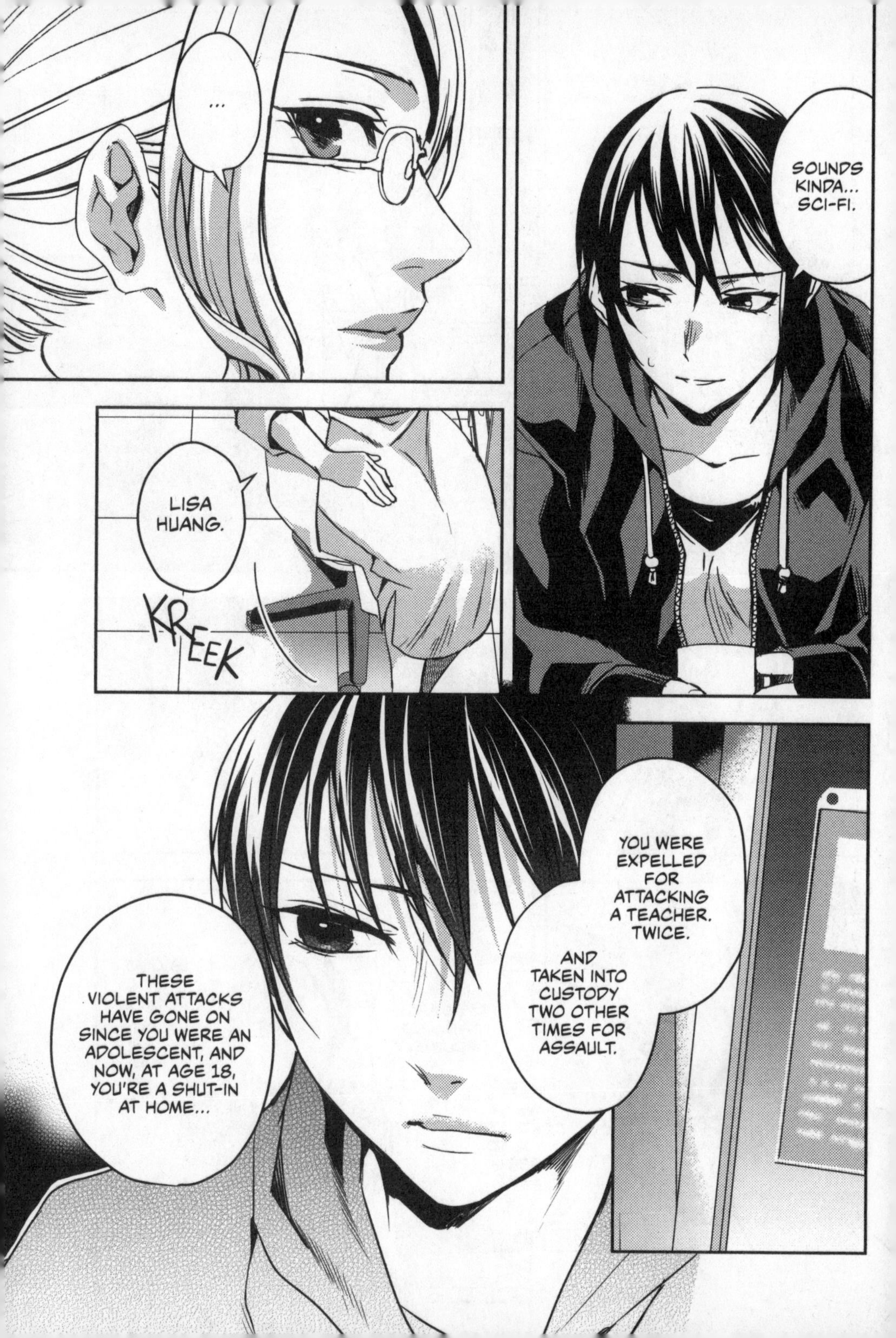
SOUNDS KINDA... SCI-FI.
...
LISA HUANG.
KREEK
YOU WERE EXPELLED FOR ATTACKING A TEACHER. TWICE.
AND TAKEN INTO CUSTODY TWO OTHER TIMES FOR ASSAULT.
THESE VIOLENT ATTACKS HAVE GONE ON SINCE YOU WERE AN ADOLESCENT, AND NOW, AT AGE 18, YOU'RE A SHUT-IN AT HOME...

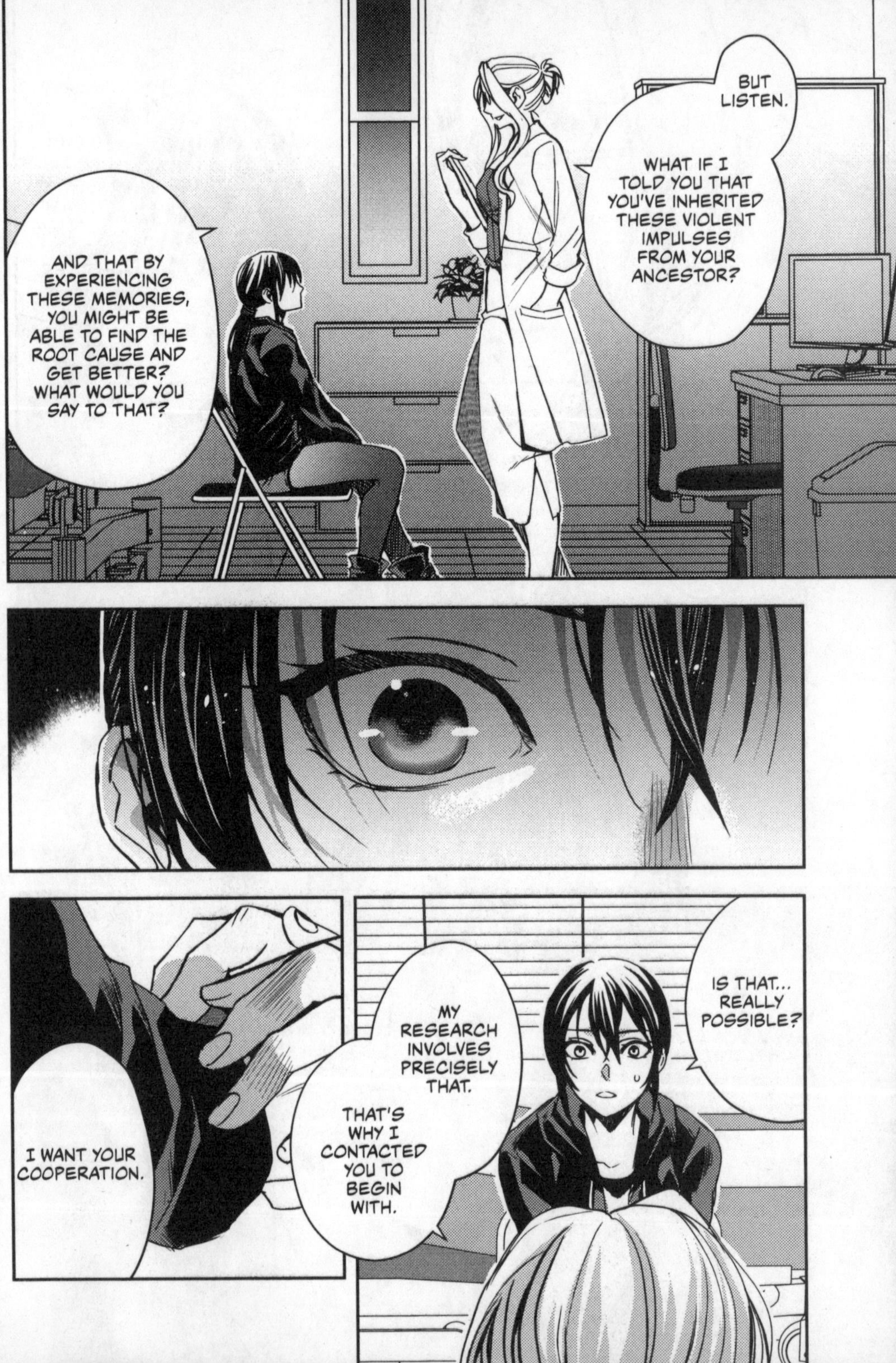
BUT LISTEN.
WHAT IF I TOLD YOU THAT YOU'VE INHERITED THESE VIOLENT IMPULSES FROM YOUR ANCESTOR?
AND THAT BY EXPERIENCING THESE MEMORIES, YOU MIGHT BE ABLE TO FIND THE ROOT CAUSE AND GET BETTER? WHAT WOULD YOU SAY TO THAT?
IS THAT... REALLY POSSIBLE?
MY RESEARCH INVOLVES PRECISELY THAT.
THAT'S WHY I CONTACTED YOU TO BEGIN WITH.
I WANT YOUR COOPERATION.

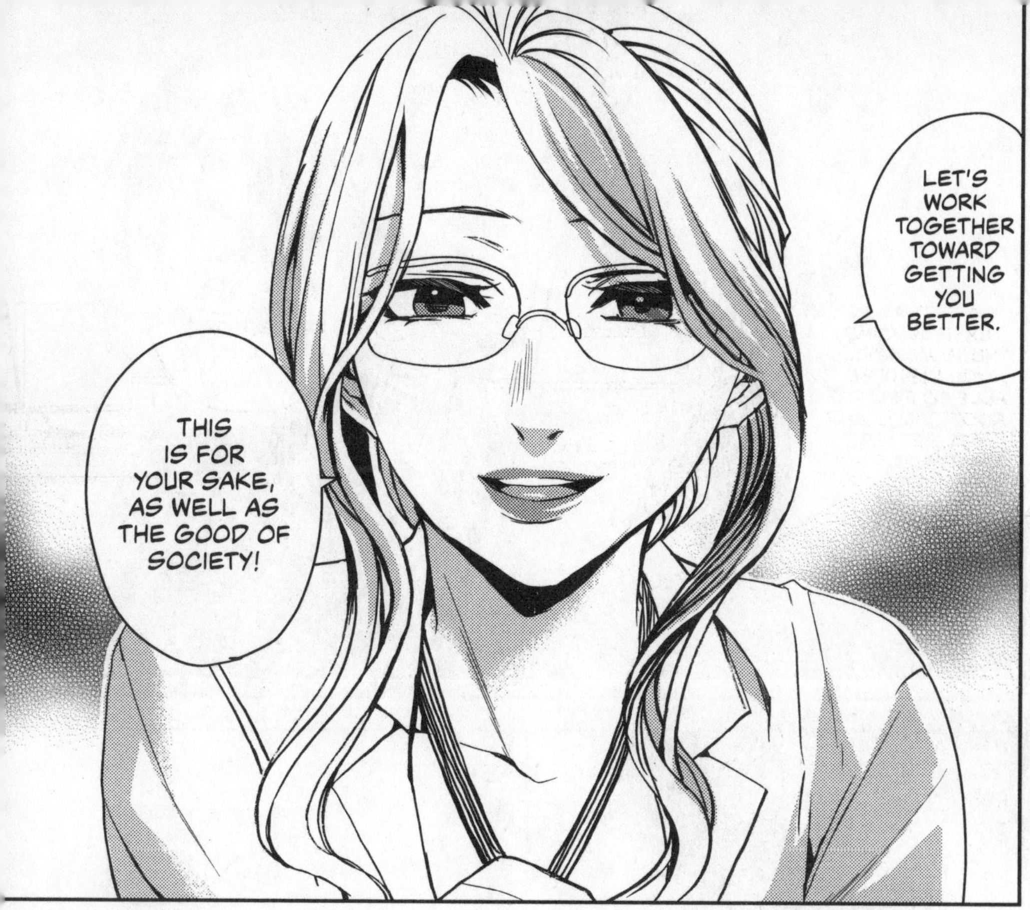
LET'S WORK TOGETHER TOWARD GETTING YOU BETTER.
THIS IS FOR YOUR SAKE, AS WELL AS THE GOOD OF SOCIETY!
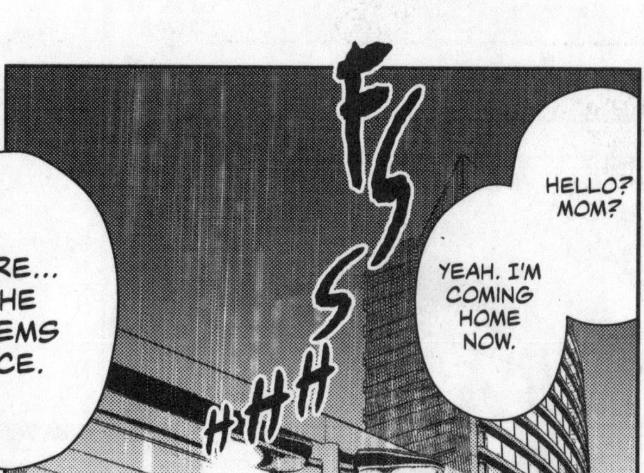
FSSHHH
HELLO? MOM?
YEAH. I'M COMING HOME NOW.
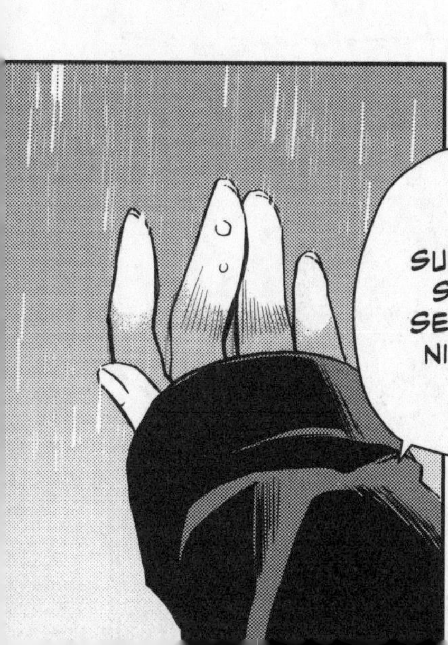
SURE... SHE SEEMS NICE.

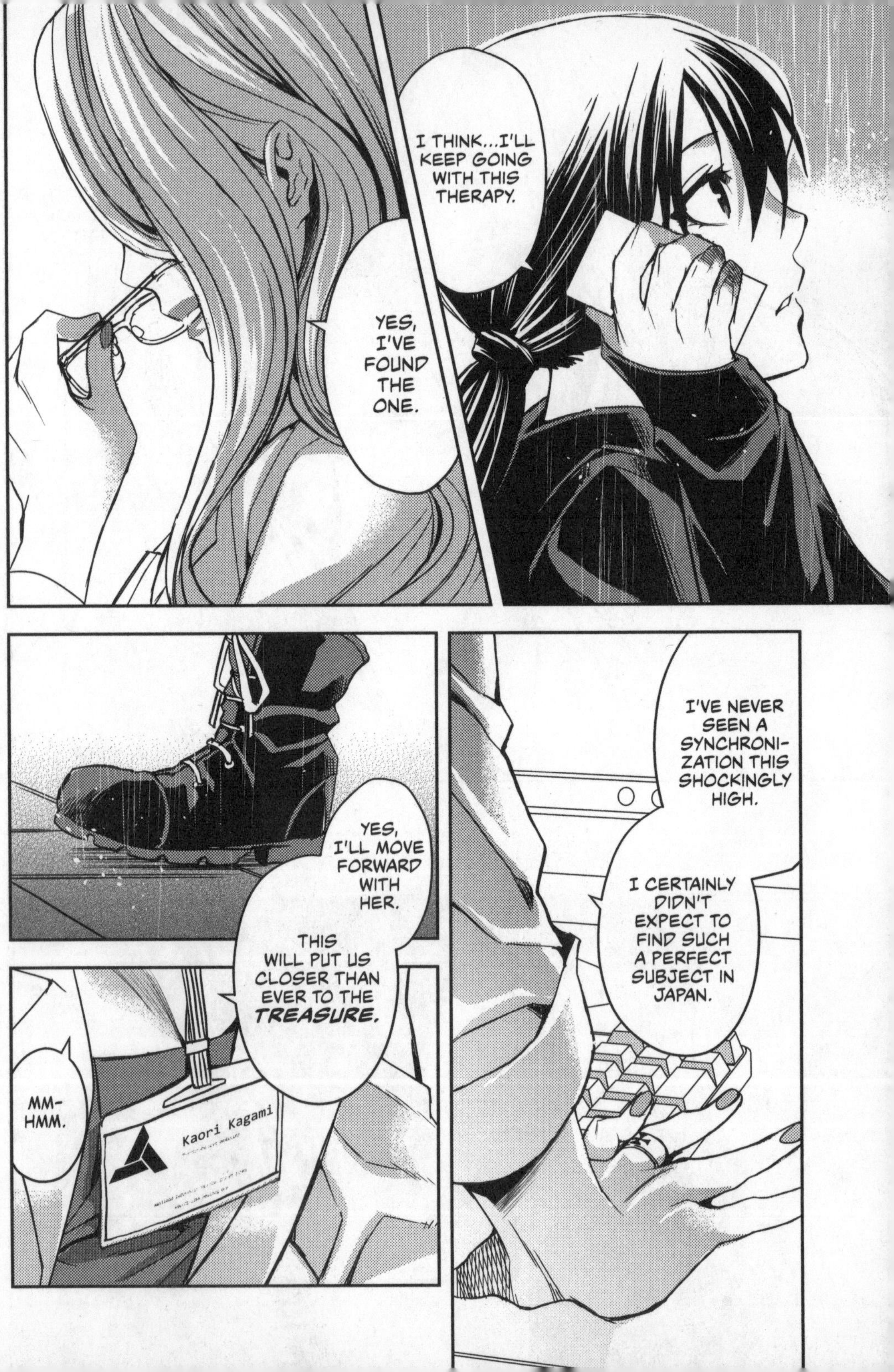
I THINK...I'LL KEEP GOING WITH THIS THERAPY.
YES, I'VE FOUND THE ONE.
I'VE NEVER SEEN A SYNCHRONIZATION THIS SHOCKINGLY HIGH.
I CERTAINLY DIDN'T EXPECT TO FIND SUCH A PERFECT SUBJECT IN JAPAN.
YES, I'LL MOVE FORWARD WITH HER.
THIS WILL PUT US CLOSER THAN EVER TO THE *TREASURE.*
MM-HMM.
Kaori Kagami

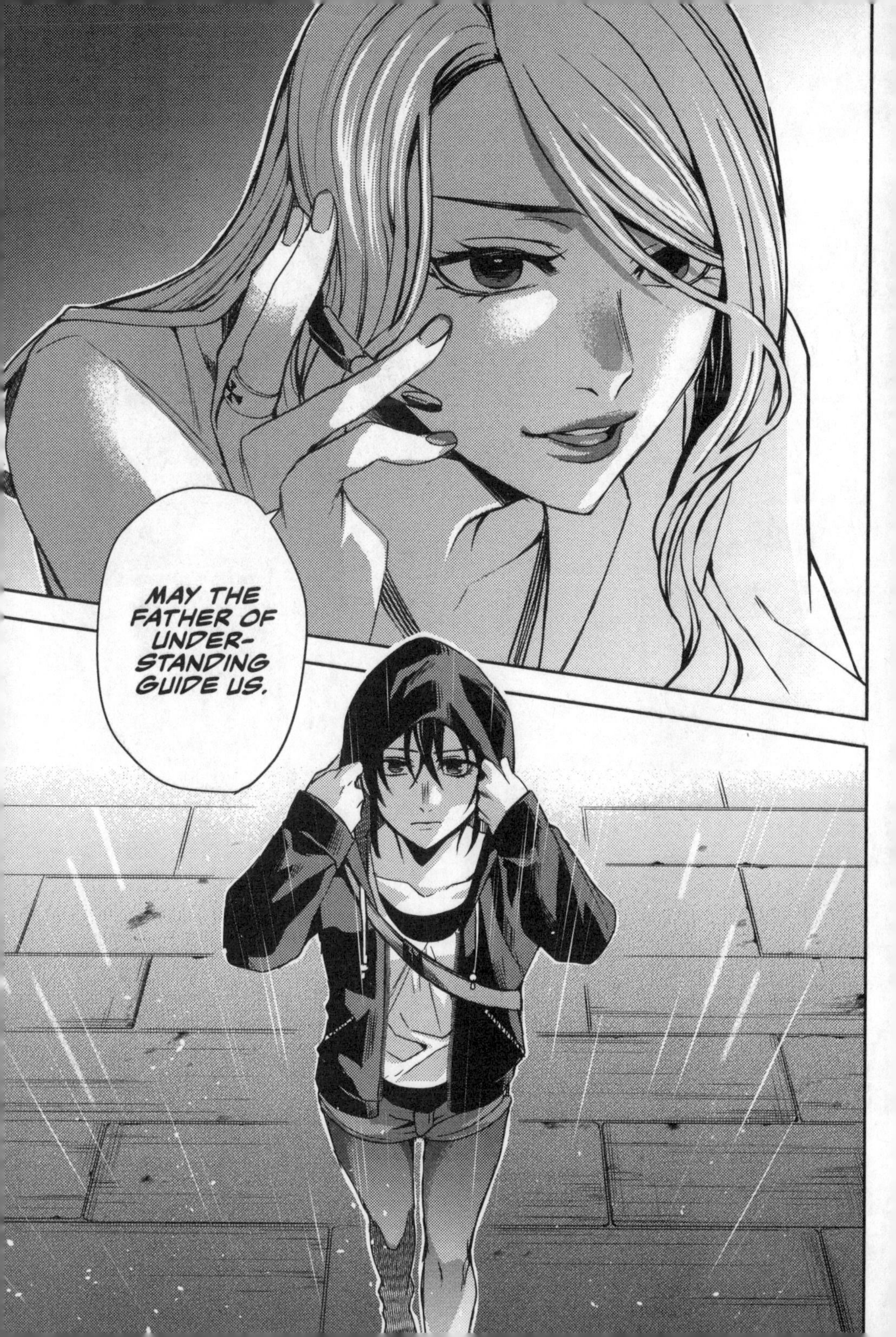
MAY THE FATHER OF UNDER-STANDING GUIDE US.

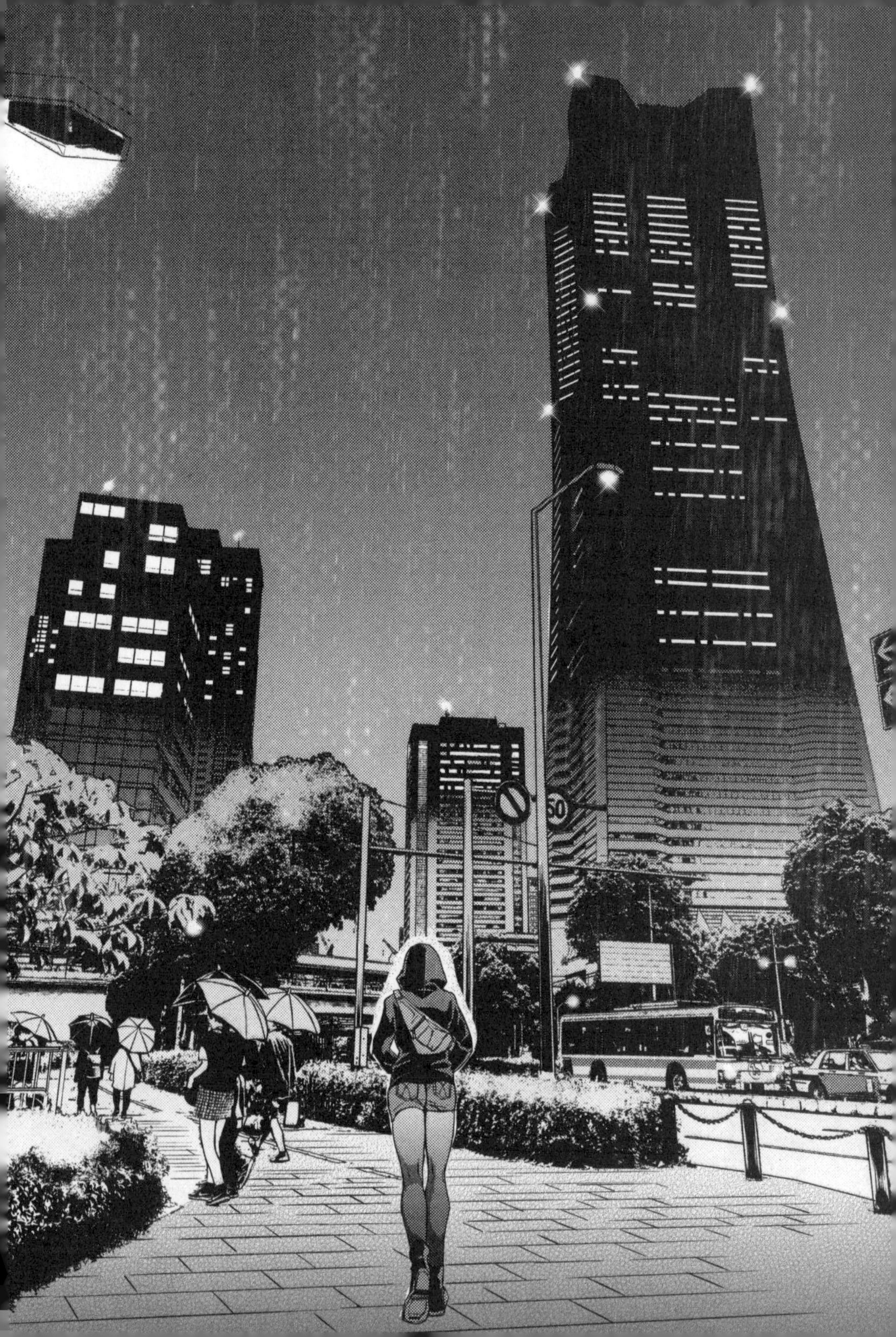
50

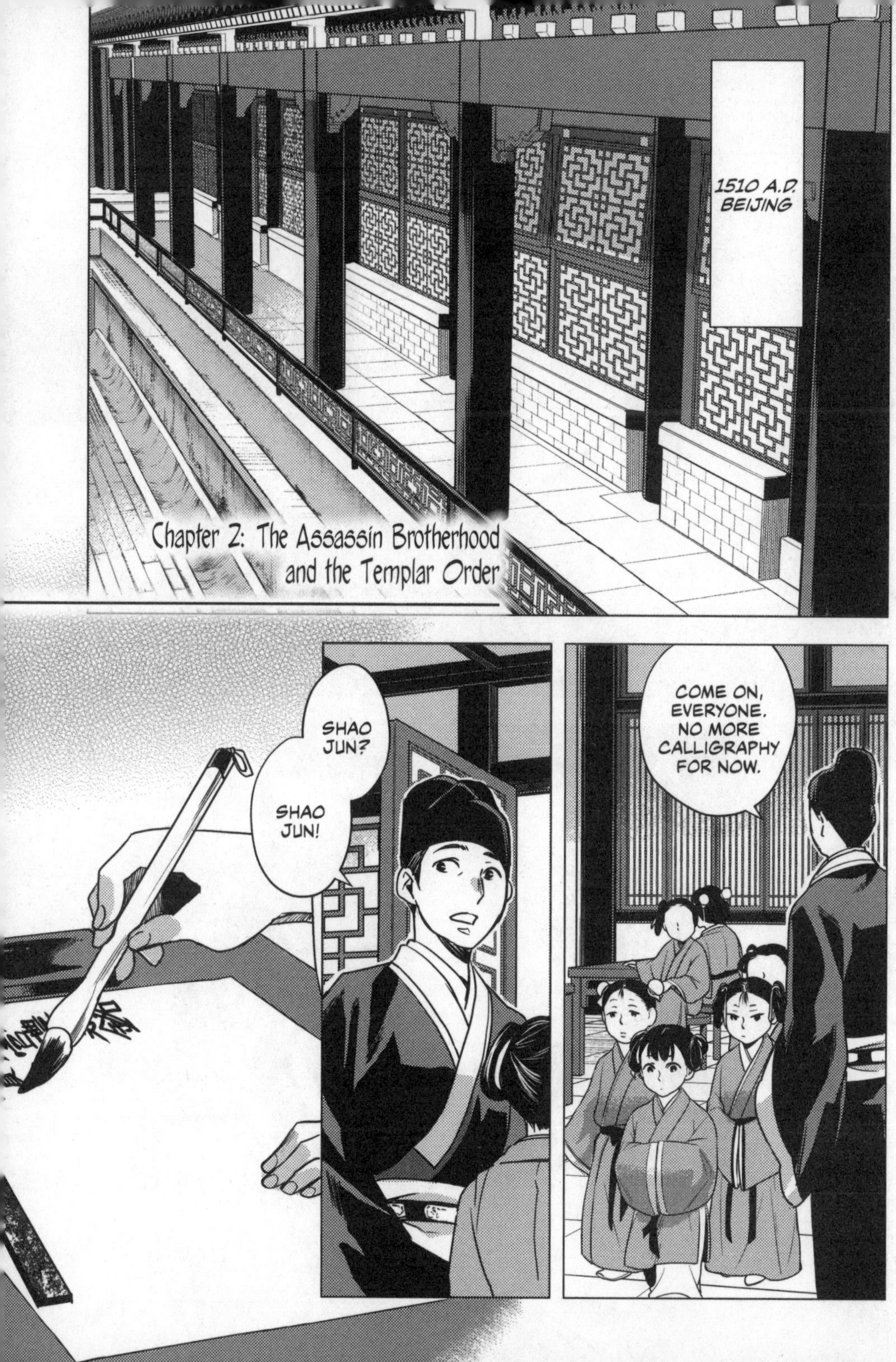
1510 A.D.
BEIJING
Chapter 2: The Assassin Brotherhood and the Templar Order
COME ON, EVERYONE. NO MORE CALLIGRAPHY FOR NOW.
SHAO JUN?
SHAO JUN!

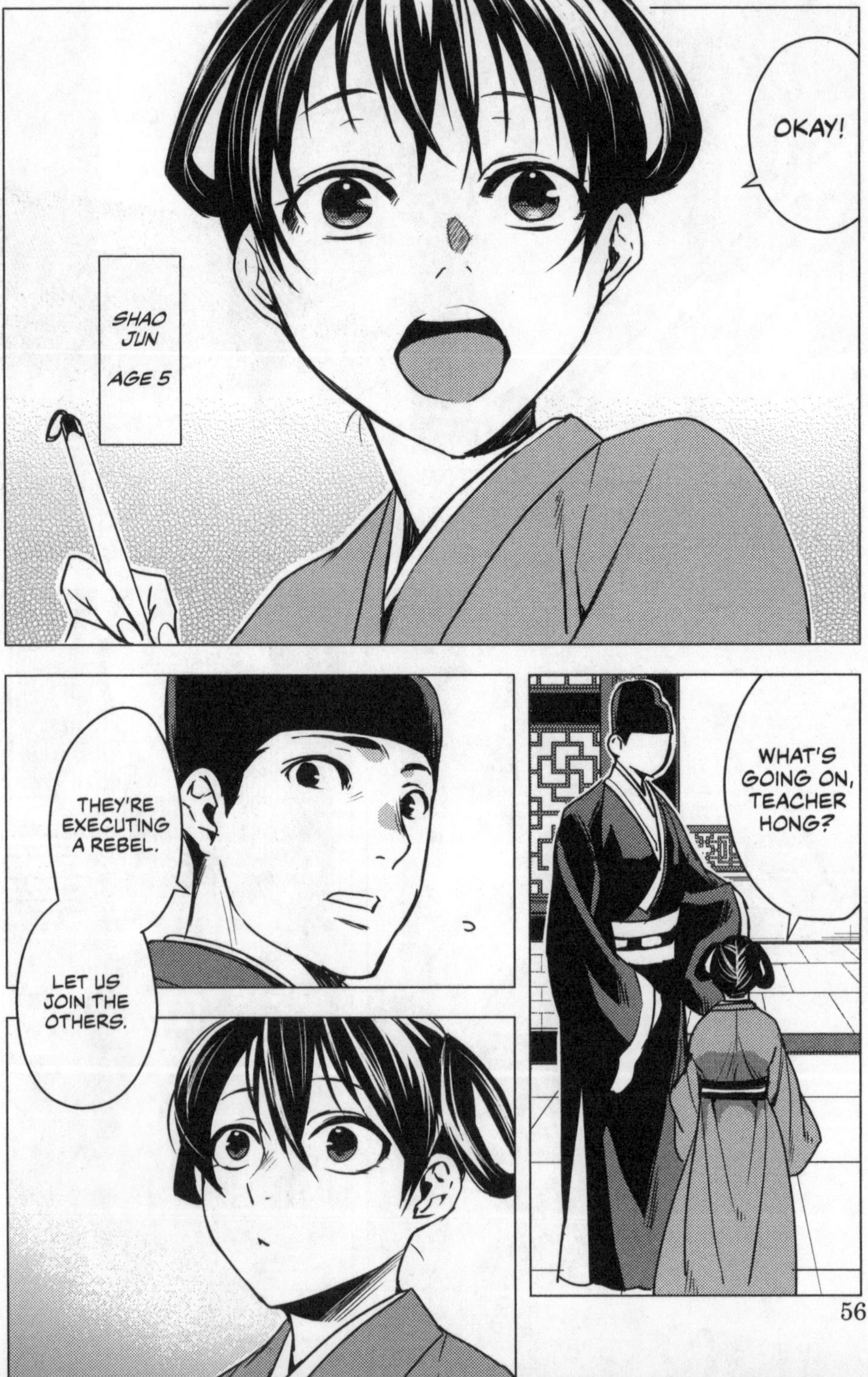
OKAY!
SHAO JUN
AGE 5
WHAT'S GOING ON, TEACHER HONG?
THEY'RE EXECUTING A REBEL.
LET US JOIN THE OTHERS.

Chapter 2: The Assassin Brotherhood and the Templar Order

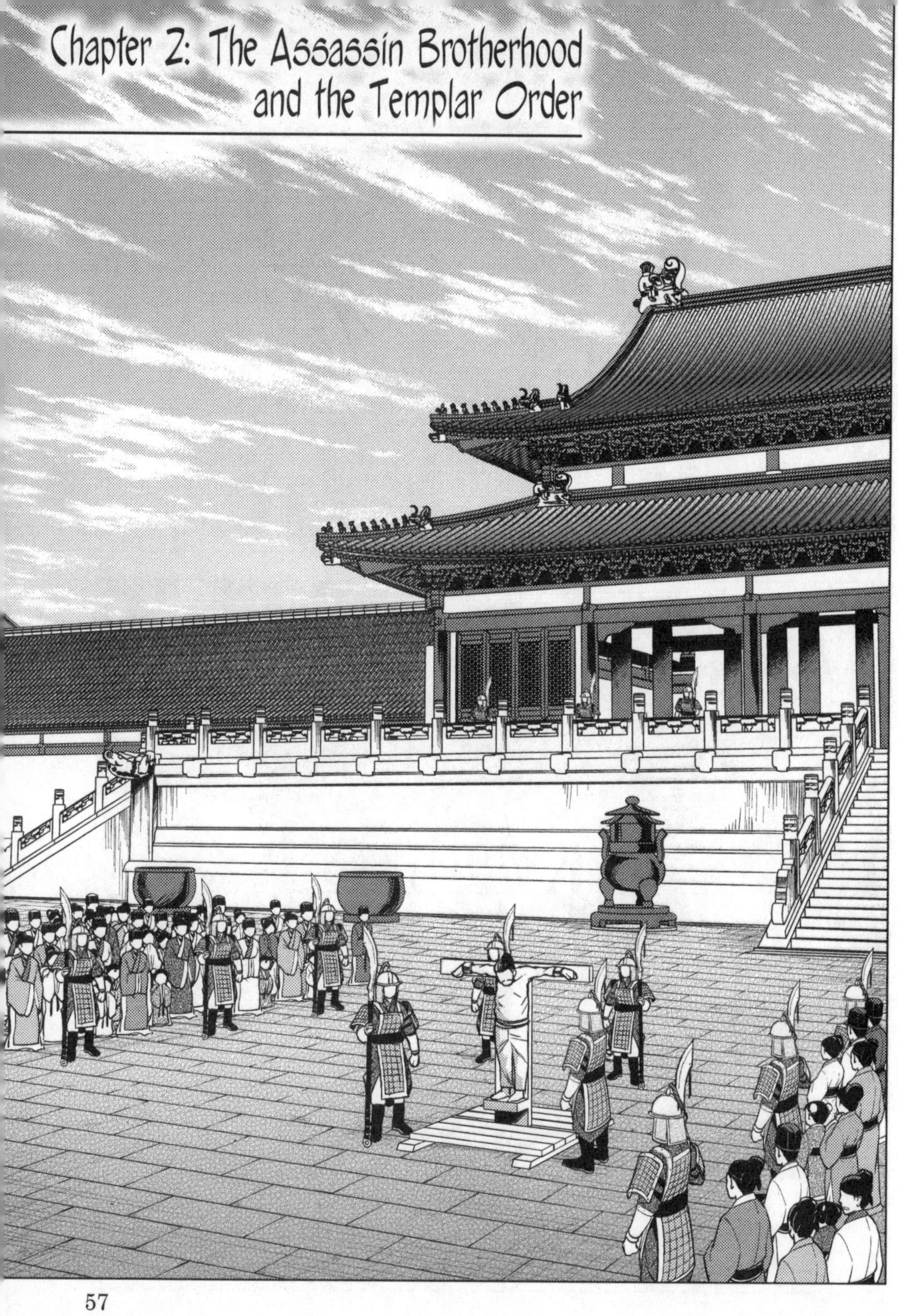

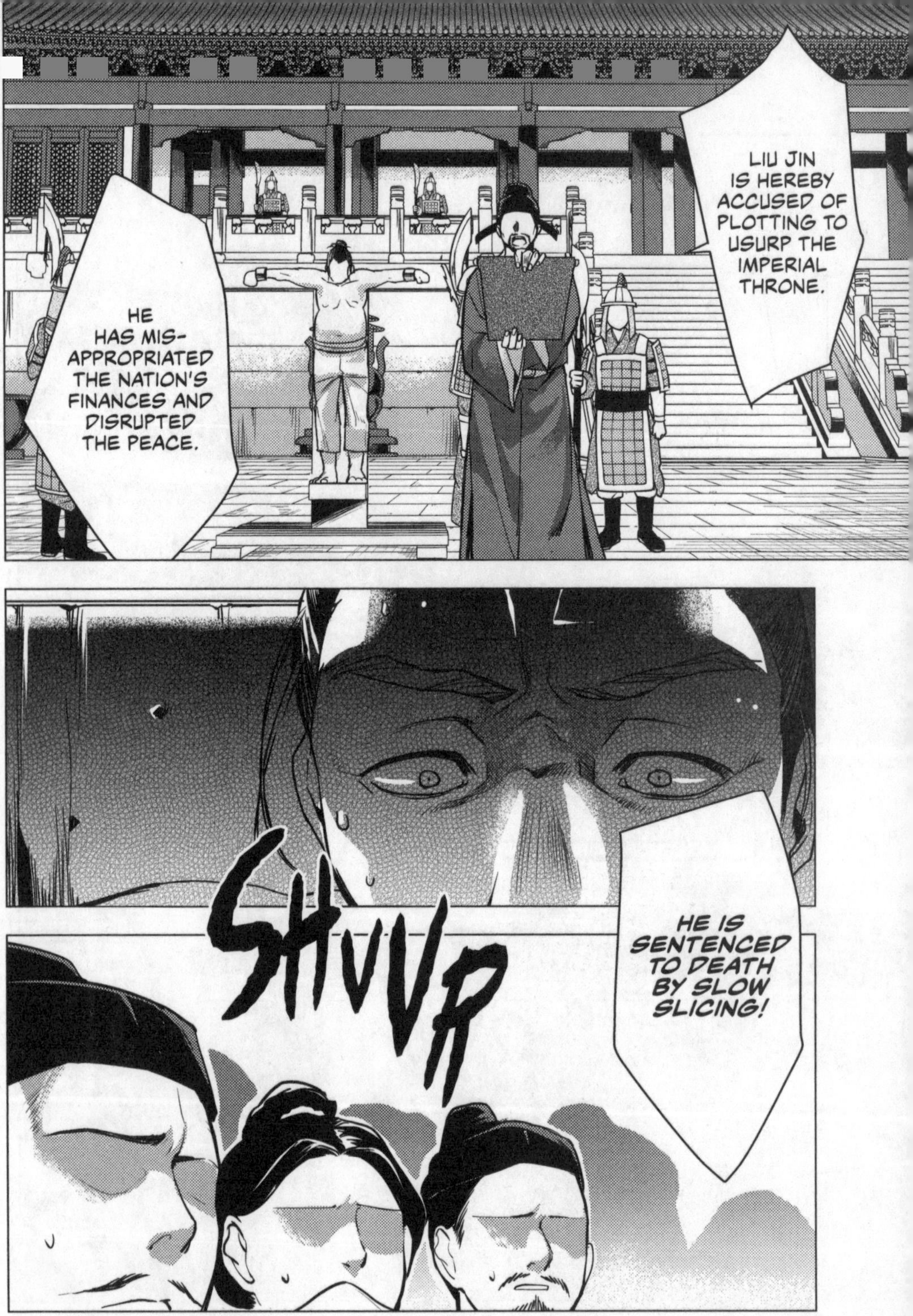
LIU JIN IS HEREBY ACCUSED OF PLOTTING TO USURP THE IMPERIAL THRONE.
HE HAS MIS-APPROPRIATED THE NATION'S FINANCES AND DISRUPTED THE PEACE.
HE IS SENTENCED TO DEATH BY SLOW SLICING!
SHVVR

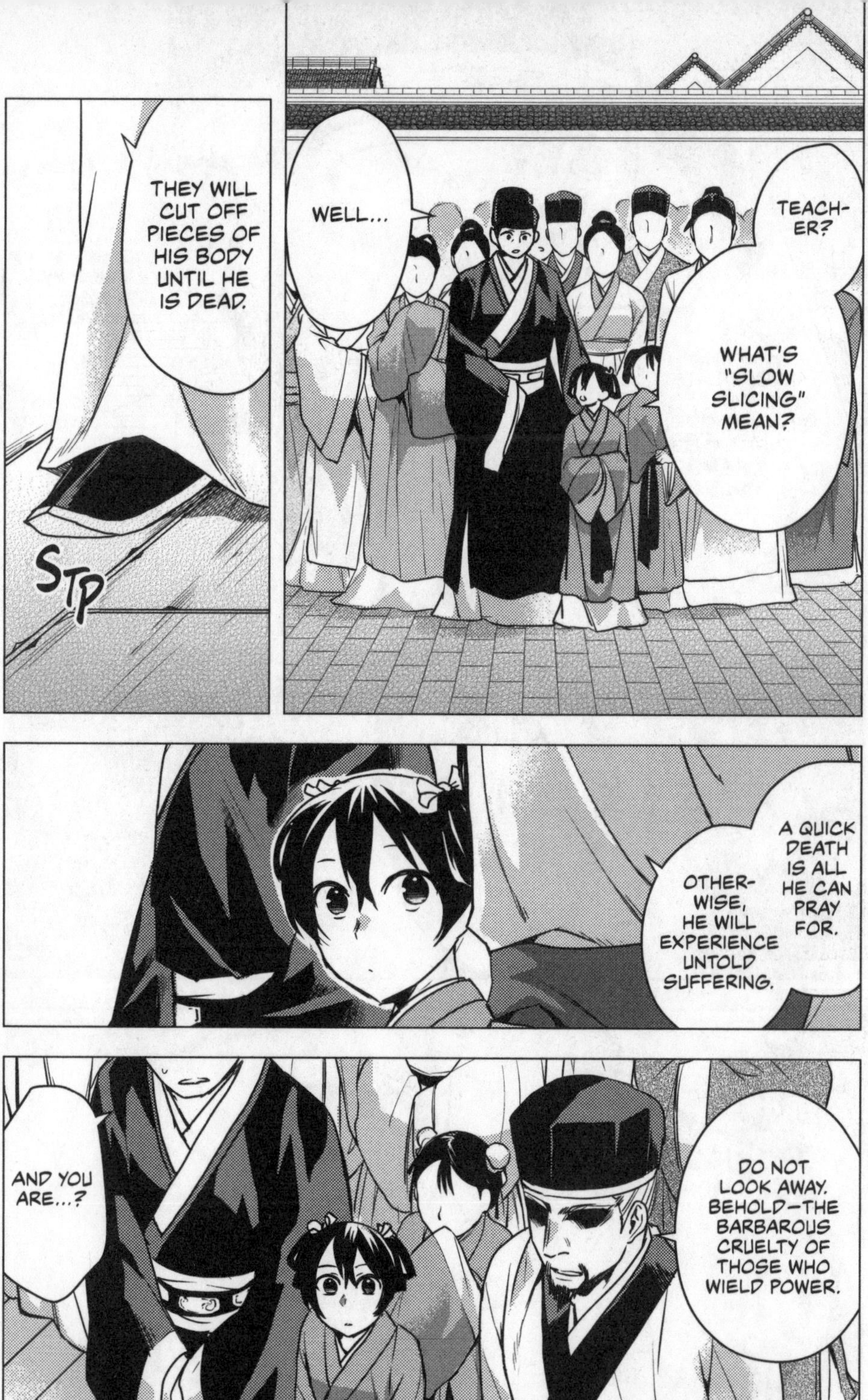
TEACHER? WHAT'S "SLOW SLICING" MEAN?
WELL...
THEY WILL CUT OFF PIECES OF HIS BODY UNTIL HE IS DEAD.
STP
A QUICK DEATH IS ALL HE CAN PRAY FOR.
OTHERWISE, HE WILL EXPERIENCE UNTOLD SUFFERING.
DO NOT LOOK AWAY. BEHOLD—THE BARBAROUS CRUELTY OF THOSE WHO WIELD POWER.
AND YOU ARE...?

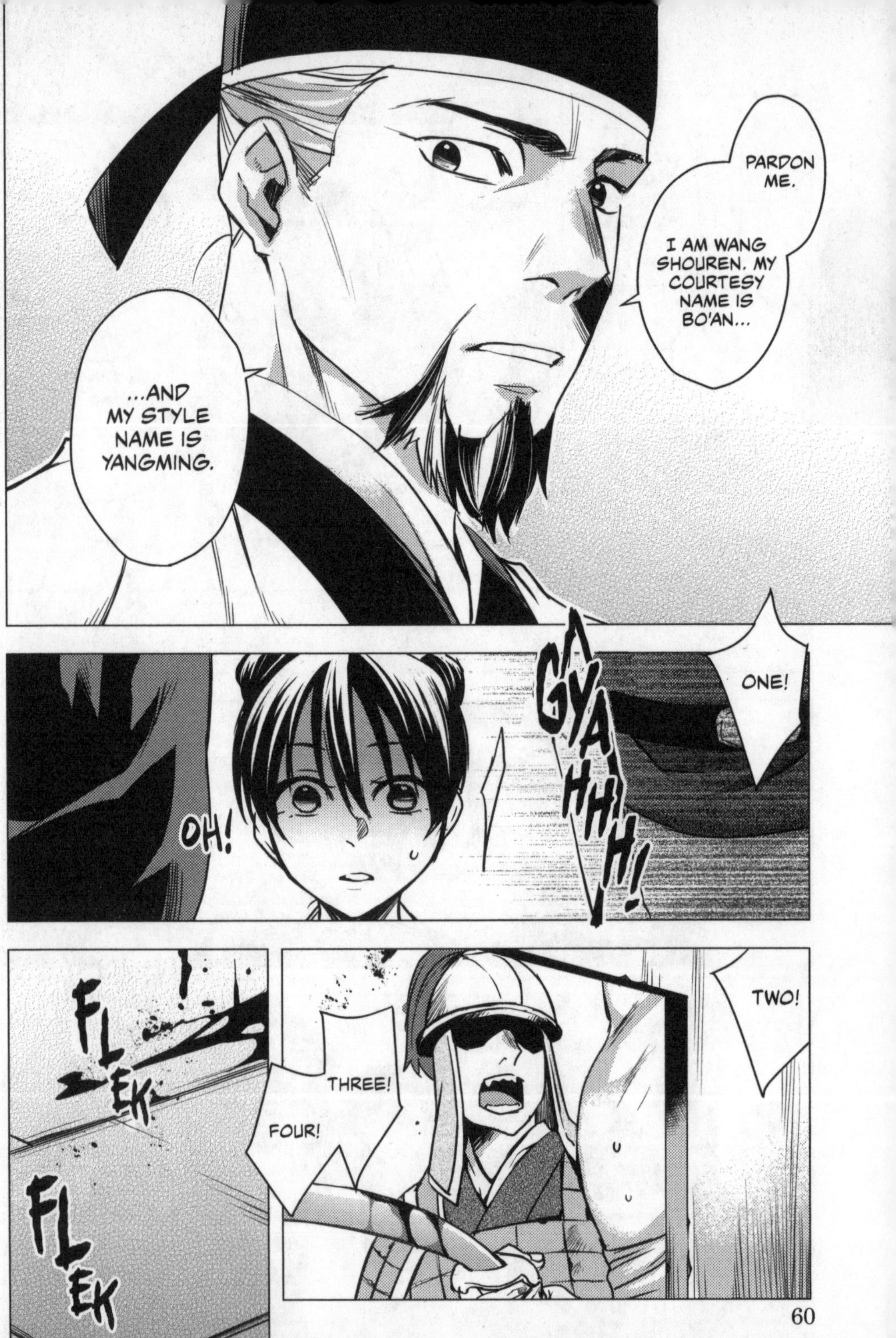
PARDON ME.
I AM WANG SHOUREN. MY COURTESY NAME IS BO'AN...
...AND MY STYLE NAME IS YANGMING.
ONE!
GYAAHHH!!
OH!
TWO!
THREE!
FOUR!
FLEK
FLEK

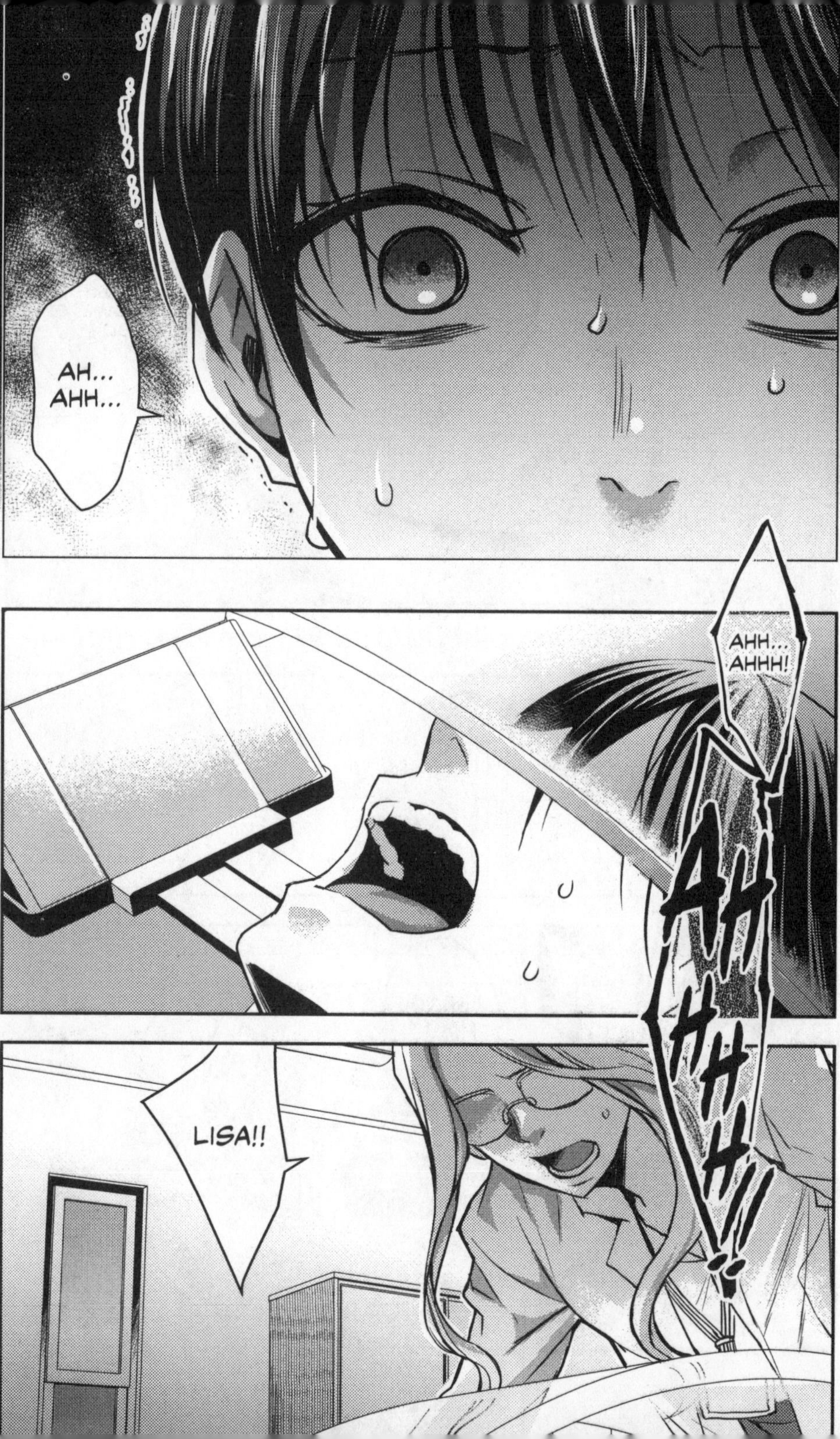
AH... AHH...
AHH... AHHH!
AHHHHH!!
LISA!!

RELAX! I'M SHUTTING IT DOWN!

LISA!

UGH!!

GASP

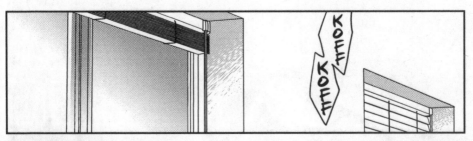

KOFF

KOFF

ARE YOU OKAY?

I'M SORRY— DID IT SUDDENLY TURN INTO SOMETHING DIFFICULT TO WATCH?

I'M... FINE.

HUFF

HUFF

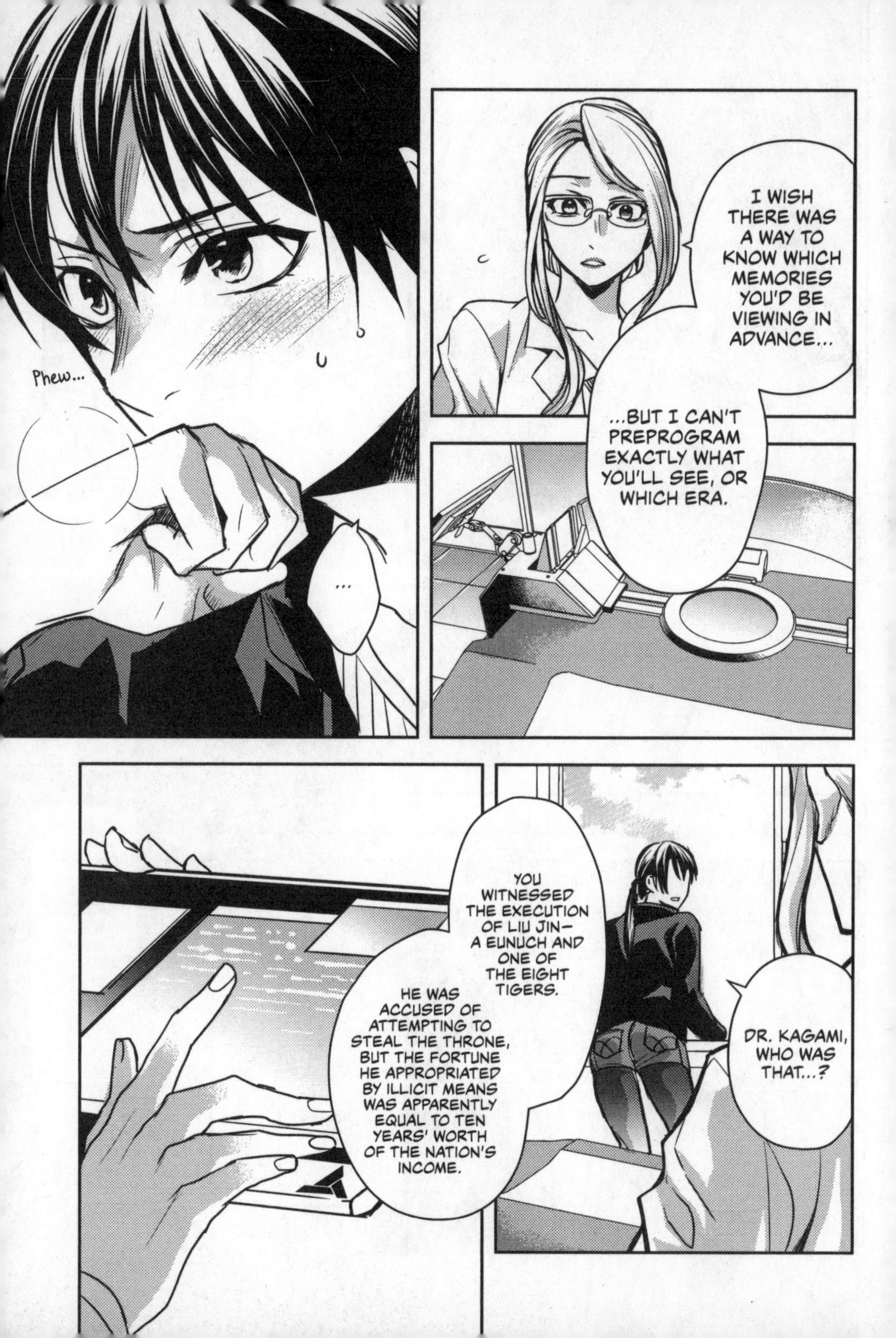
I WISH THERE WAS A WAY TO KNOW WHICH MEMORIES YOU'D BE VIEWING IN ADVANCE...
...BUT I CAN'T PREPROGRAM EXACTLY WHAT YOU'LL SEE, OR WHICH ERA.
Phew...
...
DR. KAGAMI, WHO WAS THAT...?
YOU WITNESSED THE EXECUTION OF LIU JIN—A EUNUCH AND ONE OF THE EIGHT TIGERS.
HE WAS ACCUSED OF ATTEMPTING TO STEAL THE THRONE, BUT THE FORTUNE HE APPROPRIATED BY ILLICIT MEANS WAS APPARENTLY EQUAL TO TEN YEARS' WORTH OF THE NATION'S INCOME.

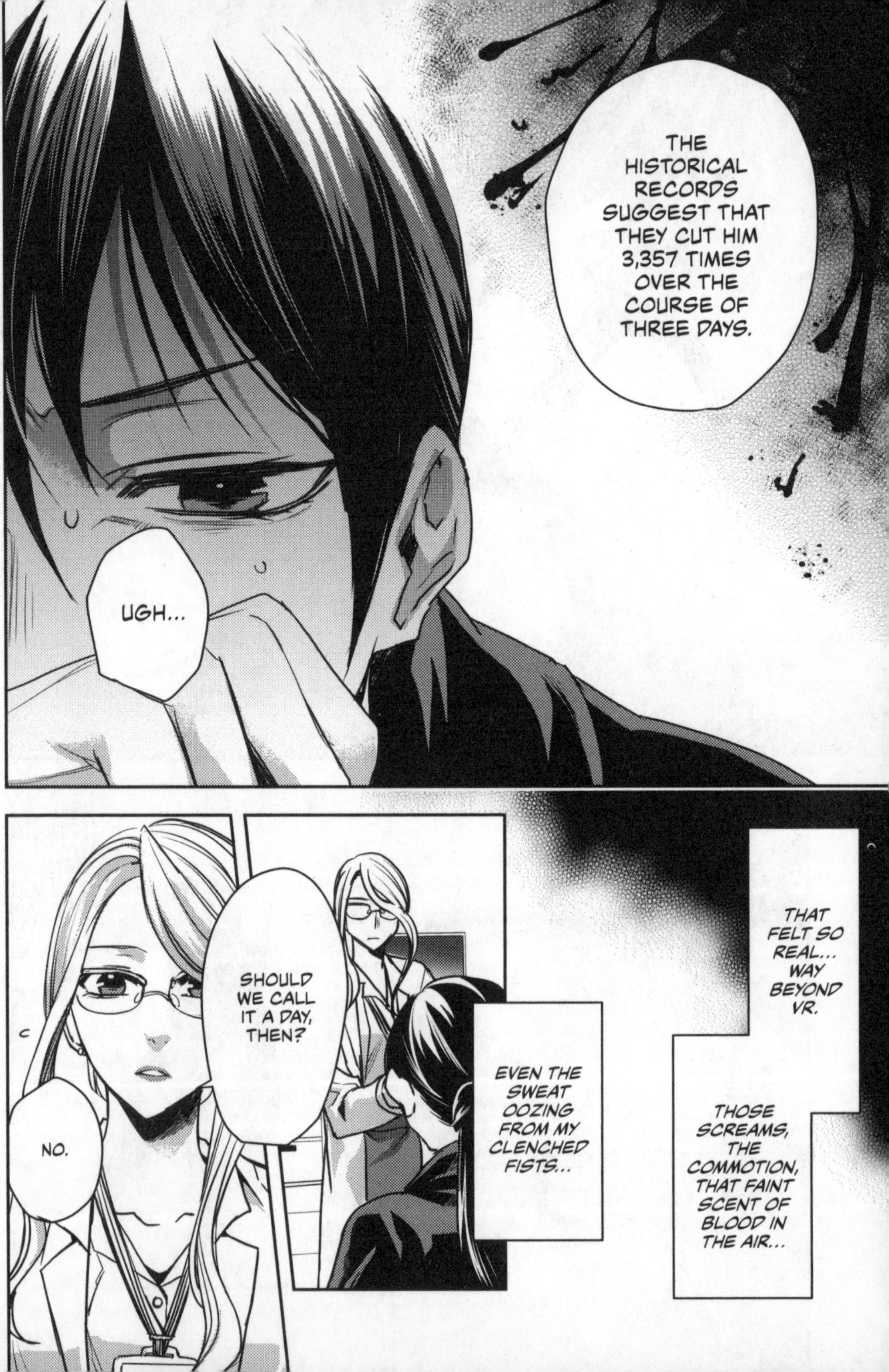
THE HISTORICAL RECORDS SUGGEST THAT THEY CUT HIM 3,357 TIMES OVER THE COURSE OF THREE DAYS.
UGH...
THAT FELT SO REAL... WAY BEYOND VR.
THOSE SCREAMS, THE COMMOTION, THAT FAINT SCENT OF BLOOD IN THE AIR...
EVEN THE SWEAT OOZING FROM MY CLENCHED FISTS...
SHOULD WE CALL IT A DAY, THEN?
NO.

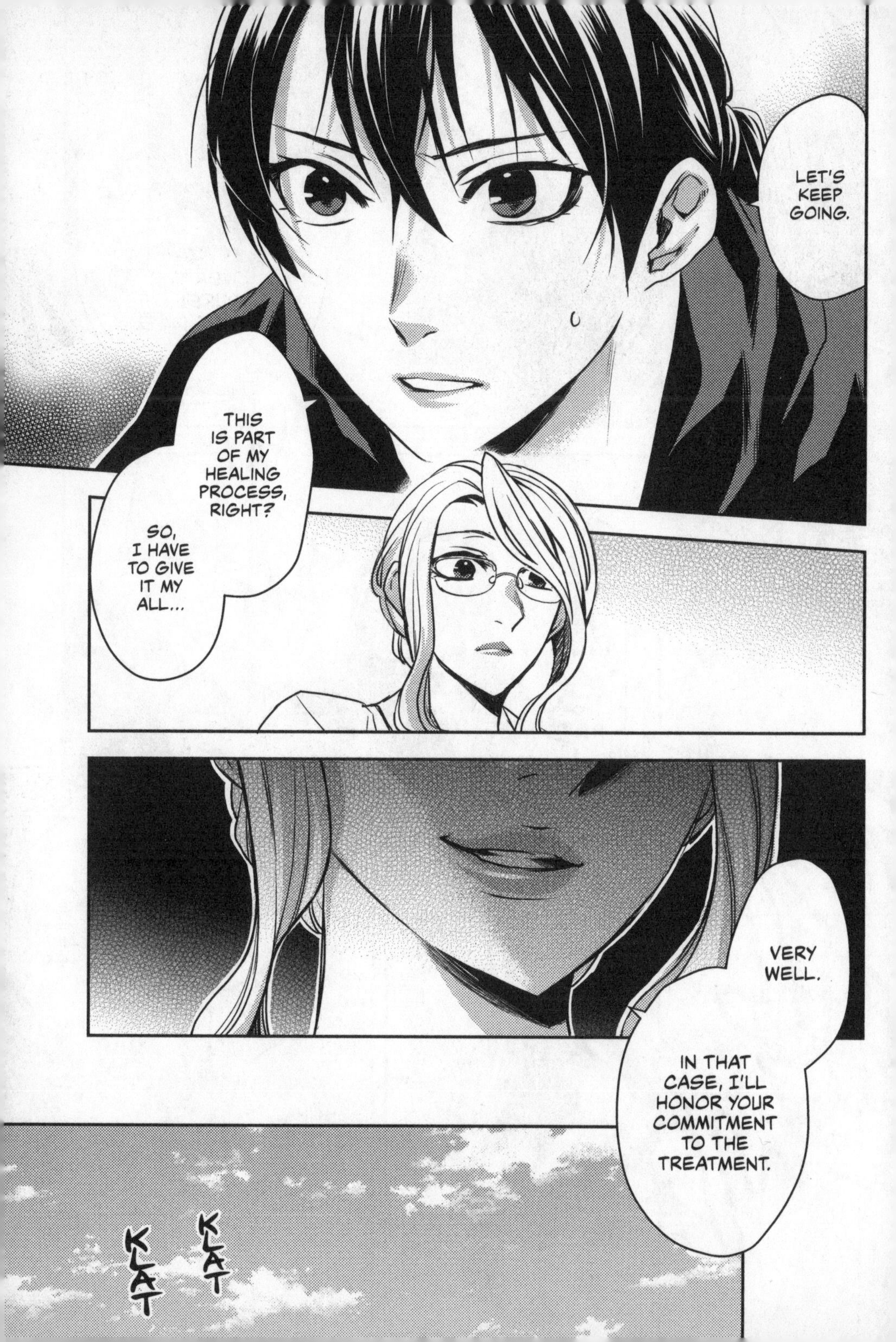
LET'S KEEP GOING.
THIS IS PART OF MY HEALING PROCESS, RIGHT?
SO, I HAVE TO GIVE IT MY ALL...
VERY WELL.
IN THAT CASE, I'LL HONOR YOUR COMMITMENT TO THE TREATMENT.
KLAT
KLAT

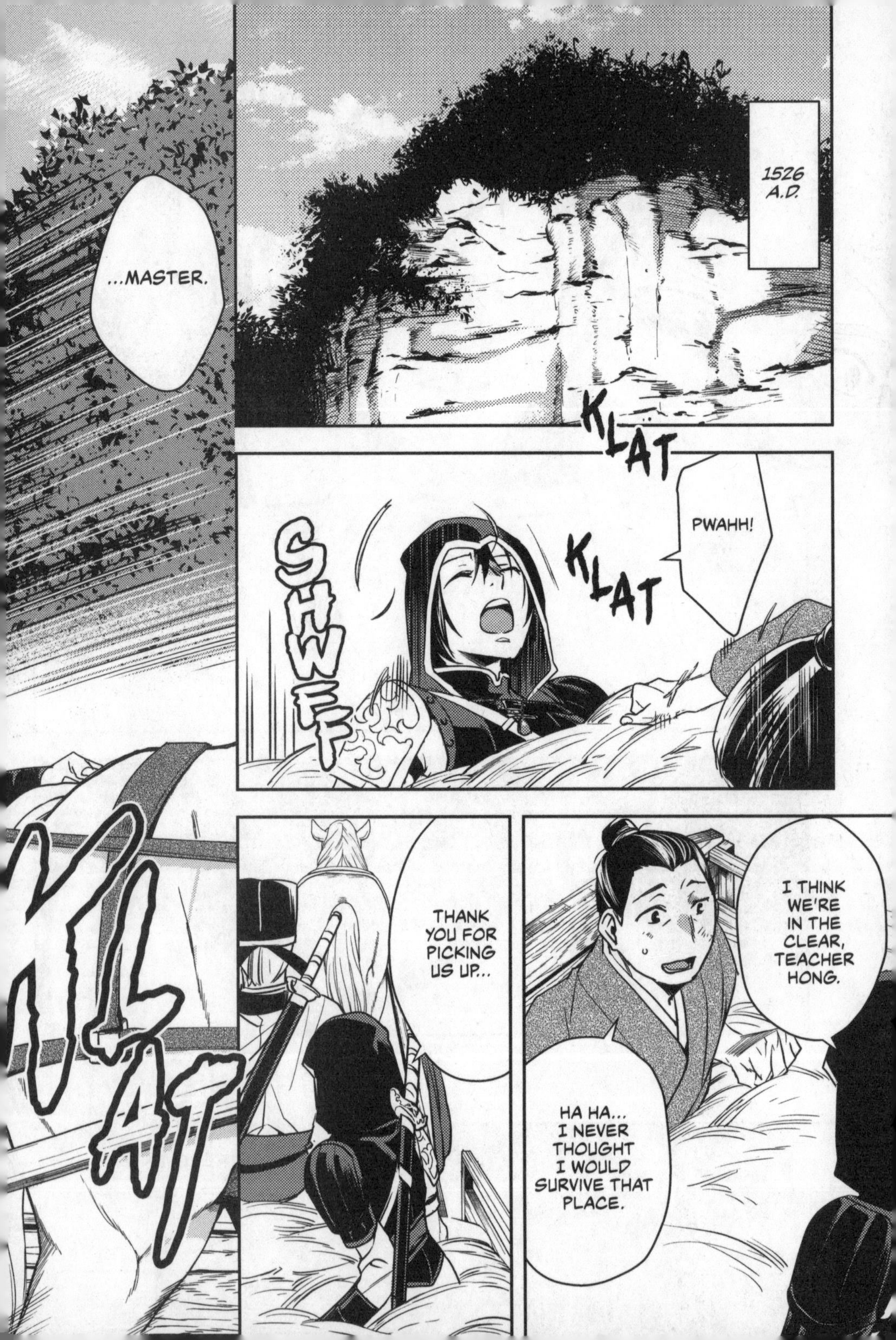
1526 A.D.
KLAT
PWAHH!
KLAT
SHWFF
I THINK WE'RE IN THE CLEAR, TEACHER HONG.
HA HA... I NEVER THOUGHT I WOULD SURVIVE THAT PLACE.
THANK YOU FOR PICKING US UP...
...MASTER.
KLAT

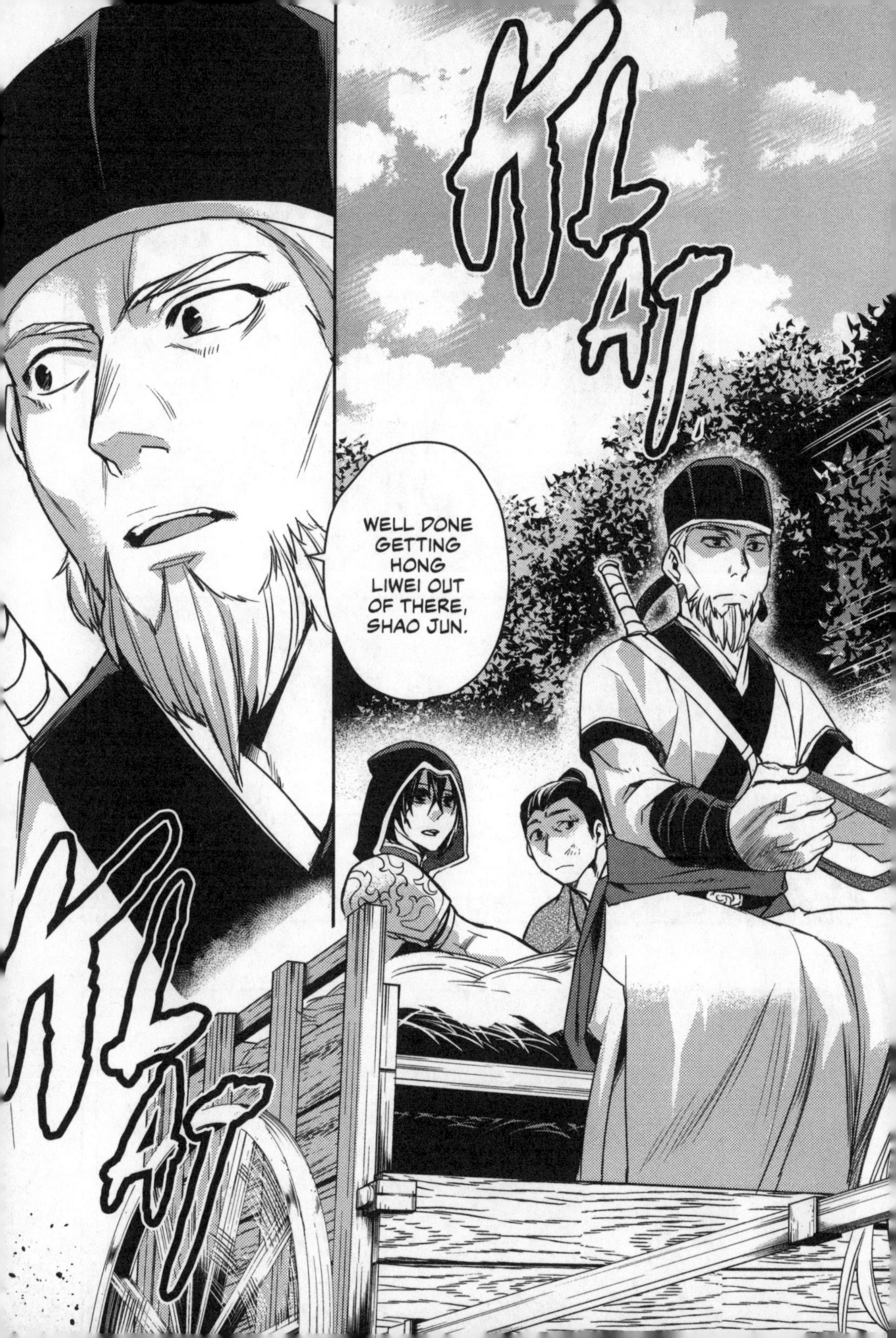
KLAT
WELL DONE GETTING HONG LIWEI OUT OF THERE, SHAO JUN.
KLAT

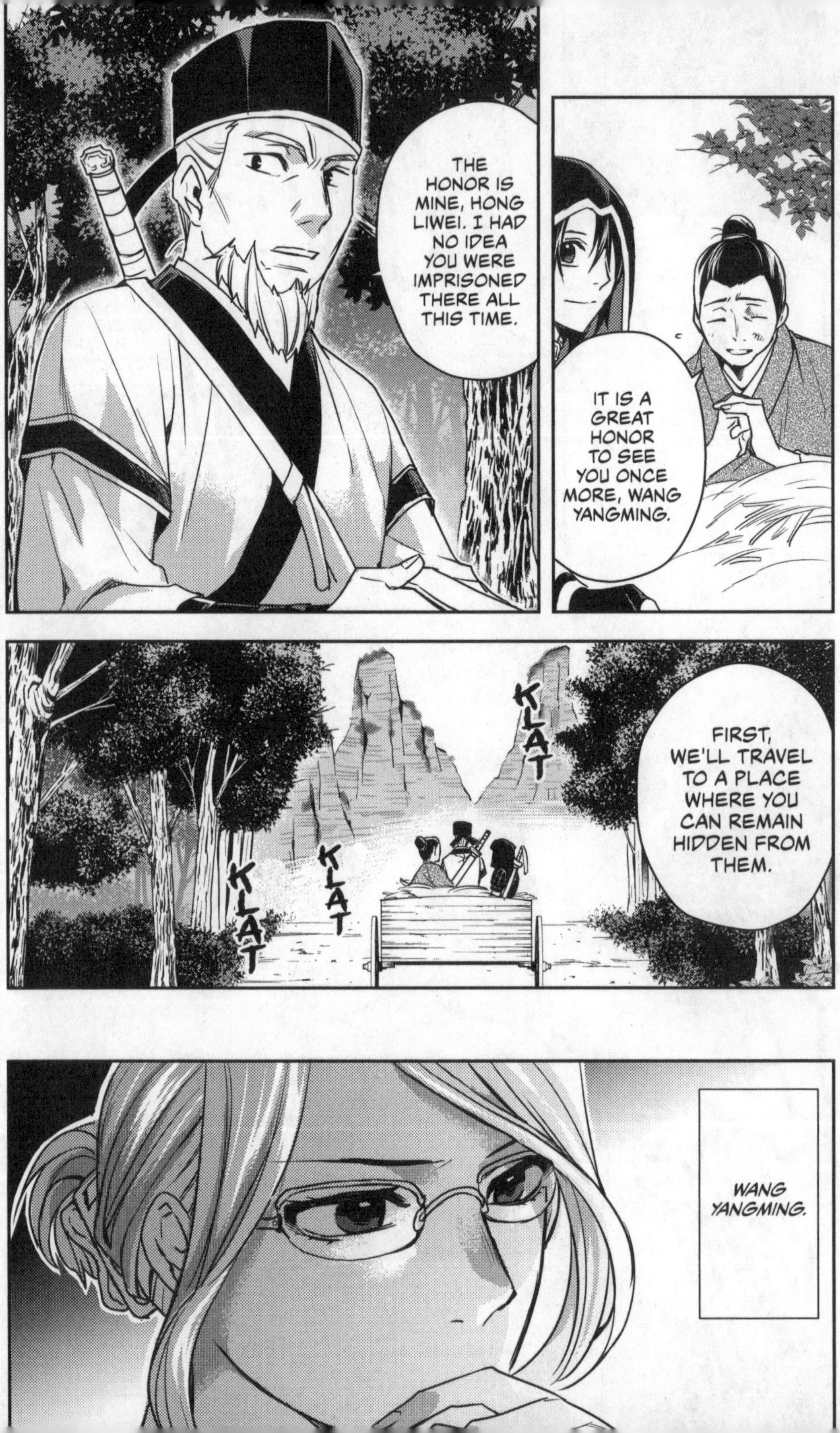
IT IS A GREAT HONOR TO SEE YOU ONCE MORE, WANG YANGMING.
THE HONOR IS MINE, HONG LIWEI. I HAD NO IDEA YOU WERE IMPRISONED THERE ALL THIS TIME.
FIRST, WE'LL TRAVEL TO A PLACE WHERE YOU CAN REMAIN HIDDEN FROM THEM.
KLAT
KLAT
KLAT
WANG YANGMING.

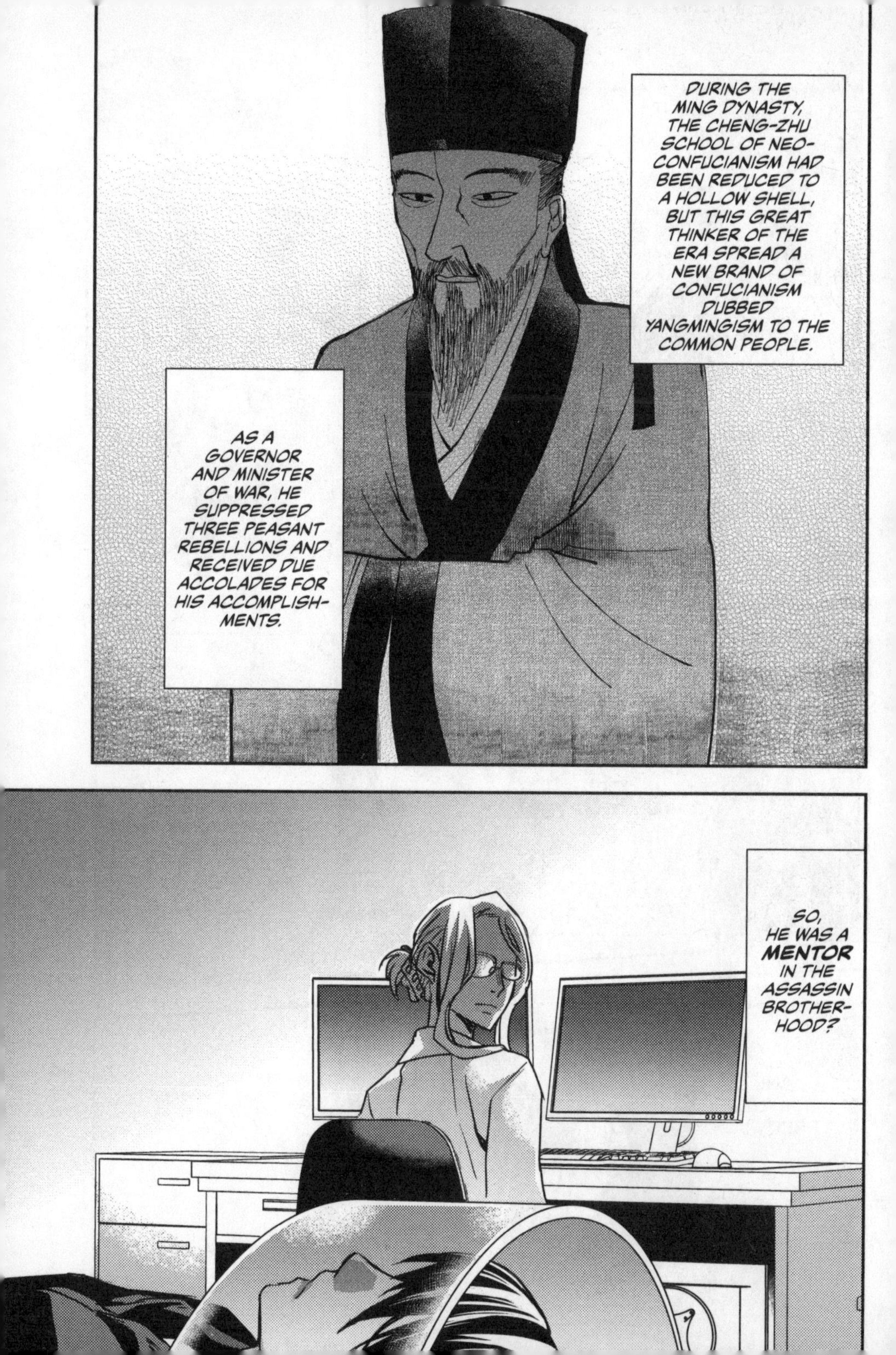
DURING THE MING DYNASTY, THE CHENG-ZHU SCHOOL OF NEO-CONFUCIANISM HAD BEEN REDUCED TO A HOLLOW SHELL, BUT THIS GREAT THINKER OF THE ERA SPREAD A NEW BRAND OF CONFUCIANISM DUBBED YANGMINGISM TO THE COMMON PEOPLE.
AS A GOVERNOR AND MINISTER OF WAR, HE SUPPRESSED THREE PEASANT REBELLIONS AND RECEIVED DUE ACCOLADES FOR HIS ACCOMPLISH-MENTS.
SO, HE WAS A **MENTOR** IN THE ASSASSIN BROTHER-HOOD?

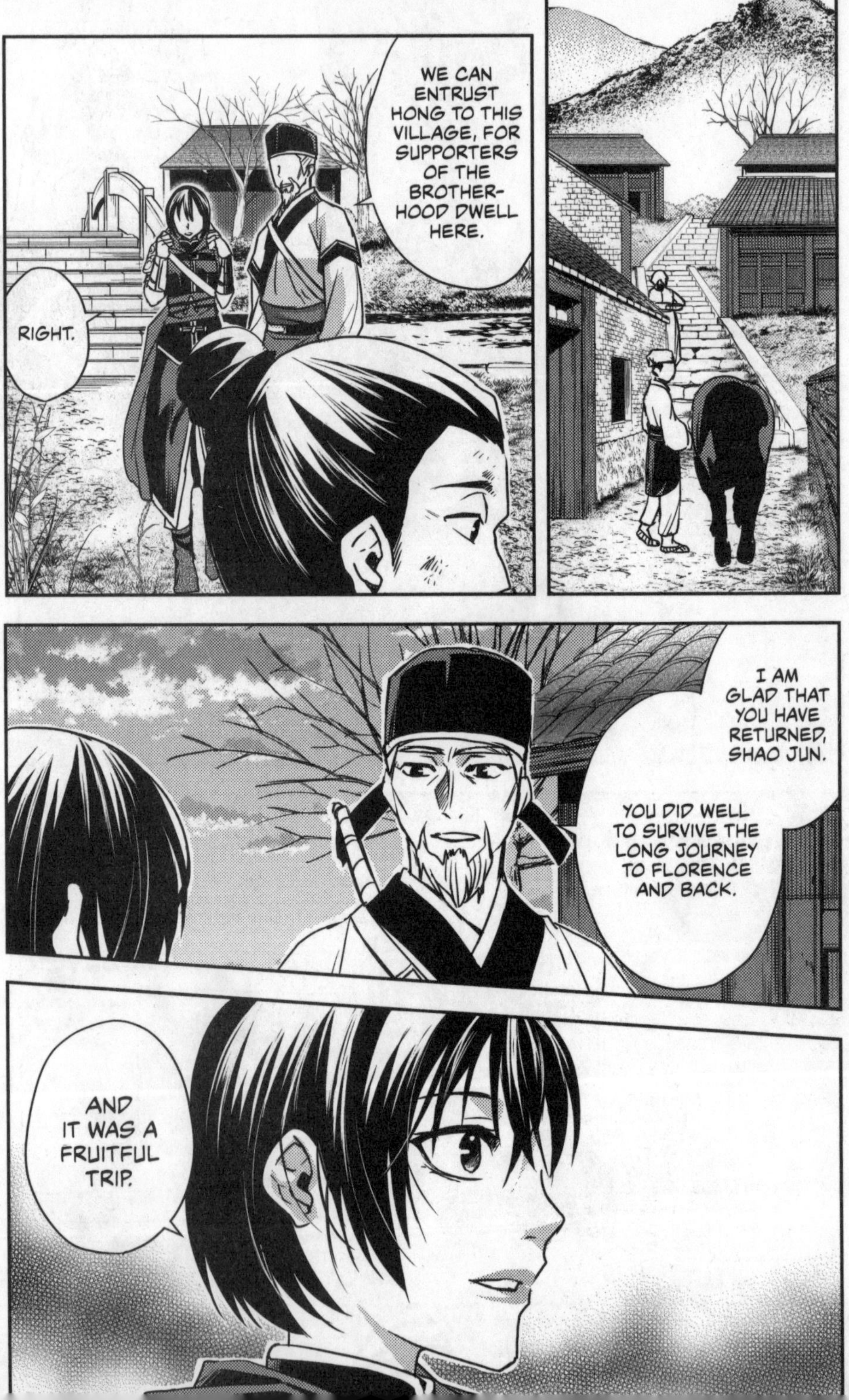
WE CAN ENTRUST HONG TO THIS VILLAGE, FOR SUPPORTERS OF THE BROTHERHOOD DWELL HERE.
RIGHT.
I AM GLAD THAT YOU HAVE RETURNED, SHAO JUN.
YOU DID WELL TO SURVIVE THE LONG JOURNEY TO FLORENCE AND BACK.
AND IT WAS A FRUITFUL TRIP.

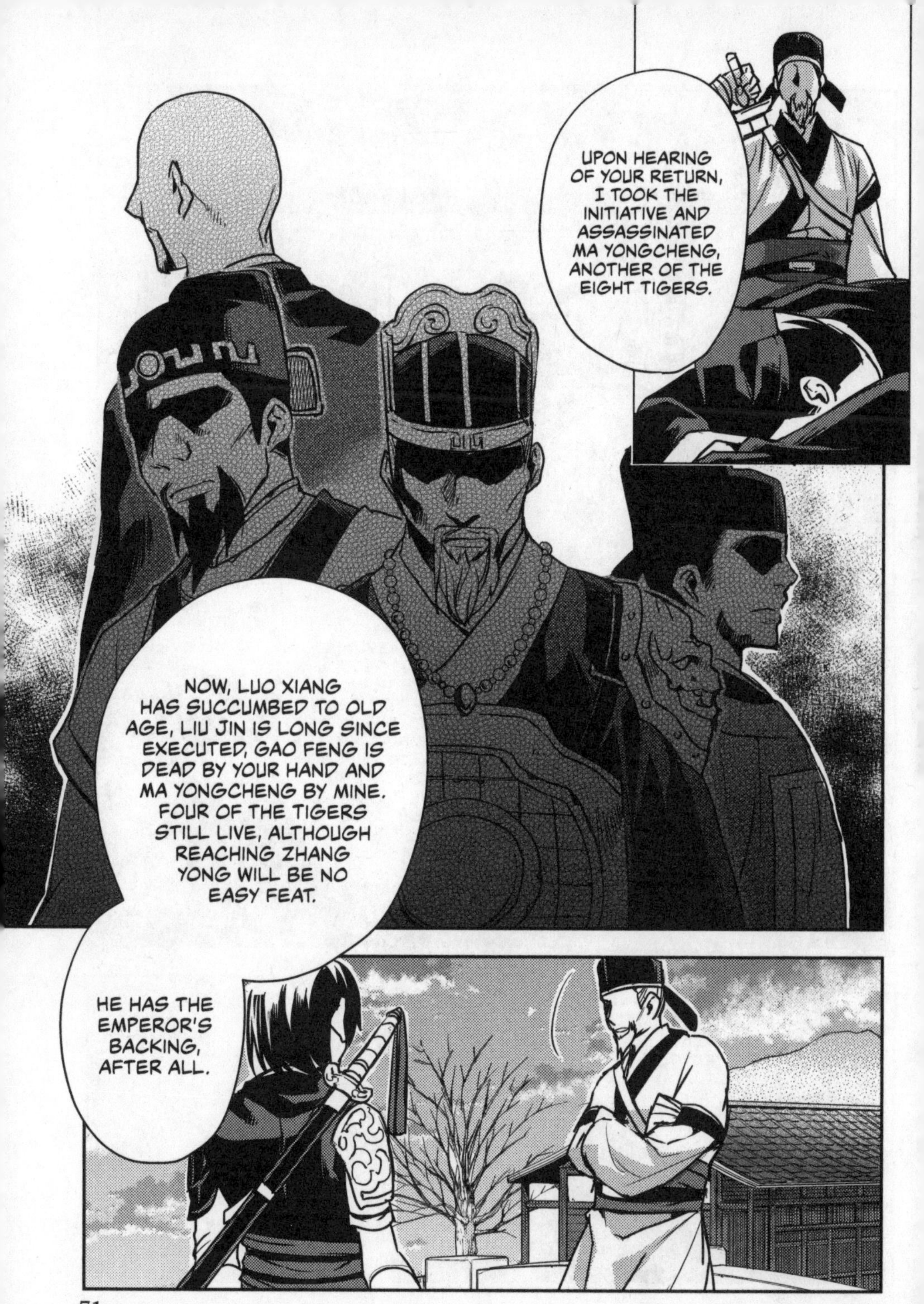
UPON HEARING OF YOUR RETURN, I TOOK THE INITIATIVE AND ASSASSINATED MA YONGCHENG, ANOTHER OF THE EIGHT TIGERS.
NOW, LUO XIANG HAS SUCCUMBED TO OLD AGE, LIU JIN IS LONG SINCE EXECUTED, GAO FENG IS DEAD BY YOUR HAND AND MA YONGCHENG BY MINE. FOUR OF THE TIGERS STILL LIVE, ALTHOUGH REACHING ZHANG YONG WILL BE NO EASY FEAT.
HE HAS THE EMPEROR'S BACKING, AFTER ALL.

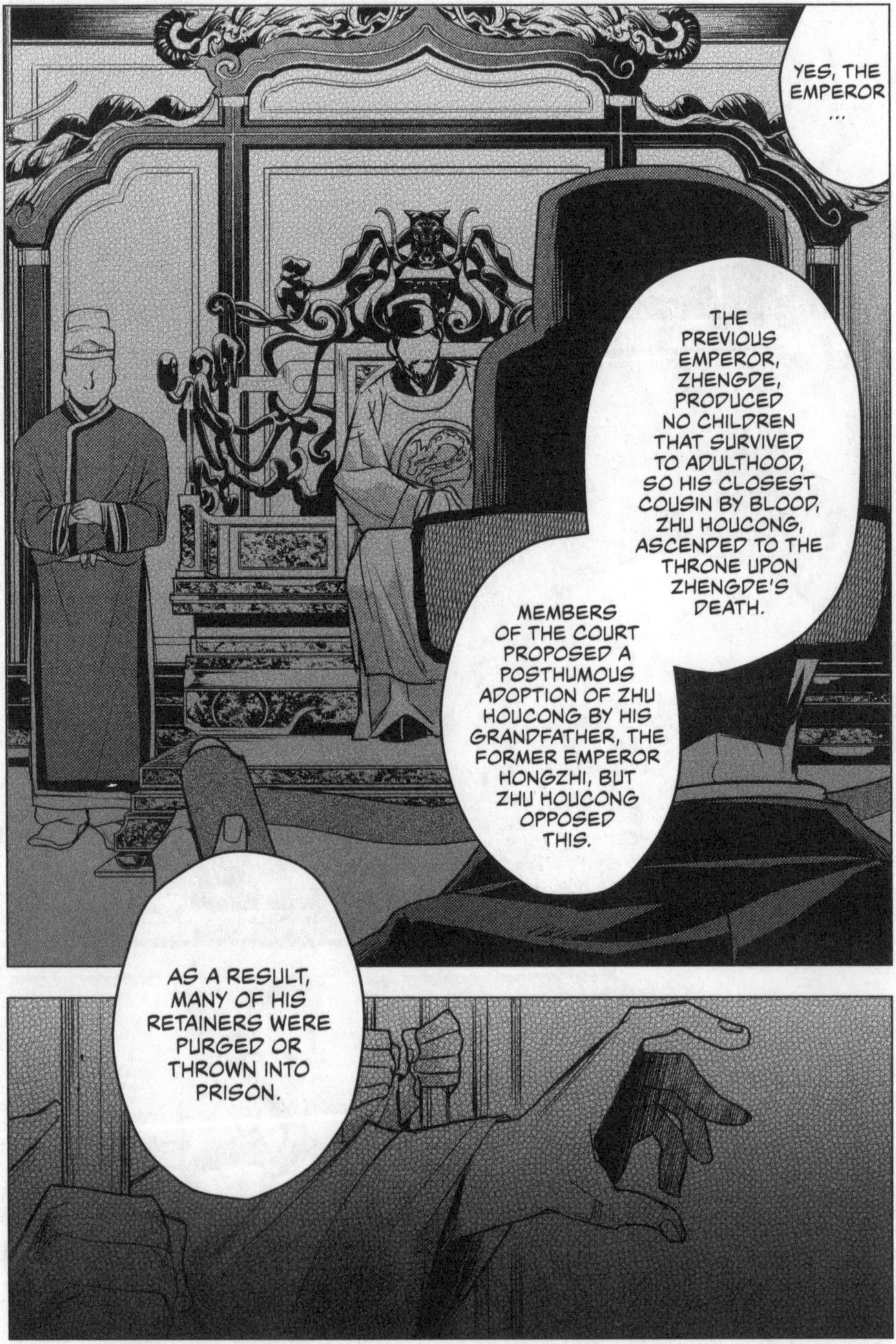
YES, THE EMPEROR ...
THE PREVIOUS EMPEROR, ZHENGDE, PRODUCED NO CHILDREN THAT SURVIVED TO ADULTHOOD, SO HIS CLOSEST COUSIN BY BLOOD, ZHU HOUCONG, ASCENDED TO THE THRONE UPON ZHENGDE'S DEATH.
MEMBERS OF THE COURT PROPOSED A POSTHUMOUS ADOPTION OF ZHU HOUCONG BY HIS GRANDFATHER, THE FORMER EMPEROR HONGZHI, BUT ZHU HOUCONG OPPOSED THIS.
AS A RESULT, MANY OF HIS RETAINERS WERE PURGED OR THROWN INTO PRISON.

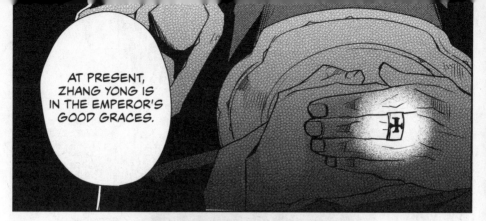

AT PRESENT, ZHANG YONG IS IN THE EMPEROR'S GOOD GRACES.

ZHANG YONG AND HIS PEOPLE HAVE USED THE TEMPLAR ORDER'S POWER TO CURRY FAVOR FROM THE EMPEROR AND ACQUIRE AUTHORITY OF THEIR OWN.

AND THE EMPEROR DARES NOT TURN ON THE TEMPLARS, FOR IT WAS THEY WHO CEMENTED HIS OWN POSITION.

ALL OF WHICH IS TO SAY, THE ENEMIES WE MUST ELIMINATE LIE DEEP WITHIN THE IMPERIAL COURT.

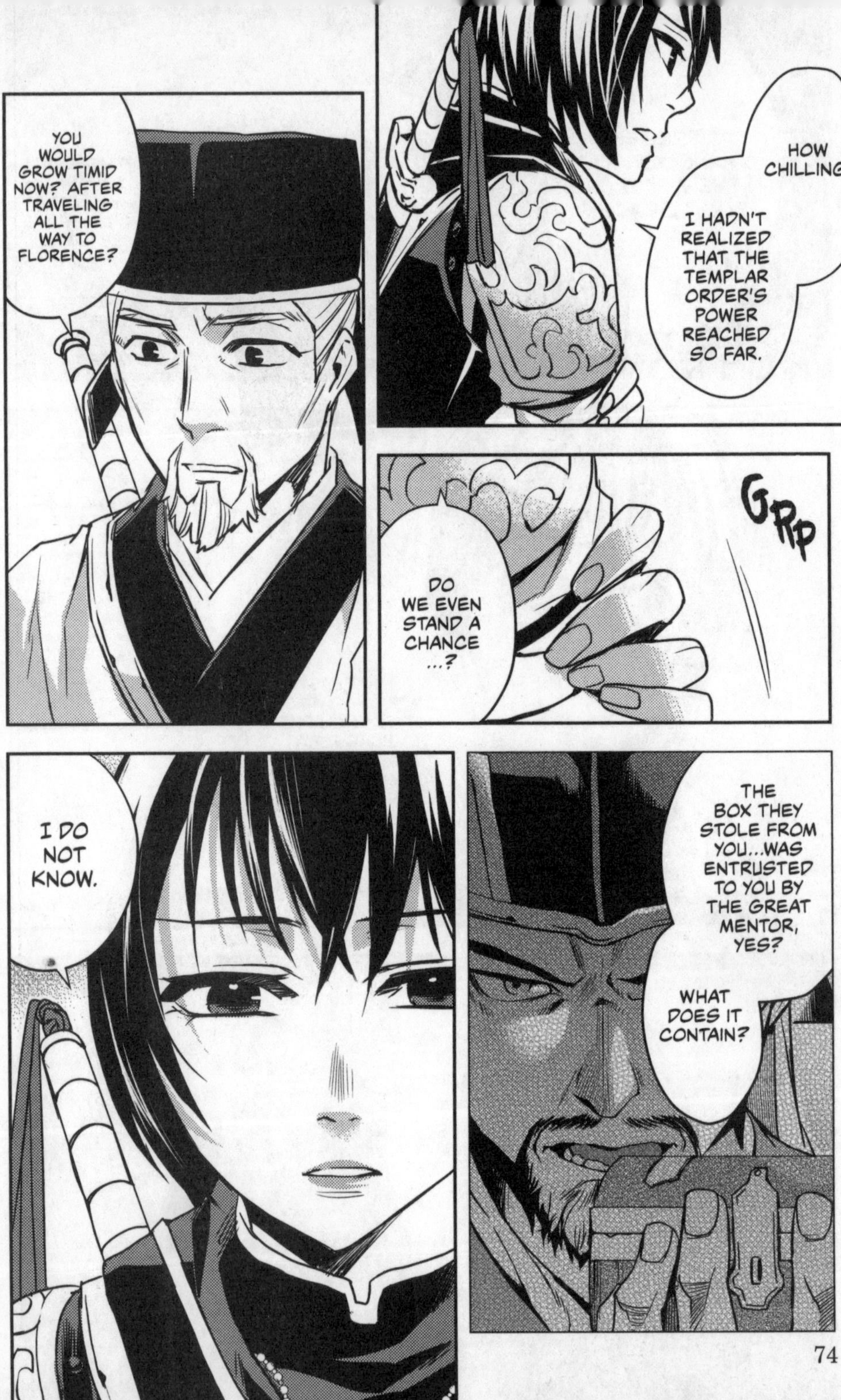
HOW CHILLING.
I HADN'T REALIZED THAT THE TEMPLAR ORDER'S POWER REACHED SO FAR.
GRP
DO WE EVEN STAND A CHANCE ...?
YOU WOULD GROW TIMID NOW? AFTER TRAVELING ALL THE WAY TO FLORENCE?
THE BOX THEY STOLE FROM YOU...WAS ENTRUSTED TO YOU BY THE GREAT MENTOR, YES?
WHAT DOES IT CONTAIN?
I DO NOT KNOW.

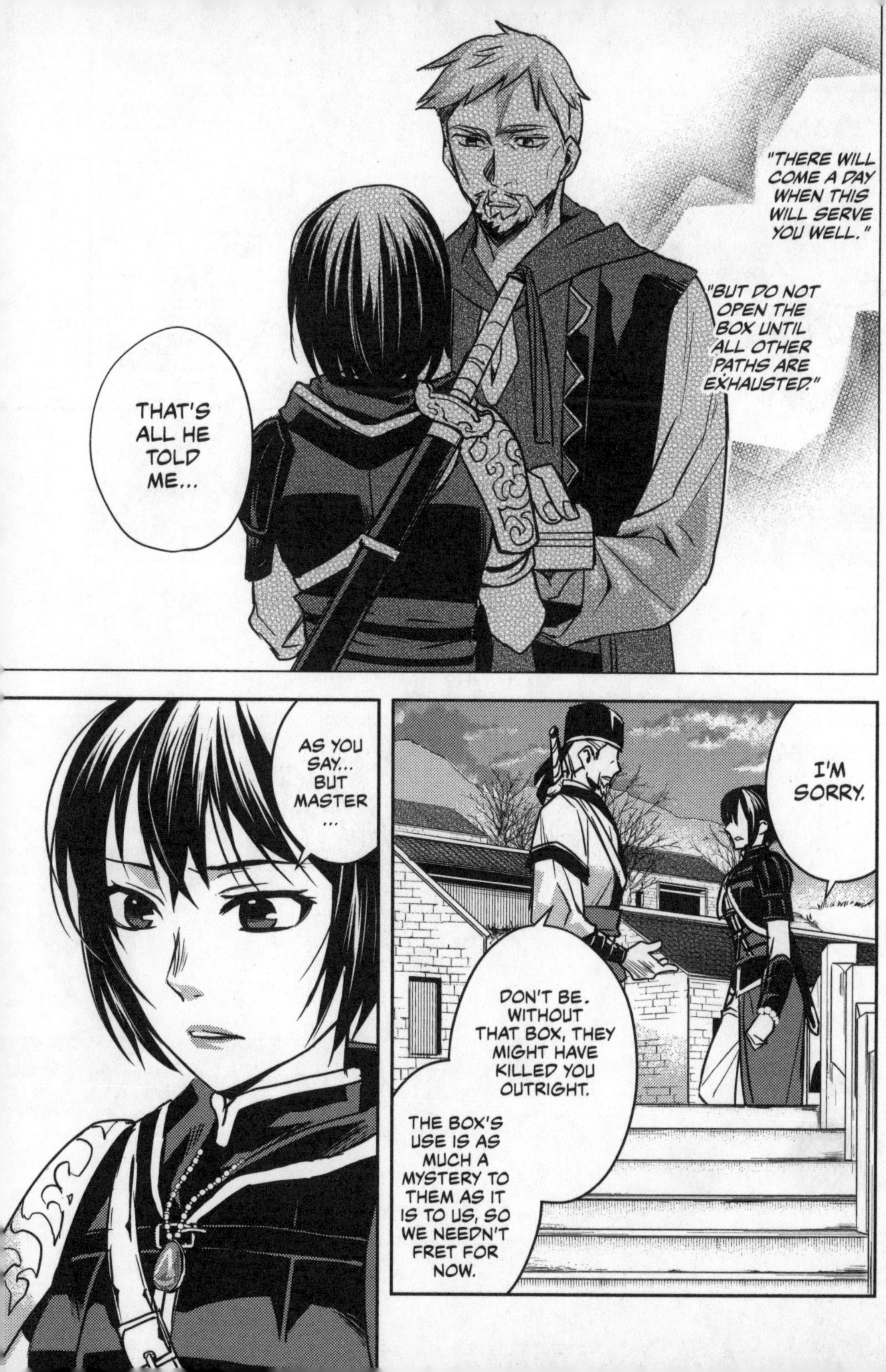
"THERE WILL COME A DAY WHEN THIS WILL SERVE YOU WELL."
"BUT DO NOT OPEN THE BOX UNTIL ALL OTHER PATHS ARE EXHAUSTED."
THAT'S ALL HE TOLD ME...
I'M SORRY.
DON'T BE. WITHOUT THAT BOX, THEY MIGHT HAVE KILLED YOU OUTRIGHT.
THE BOX'S USE IS AS MUCH A MYSTERY TO THEM AS IT IS TO US, SO WE NEEDN'T FRET FOR NOW.
AS YOU SAY... BUT MASTER ...

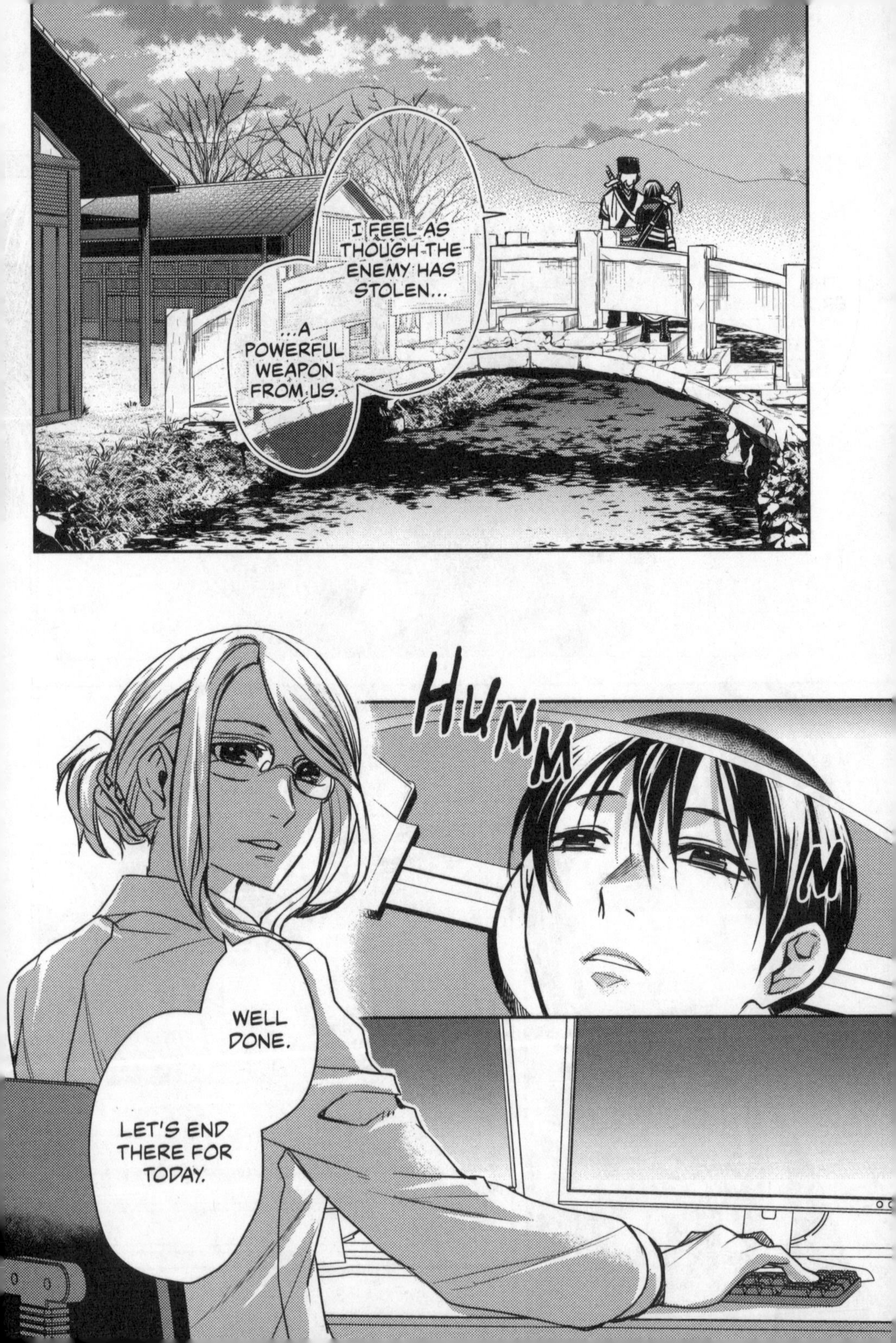
I FEEL AS THOUGH THE ENEMY HAS STOLEN...
...A POWERFUL WEAPON FROM US.
HUMMM
WELL DONE.
LET'S END THERE FOR TODAY.

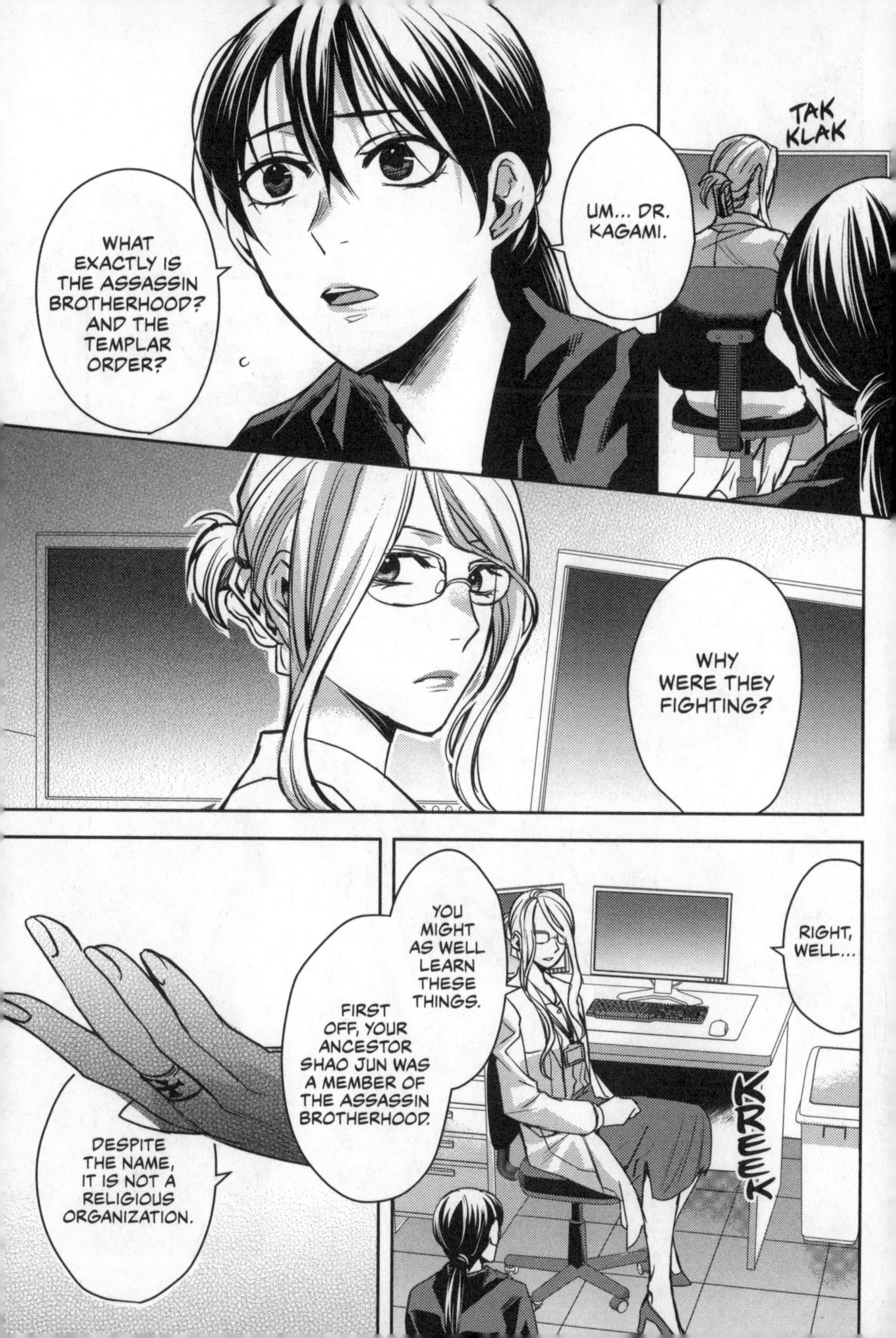
TAK KLAK
UM... DR. KAGAMI.
WHAT EXACTLY IS THE ASSASSIN BROTHERHOOD? AND THE TEMPLAR ORDER?
WHY WERE THEY FIGHTING?
RIGHT, WELL...
KREEK
YOU MIGHT AS WELL LEARN THESE THINGS.
FIRST OFF, YOUR ANCESTOR SHAO JUN WAS A MEMBER OF THE ASSASSIN BROTHERHOOD.
DESPITE THE NAME, IT IS NOT A RELIGIOUS ORGANIZATION.

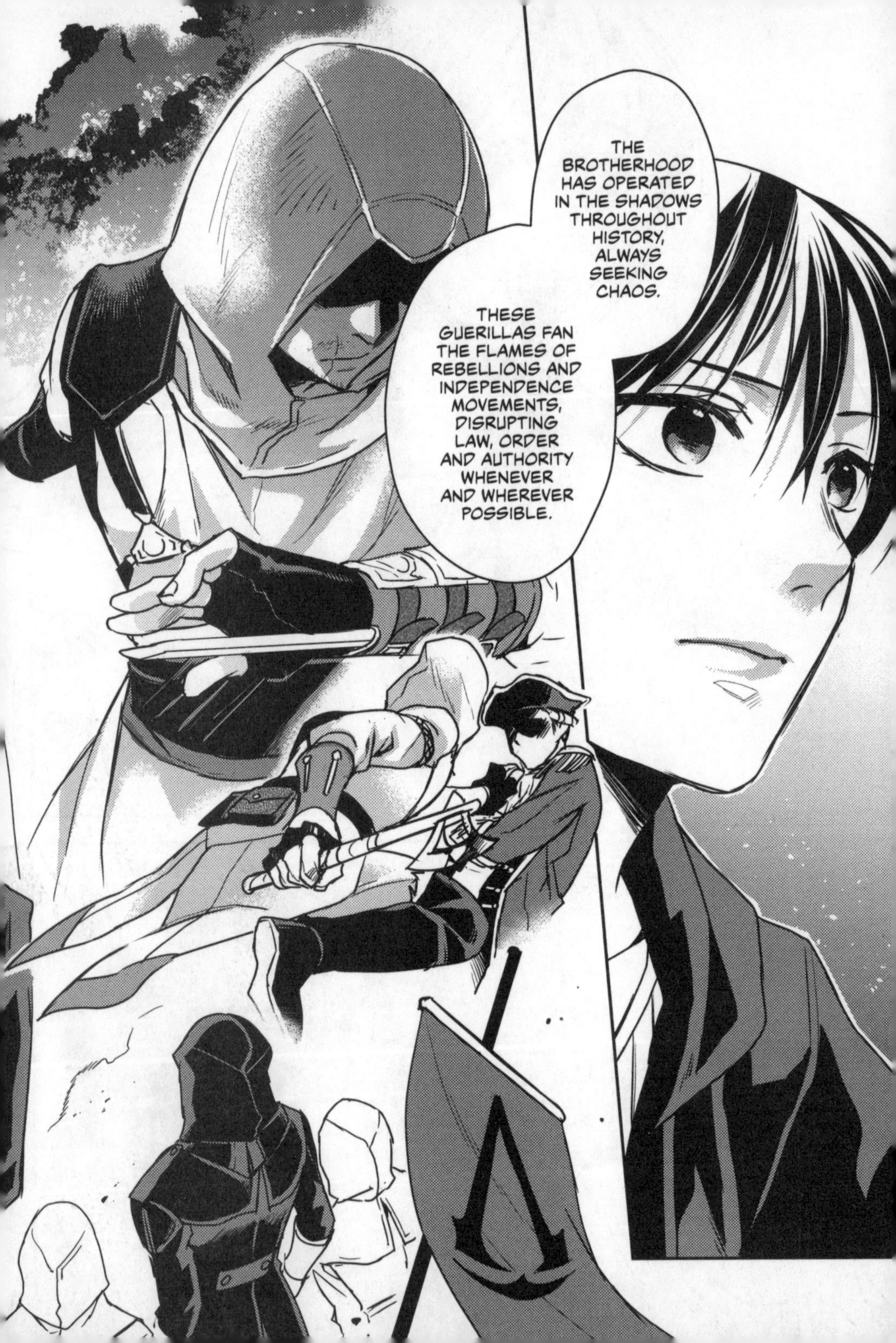
THE BROTHERHOOD HAS OPERATED IN THE SHADOWS THROUGHOUT HISTORY, ALWAYS SEEKING CHAOS.
THESE GUERILLAS FAN THE FLAMES OF REBELLIONS AND INDEPENDENCE MOVEMENTS, DISRUPTING LAW, ORDER AND AUTHORITY WHENEVER AND WHEREVER POSSIBLE.

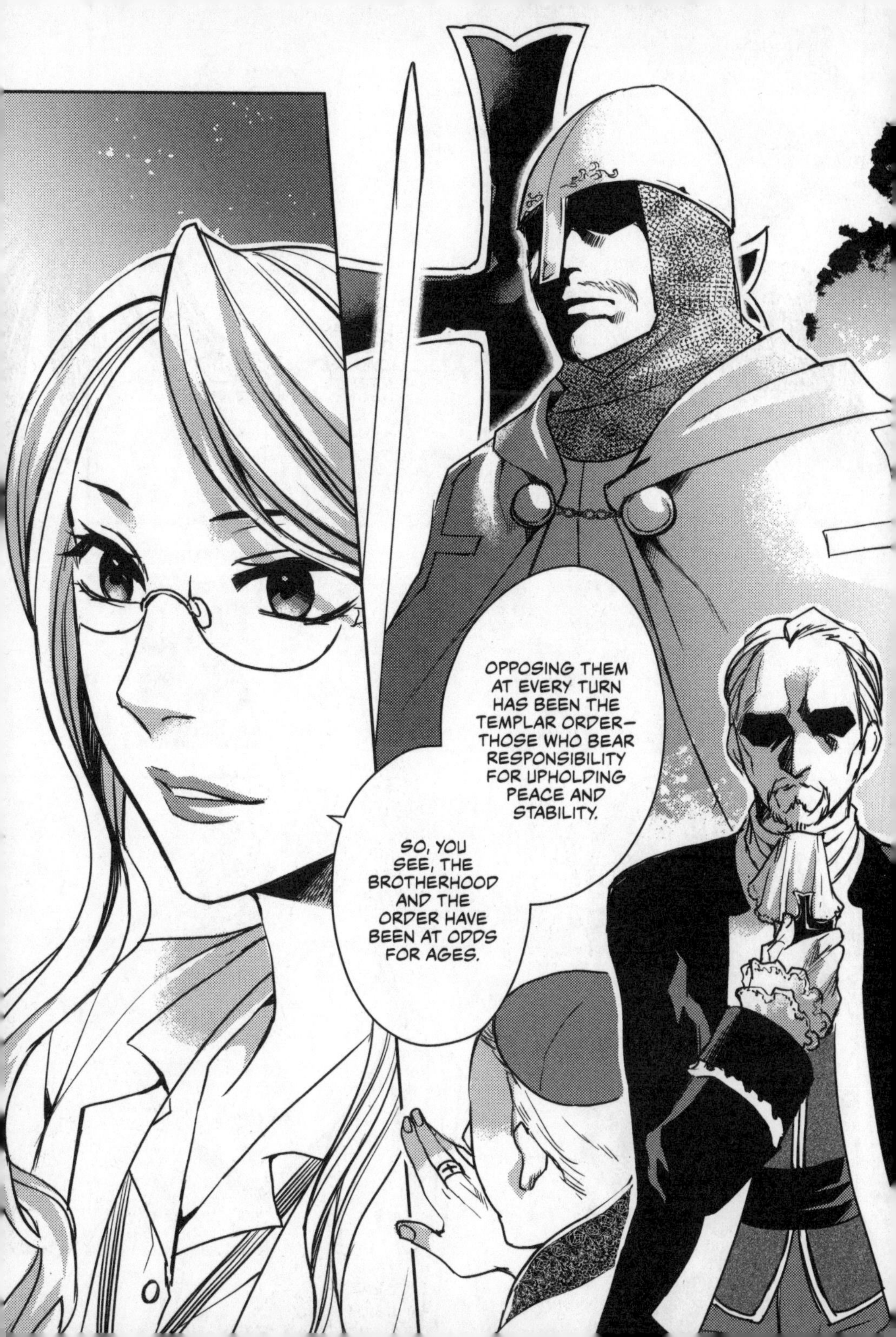
OPPOSING THEM AT EVERY TURN HAS BEEN THE TEMPLAR ORDER— THOSE WHO BEAR RESPONSIBILITY FOR UPHOLDING PEACE AND STABILITY.
SO, YOU SEE, THE BROTHERHOOD AND THE ORDER HAVE BEEN AT ODDS FOR AGES.

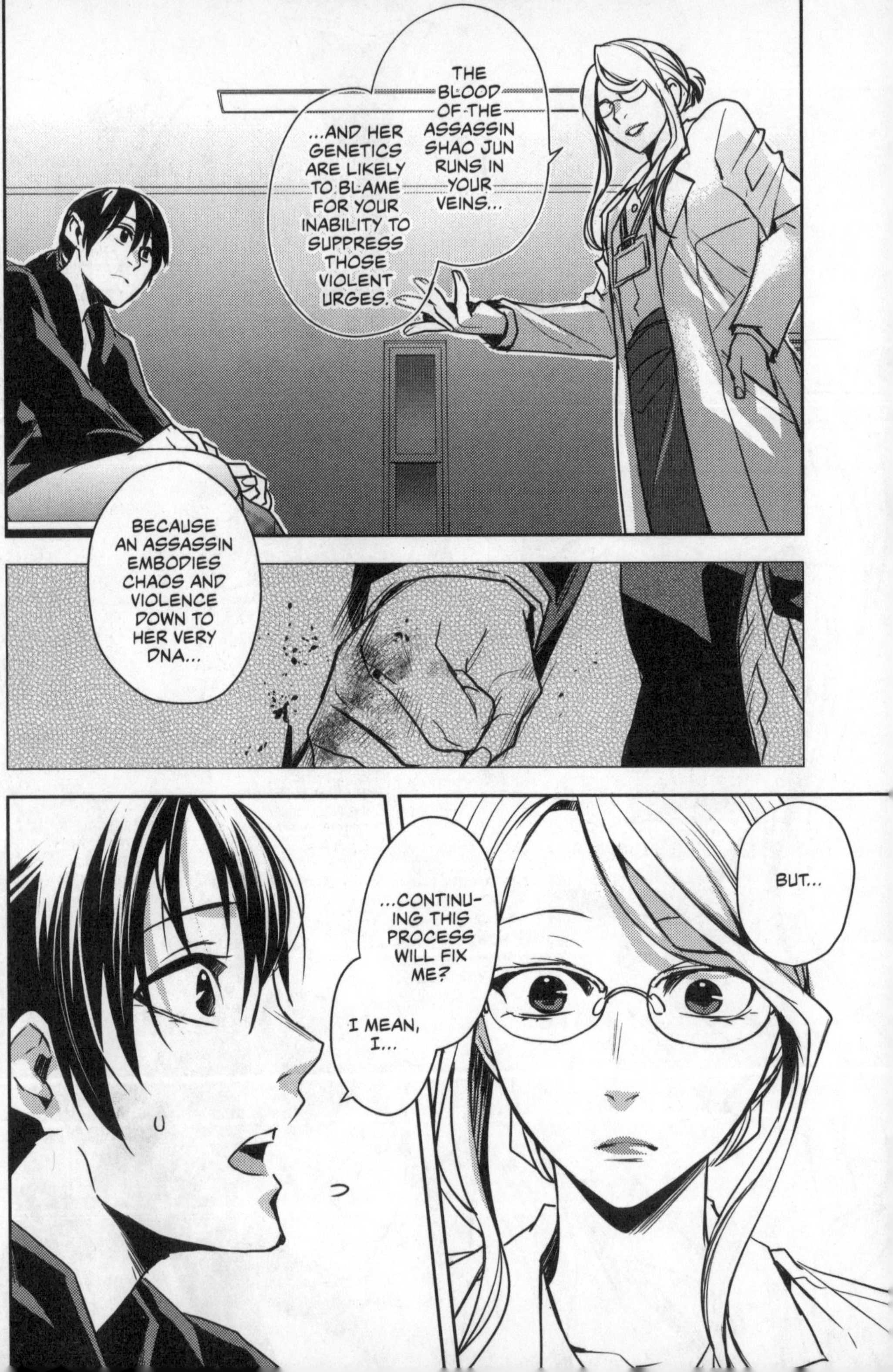
THE BLOOD OF THE ASSASSIN SHAO JUN RUNS IN YOUR VEINS...
...AND HER GENETICS ARE LIKELY TO BLAME FOR YOUR INABILITY TO SUPPRESS THOSE VIOLENT URGES.
BECAUSE AN ASSASSIN EMBODIES CHAOS AND VIOLENCE DOWN TO HER VERY DNA...
BUT...
...CONTINUING THIS PROCESS WILL FIX ME?
I MEAN, I...

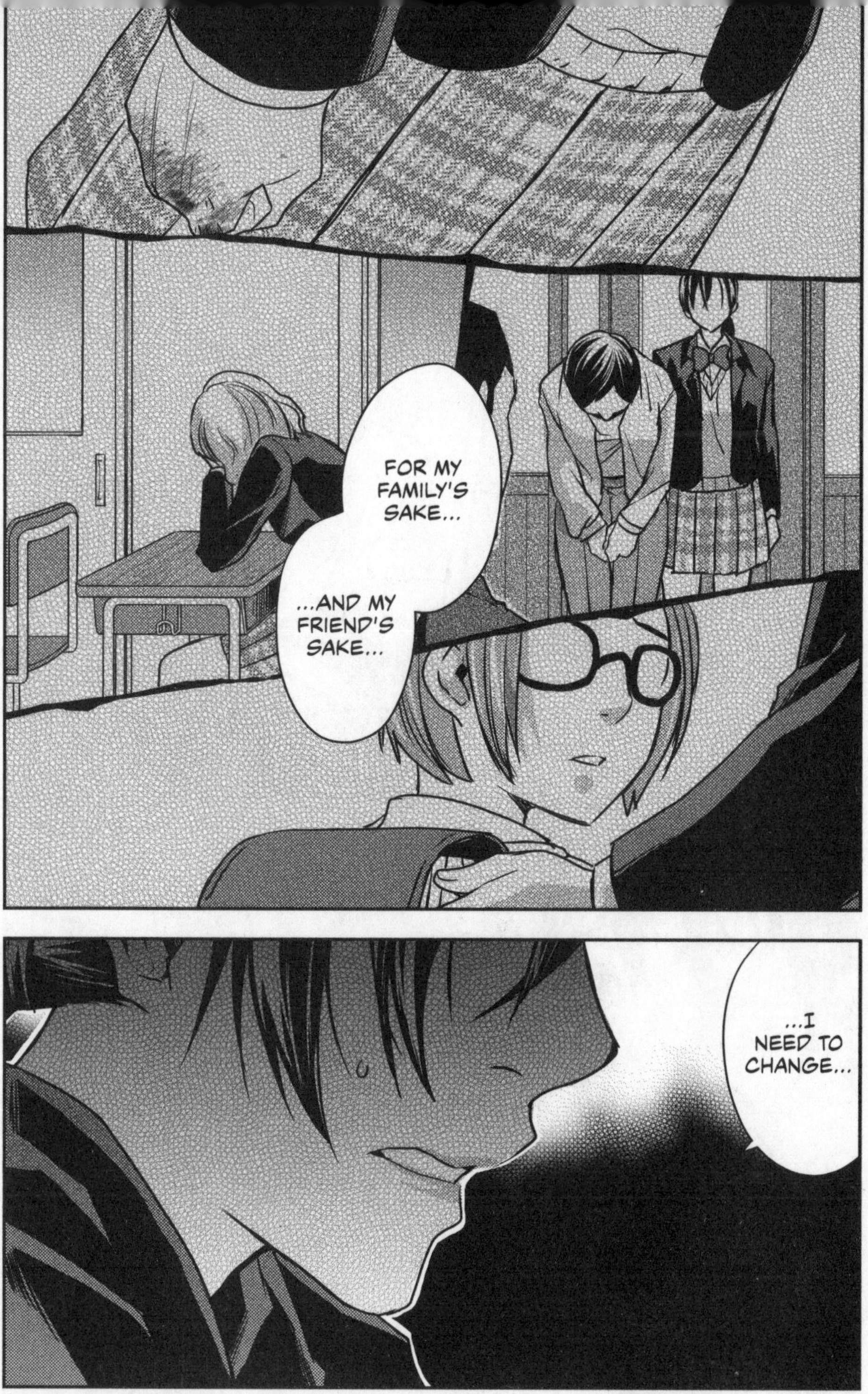
FOR MY FAMILY'S SAKE...
...AND MY FRIEND'S SAKE...
...I NEED TO CHANGE...

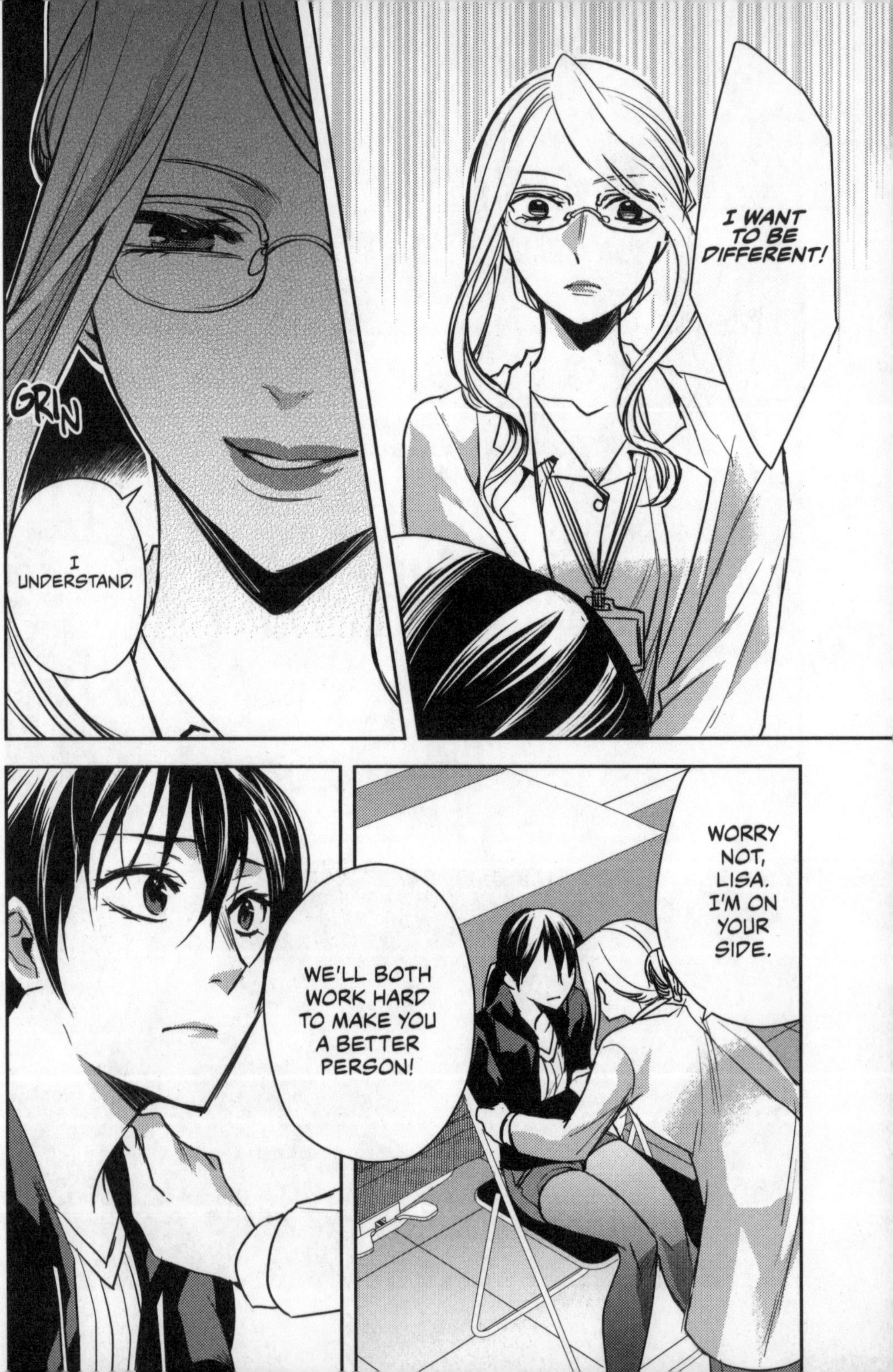
I WANT TO BE DIFFERENT!
GRIN
I UNDERSTAND.
WORRY NOT, LISA. I'M ON YOUR SIDE.
WE'LL BOTH WORK HARD TO MAKE YOU A BETTER PERSON!

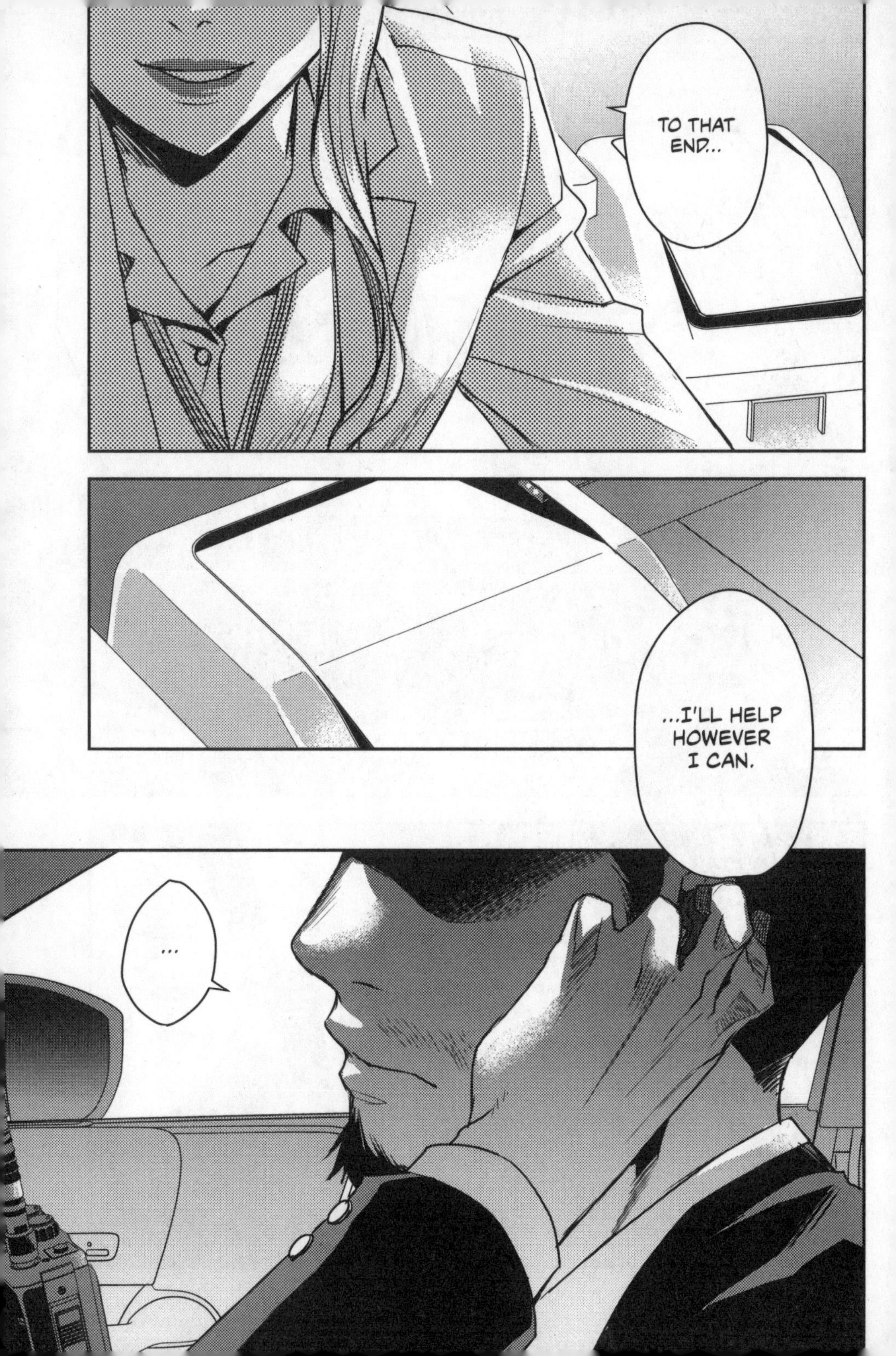
TO THAT END...
...I'LL HELP HOWEVER I CAN.
...

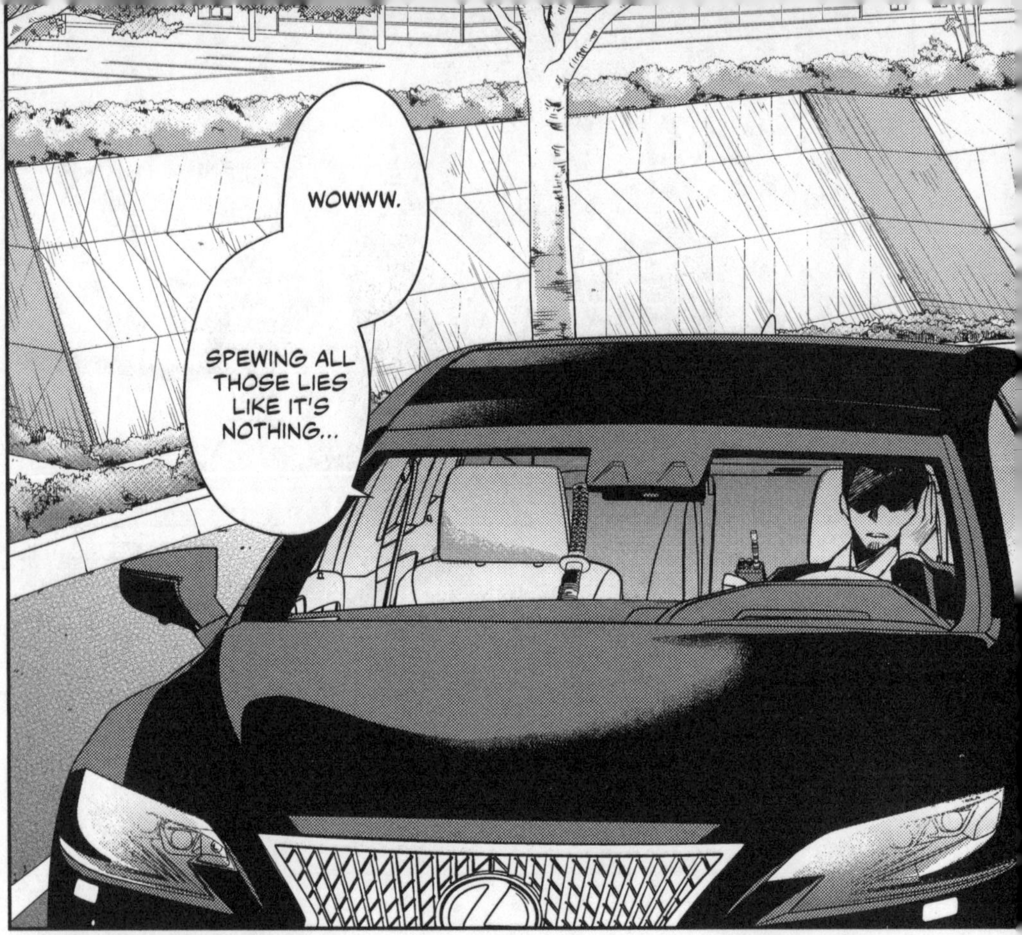
WOWWW.
SPEWING ALL THOSE LIES LIKE IT'S NOTHING...

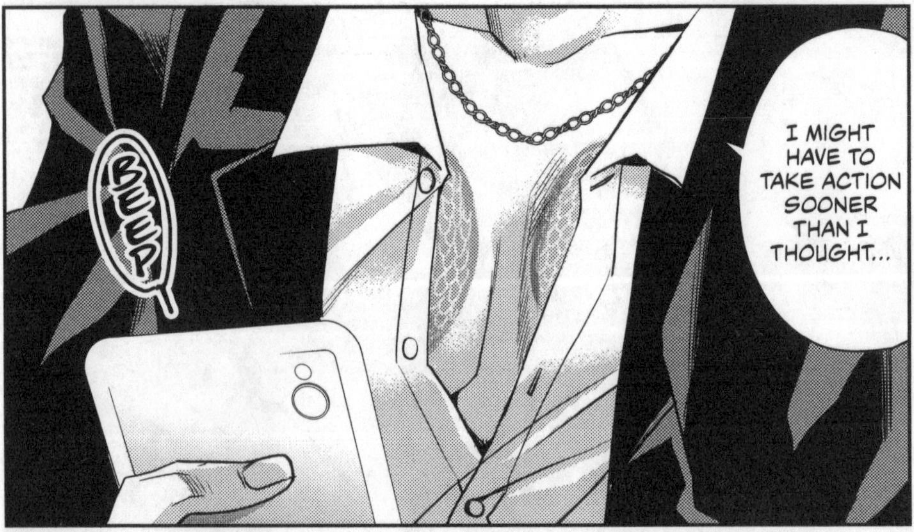
I MIGHT HAVE TO TAKE ACTION SOONER THAN I THOUGHT...
BEEP

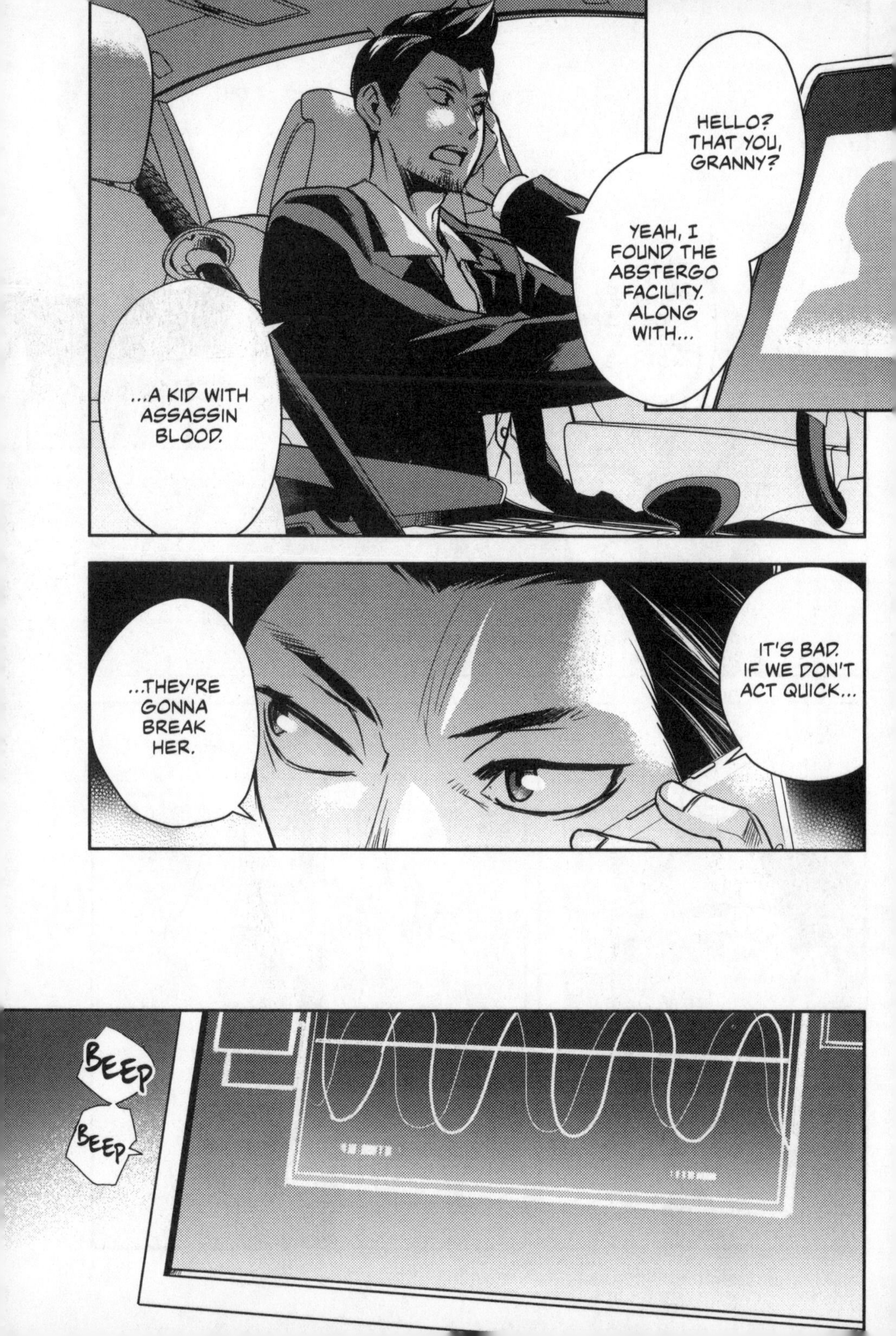
HELLO? THAT YOU, GRANNY?
YEAH, I FOUND THE ABSTERGO FACILITY. ALONG WITH...
...A KID WITH ASSASSIN BLOOD.
IT'S BAD. IF WE DON'T ACT QUICK...
...THEY'RE GONNA BREAK HER.
BEEP
BEEP

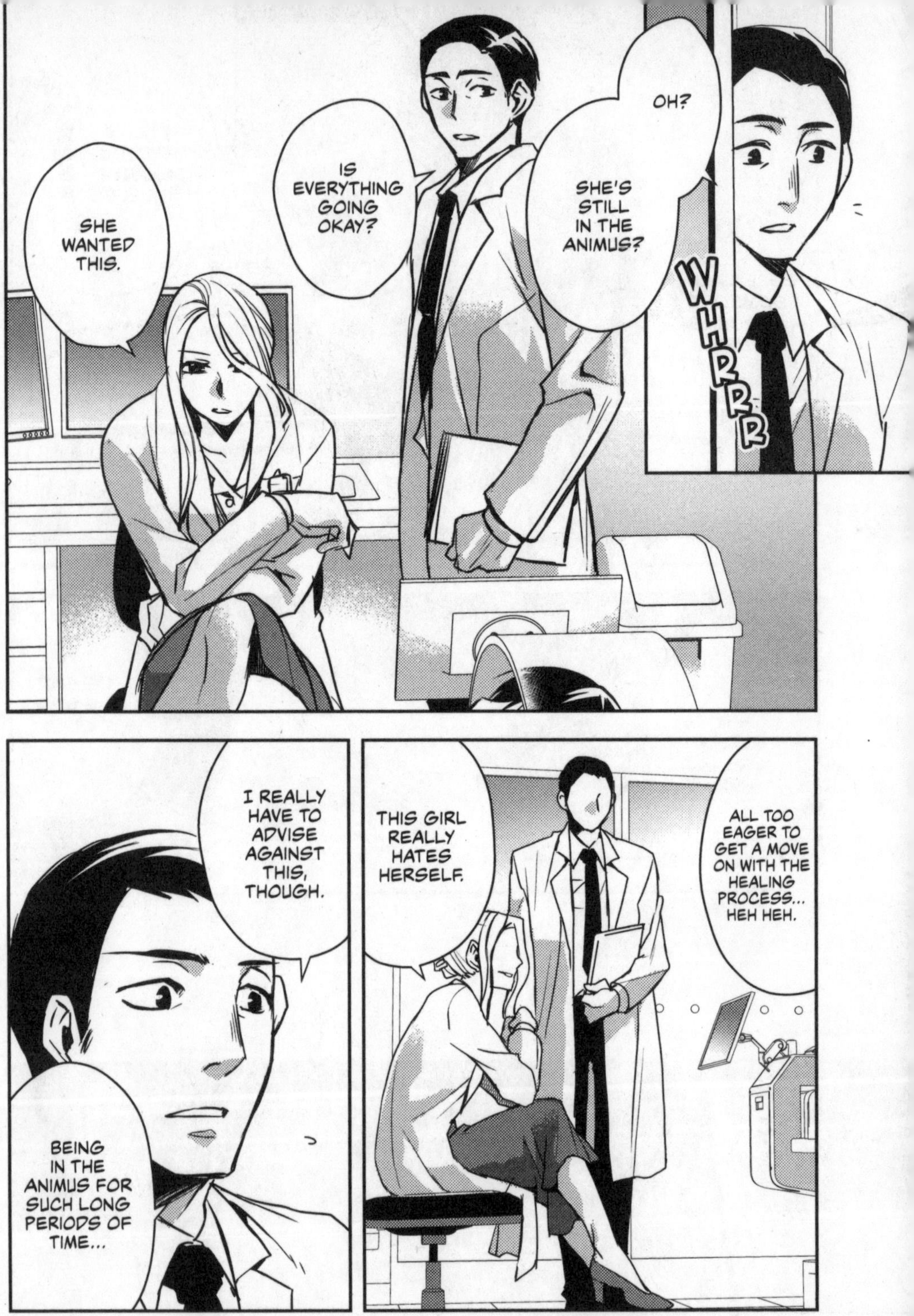
OH?
SHE'S STILL IN THE ANIMUS?
WHRRR
IS EVERYTHING GOING OKAY?
SHE WANTED THIS.
ALL TOO EAGER TO GET A MOVE ON WITH THE HEALING PROCESS... HEH HEH.
THIS GIRL REALLY HATES HERSELF.
I REALLY HAVE TO ADVISE AGAINST THIS, THOUGH.
BEING IN THE ANIMUS FOR SUCH LONG PERIODS OF TIME...

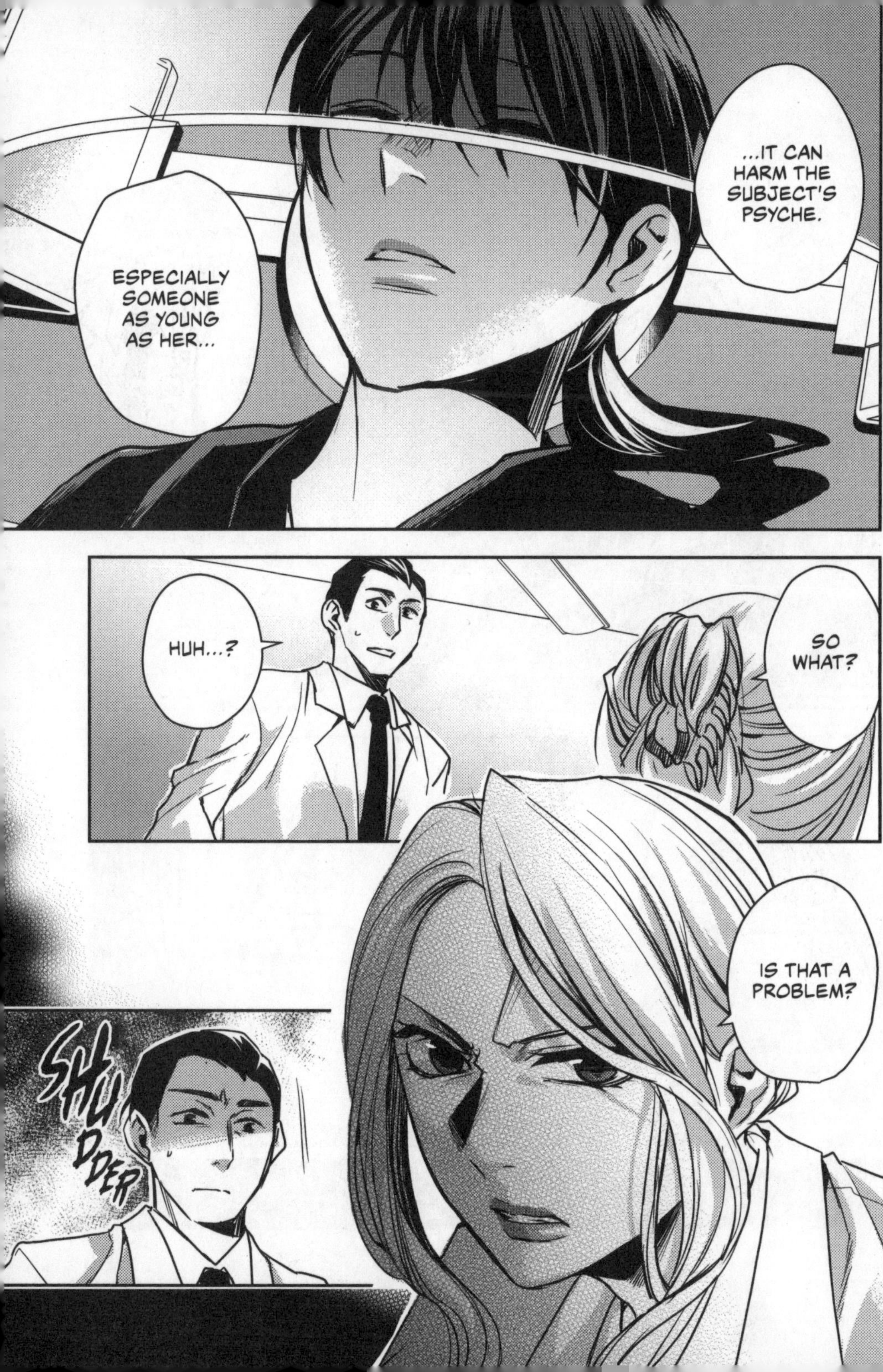
...IT CAN HARM THE SUBJECT'S PSYCHE.
ESPECIALLY SOMEONE AS YOUNG AS HER...
SO WHAT?
HUH...?
IS THAT A PROBLEM?
SHUDDER

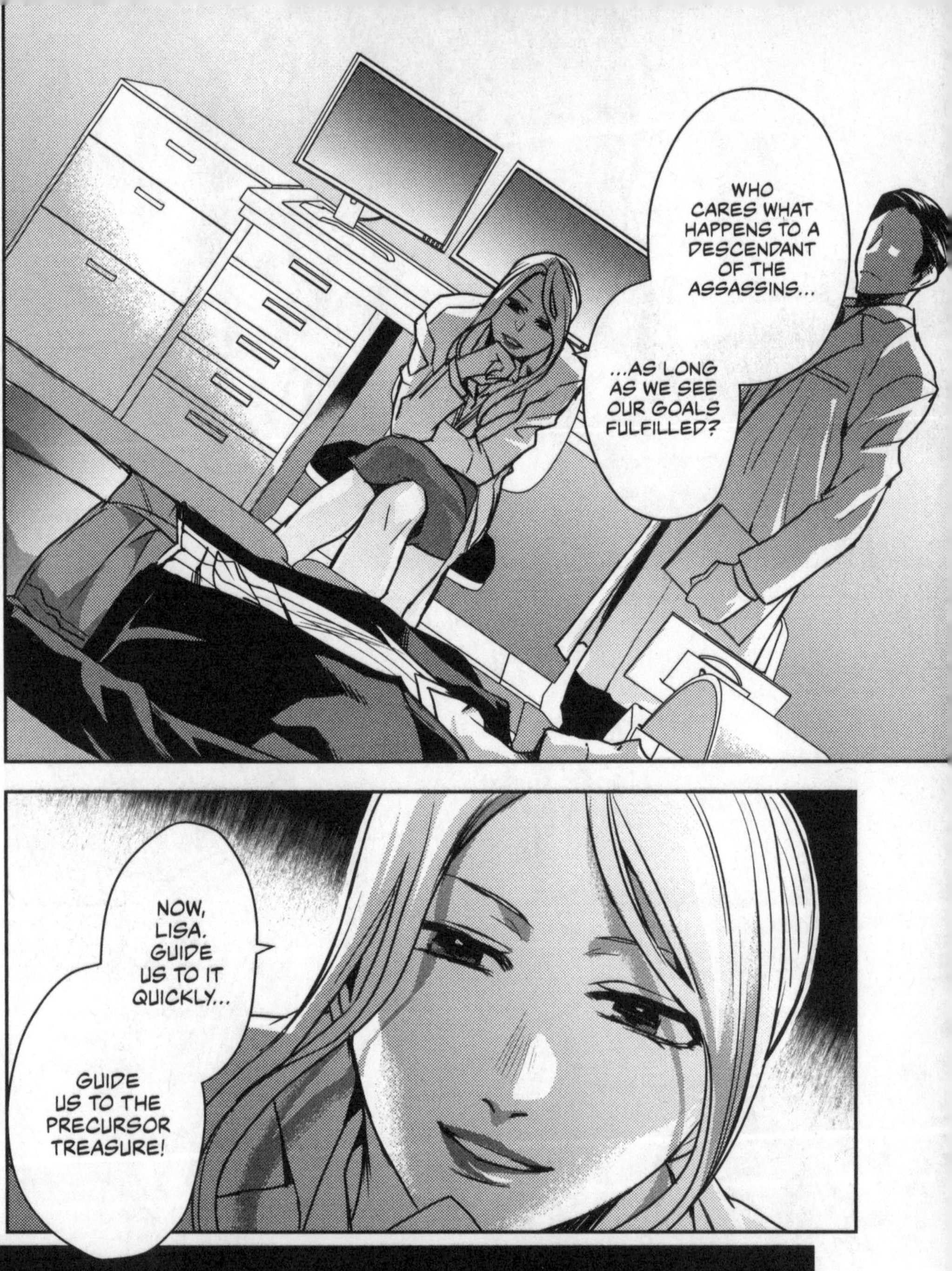
WHO CARES WHAT HAPPENS TO A DESCENDANT OF THE ASSASSINS...
...AS LONG AS WE SEE OUR GOALS FULFILLED?
NOW, LISA. GUIDE US TO IT QUICKLY...
GUIDE US TO THE PRECURSOR TREASURE!

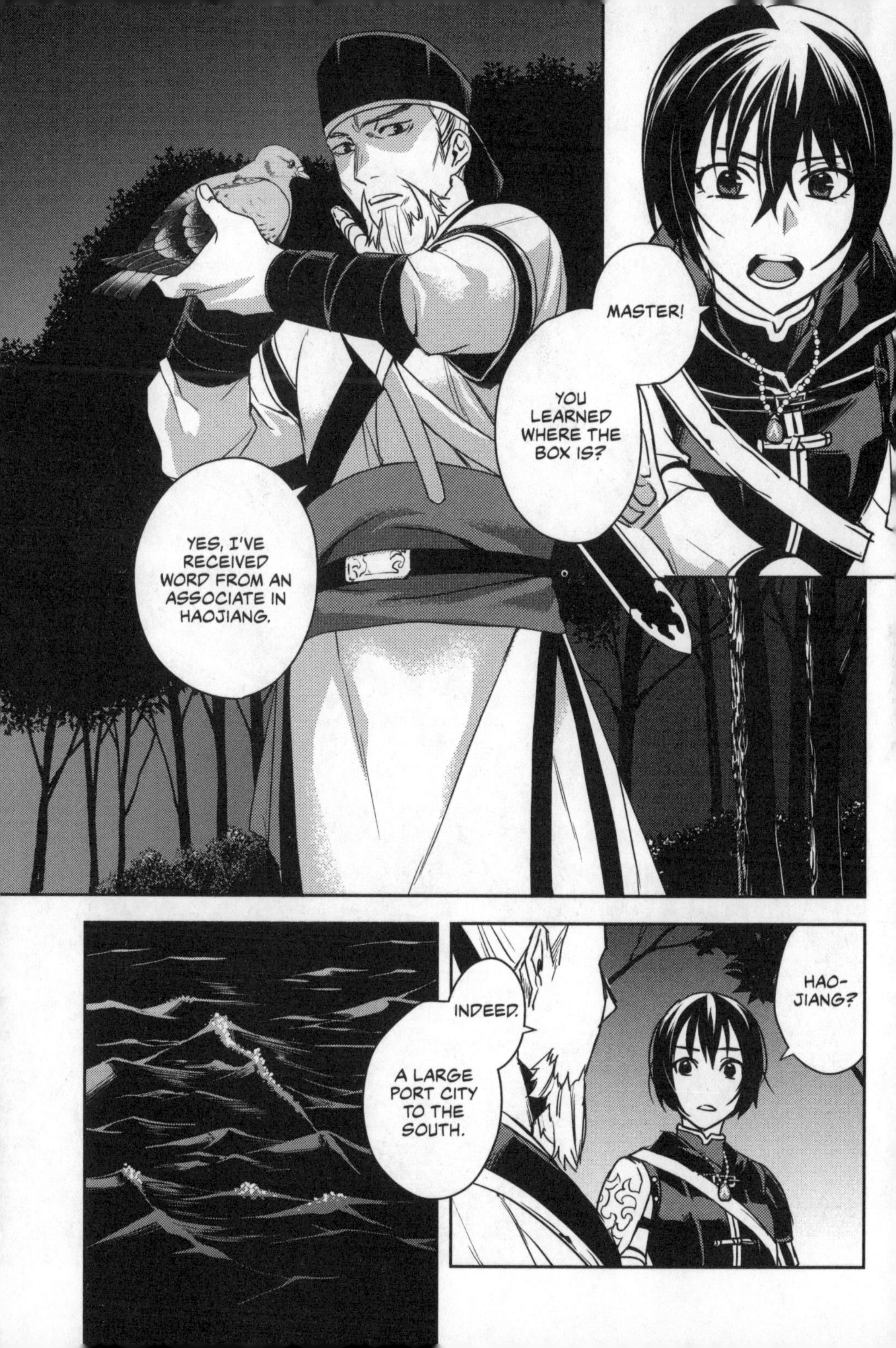
MASTER!
YOU LEARNED WHERE THE BOX IS?
YES, I'VE RECEIVED WORD FROM AN ASSOCIATE IN HAOJIANG.
HAO-JIANG?
INDEED.
A LARGE PORT CITY TO THE SOUTH.

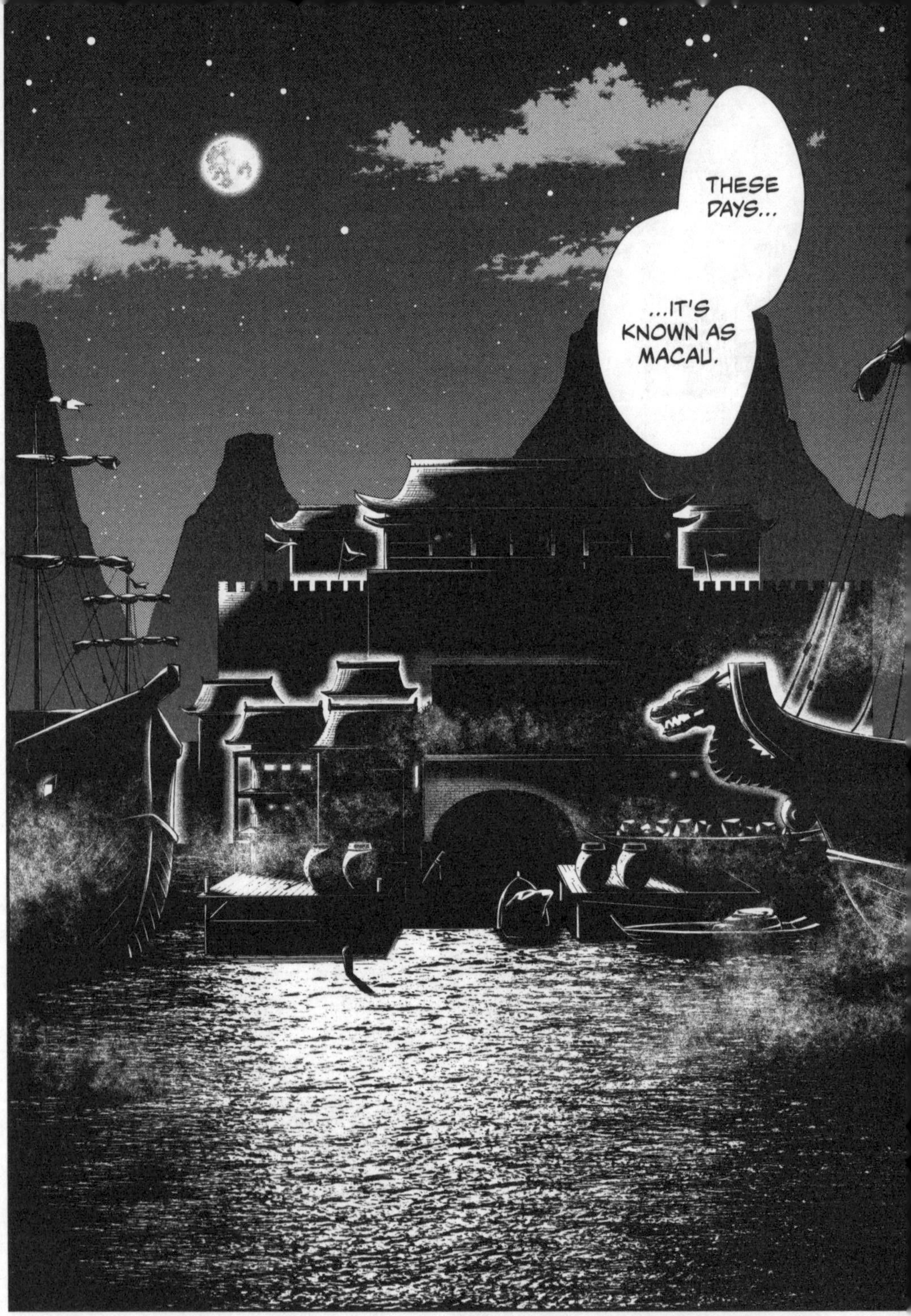
THESE DAYS...
...IT'S KNOWN AS MACAU.

Chapter 3: Port

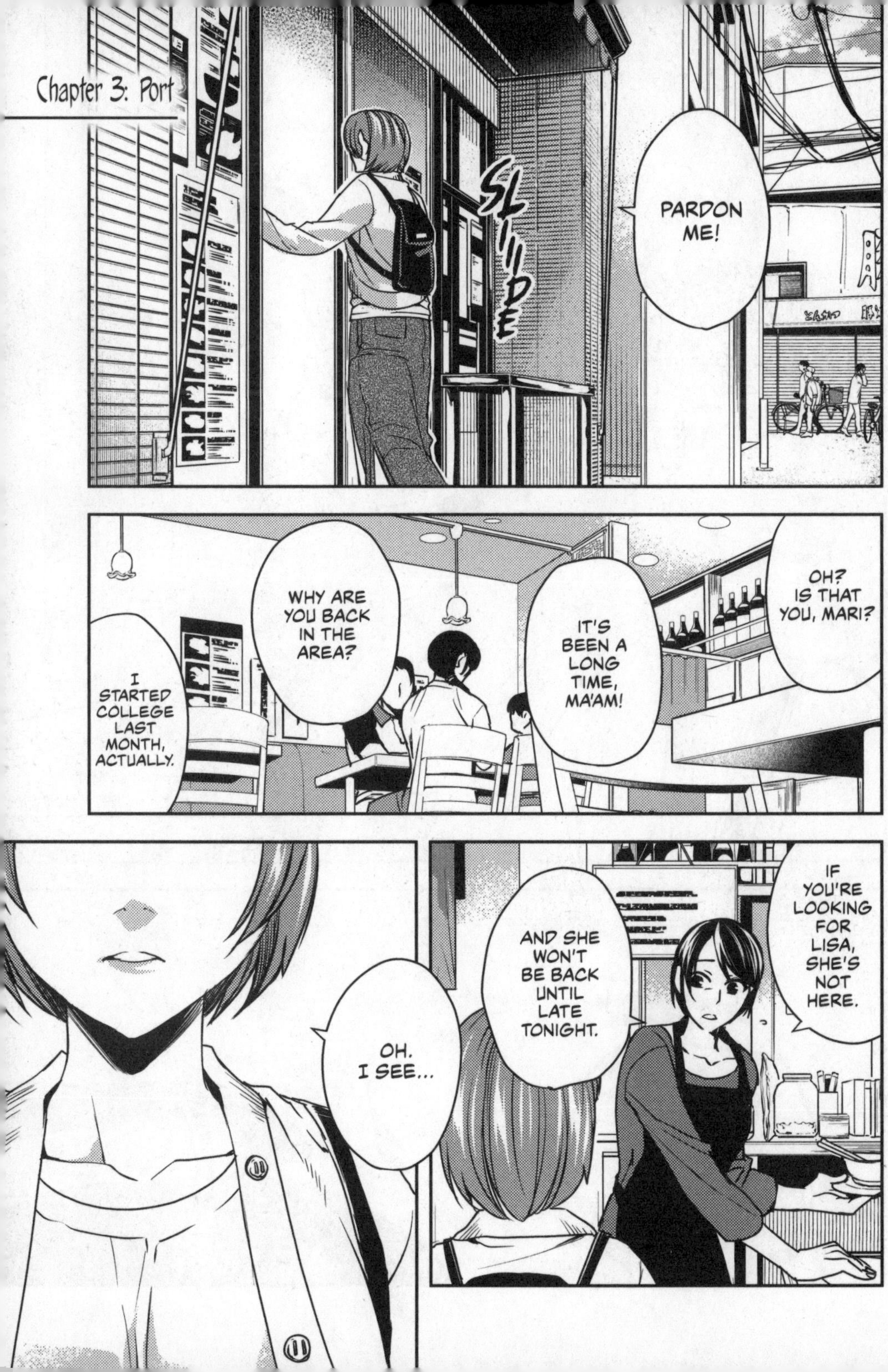

SLIIDE
PARDON ME!
OH? IS THAT YOU, MARI?
IT'S BEEN A LONG TIME, MA'AM!
WHY ARE YOU BACK IN THE AREA?
I STARTED COLLEGE LAST MONTH, ACTUALLY.
IF YOU'RE LOOKING FOR LISA, SHE'S NOT HERE.
AND SHE WON'T BE BACK UNTIL LATE TONIGHT.
OH. I SEE...

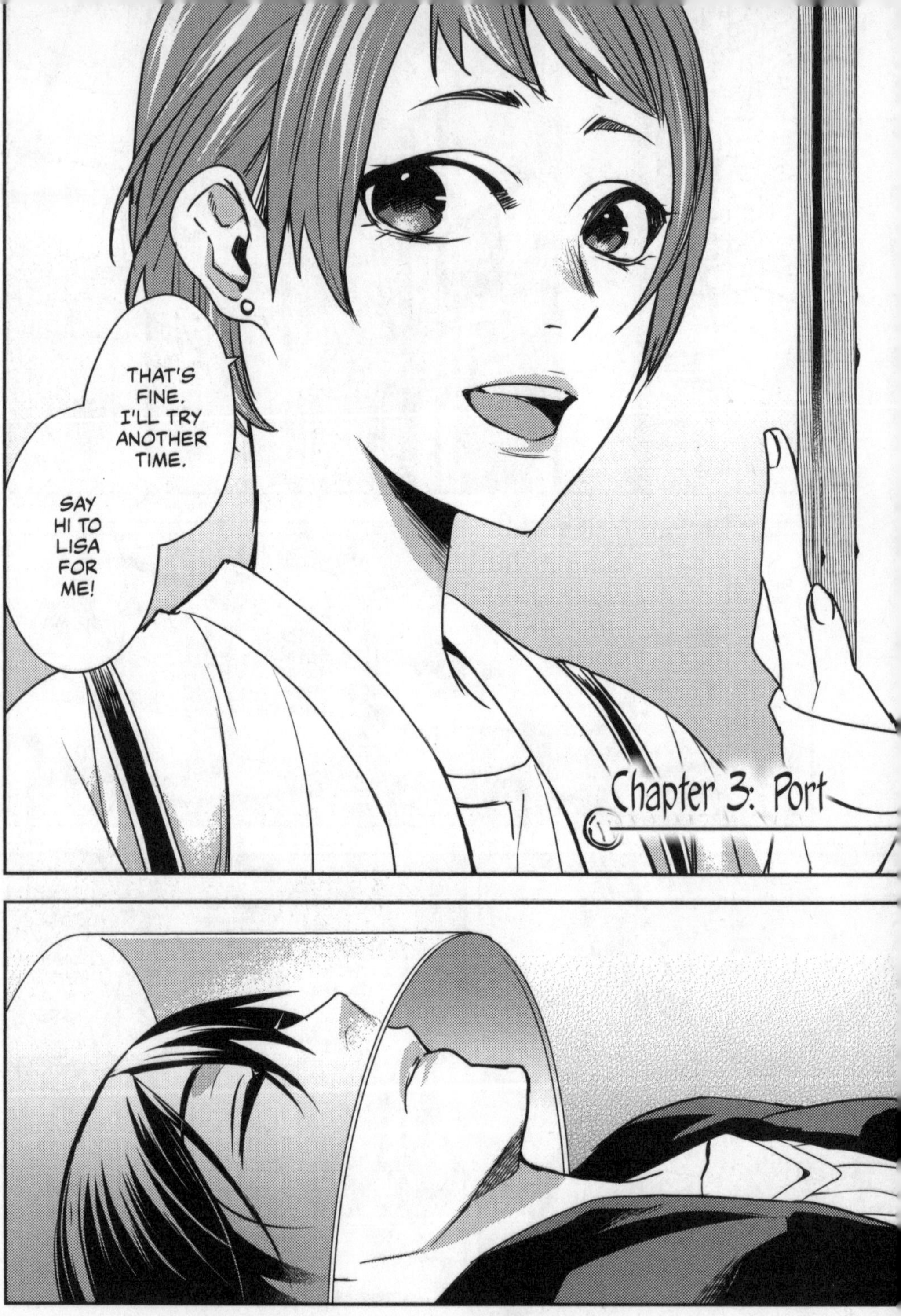
THAT'S FINE. I'LL TRY ANOTHER TIME.
SAY HI TO LISA FOR ME!
Chapter 3: Port

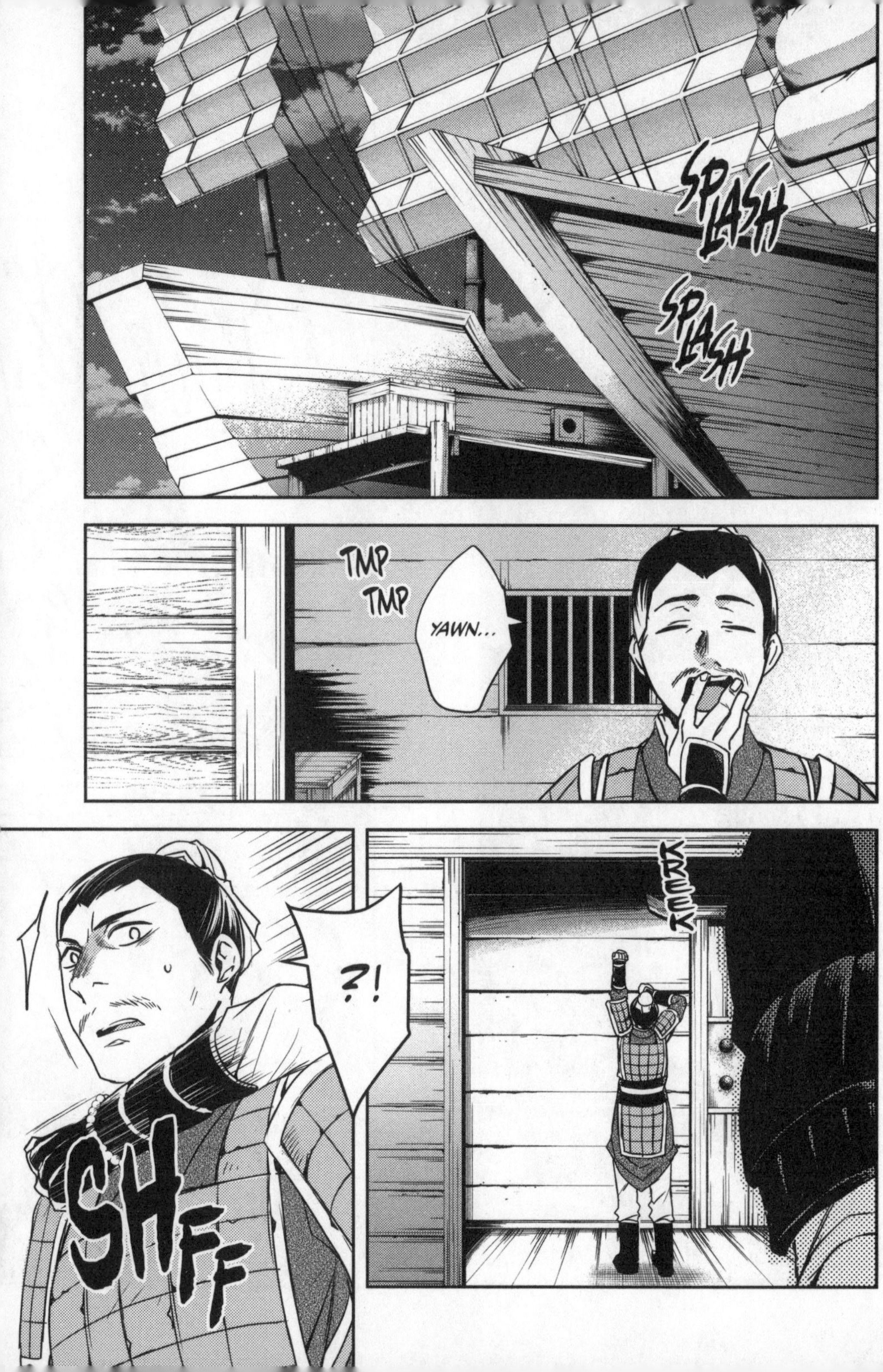
SPLASH
SPLASH
TMP TMP
YAWN...
KREEK
?!
SHFF

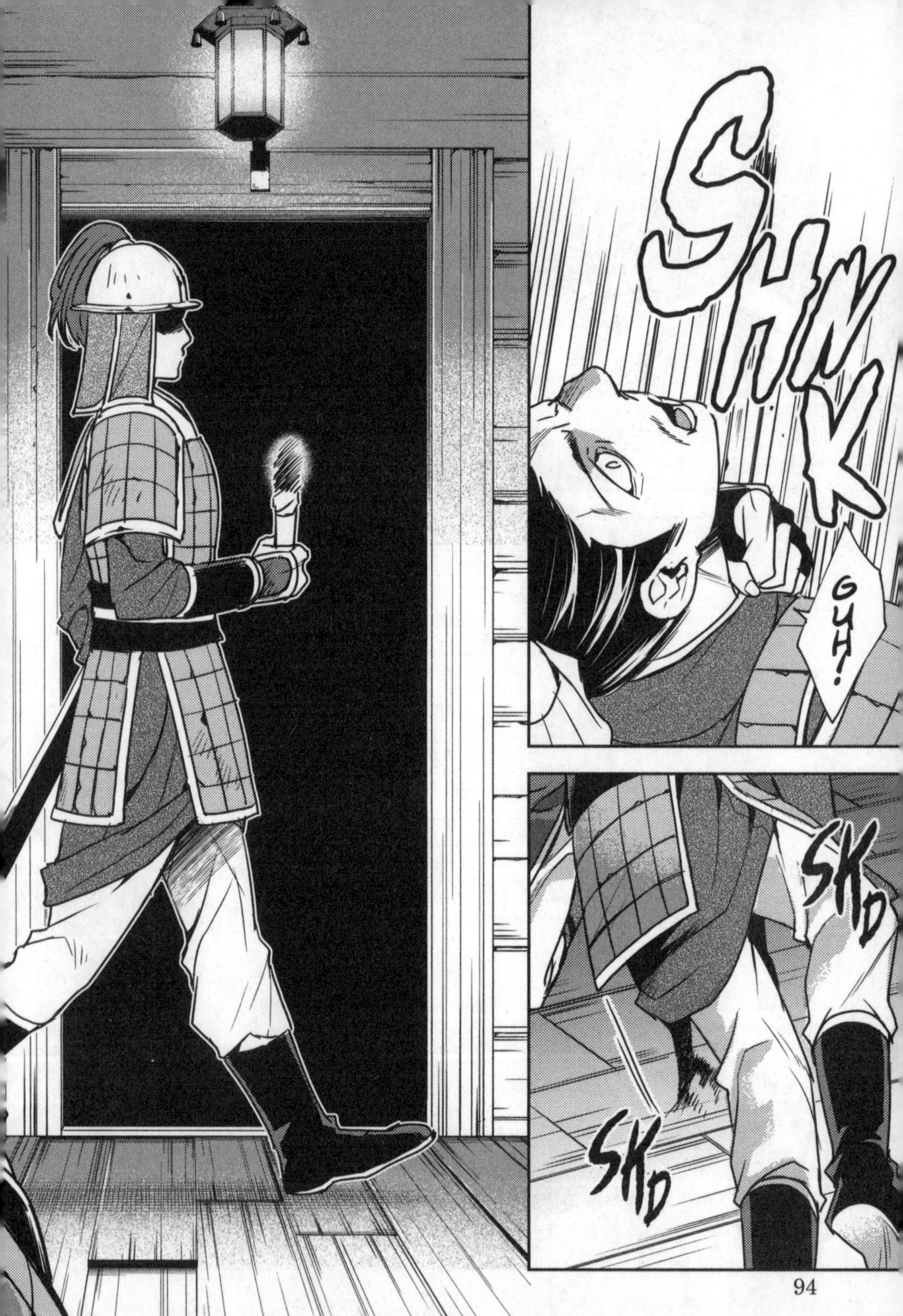
SHNK
GUH!
SKD
SKD

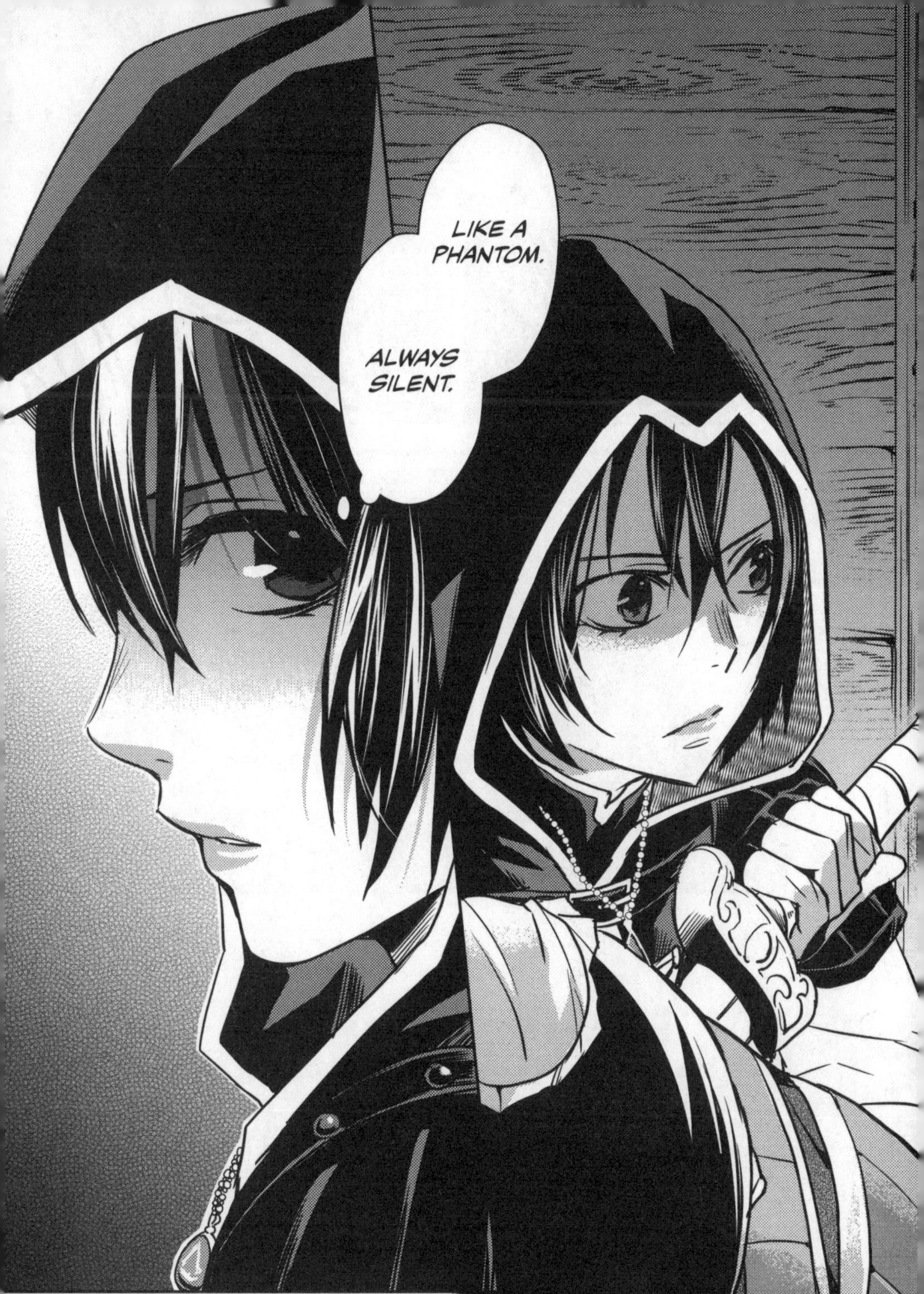
LIKE A PHANTOM.
ALWAYS SILENT.

I HAVE TO TAKE HIM OUT BEFORE THEY'RE ALERTED TO MY PRESENCE.

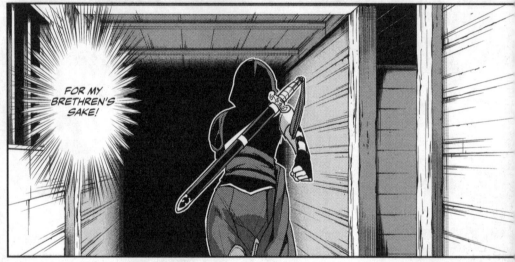

FOR MY BRETHREN'S SAKE!

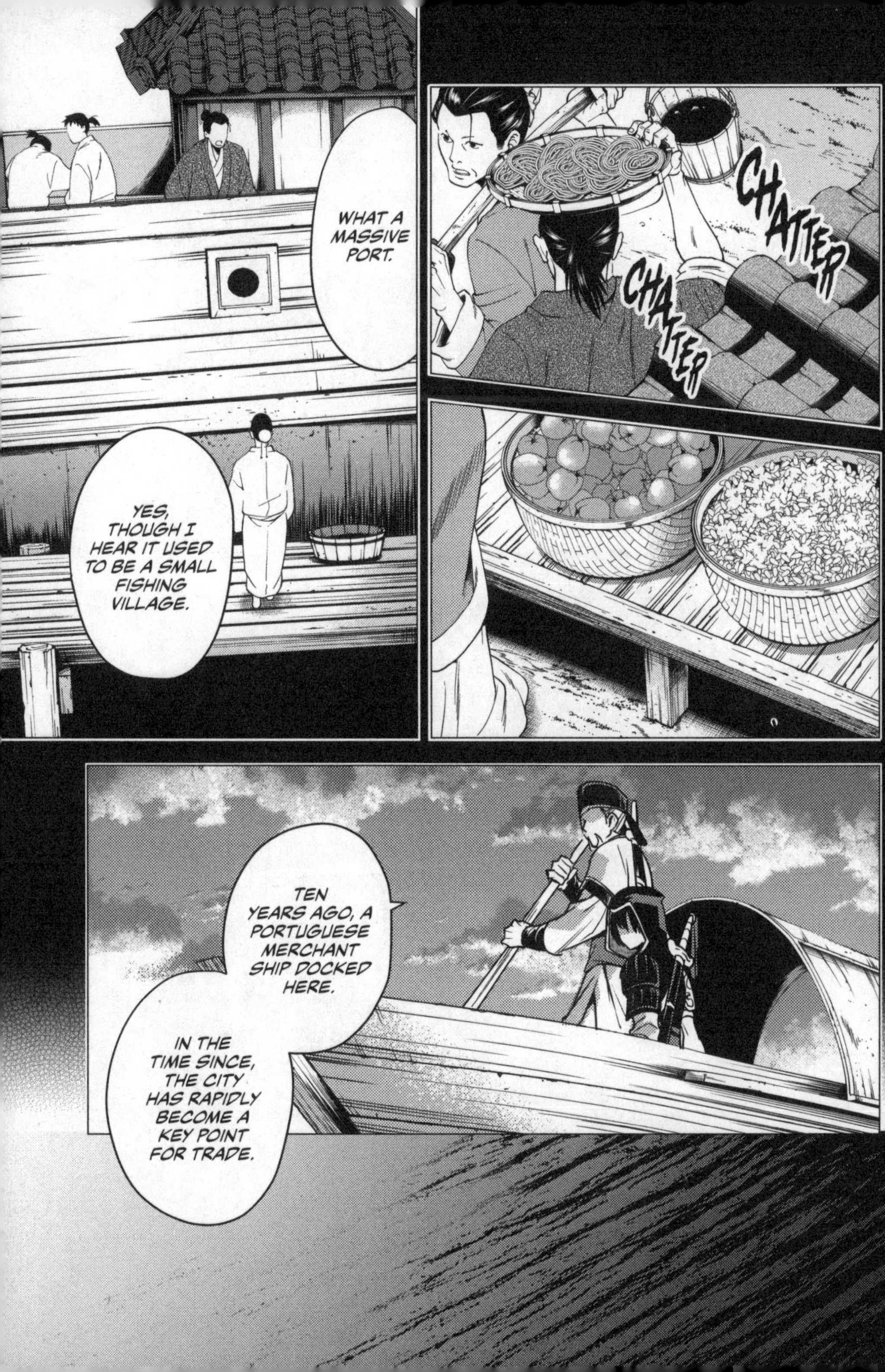
CHATTER
CHATTER
WHAT A MASSIVE PORT.
YES, THOUGH I HEAR IT USED TO BE A SMALL FISHING VILLAGE.
TEN YEARS AGO, A PORTUGUESE MERCHANT SHIP DOCKED HERE.
IN THE TIME SINCE, THE CITY HAS RAPIDLY BECOME A KEY POINT FOR TRADE.

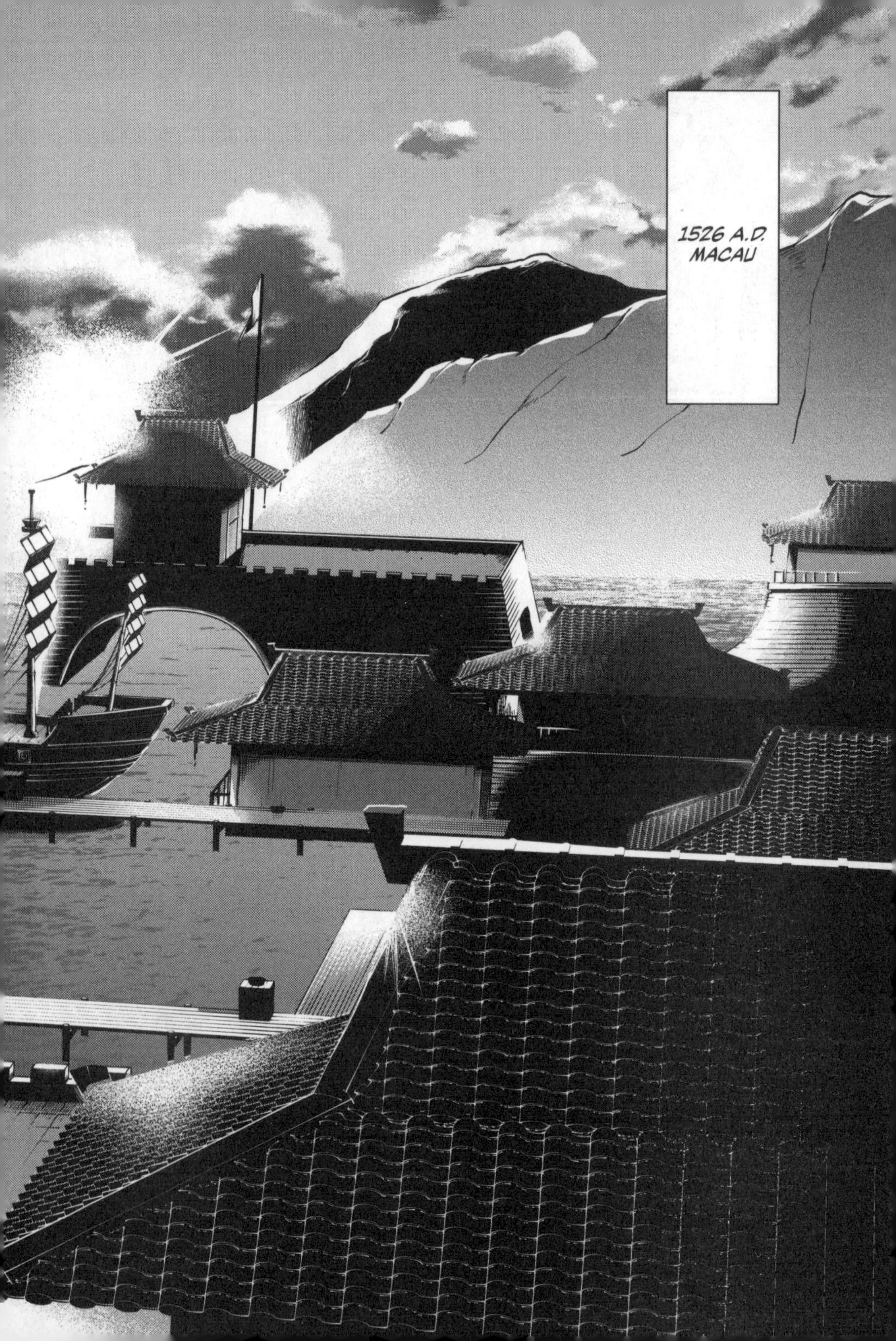
1526 A.D.
MACAU

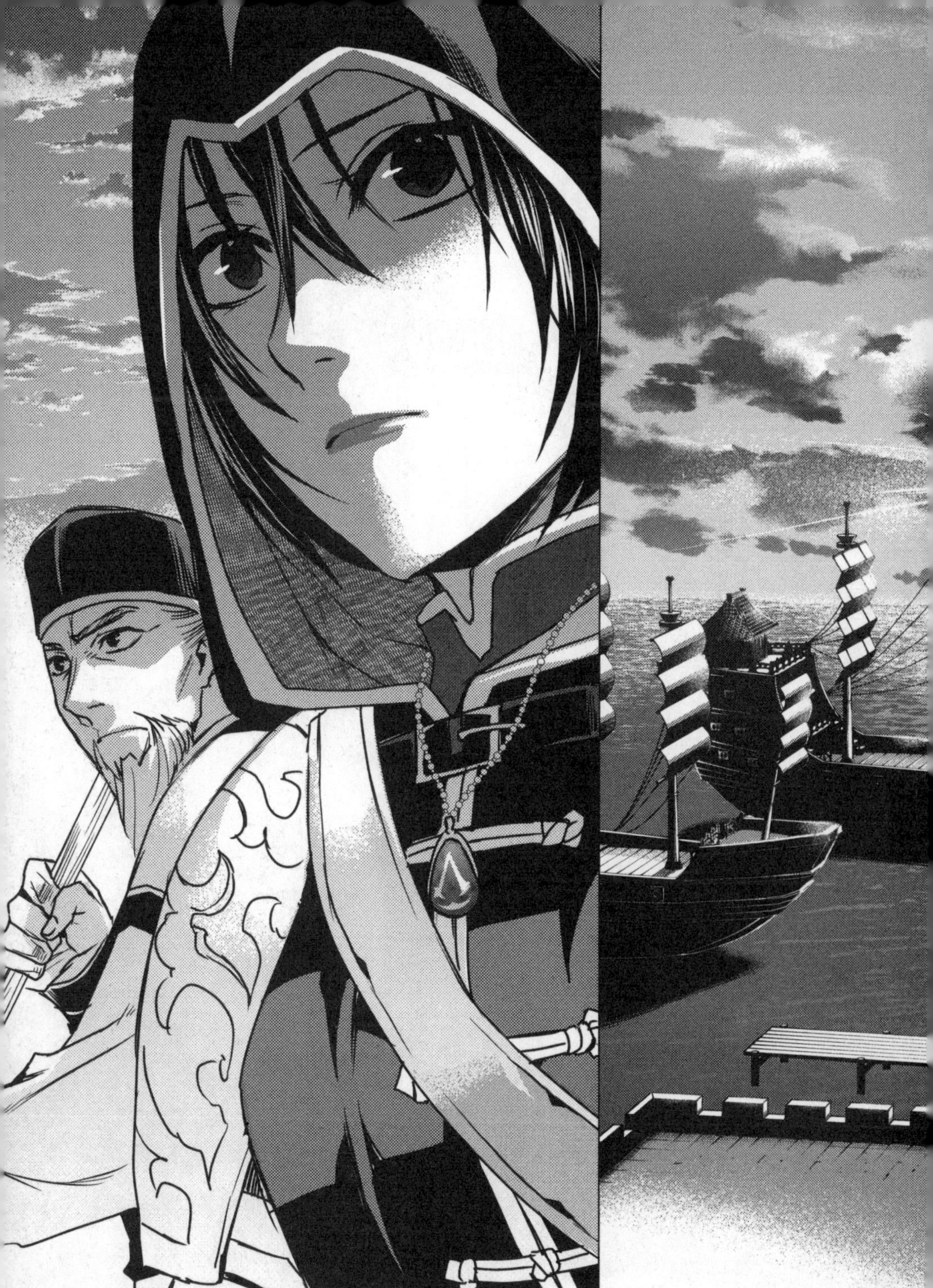

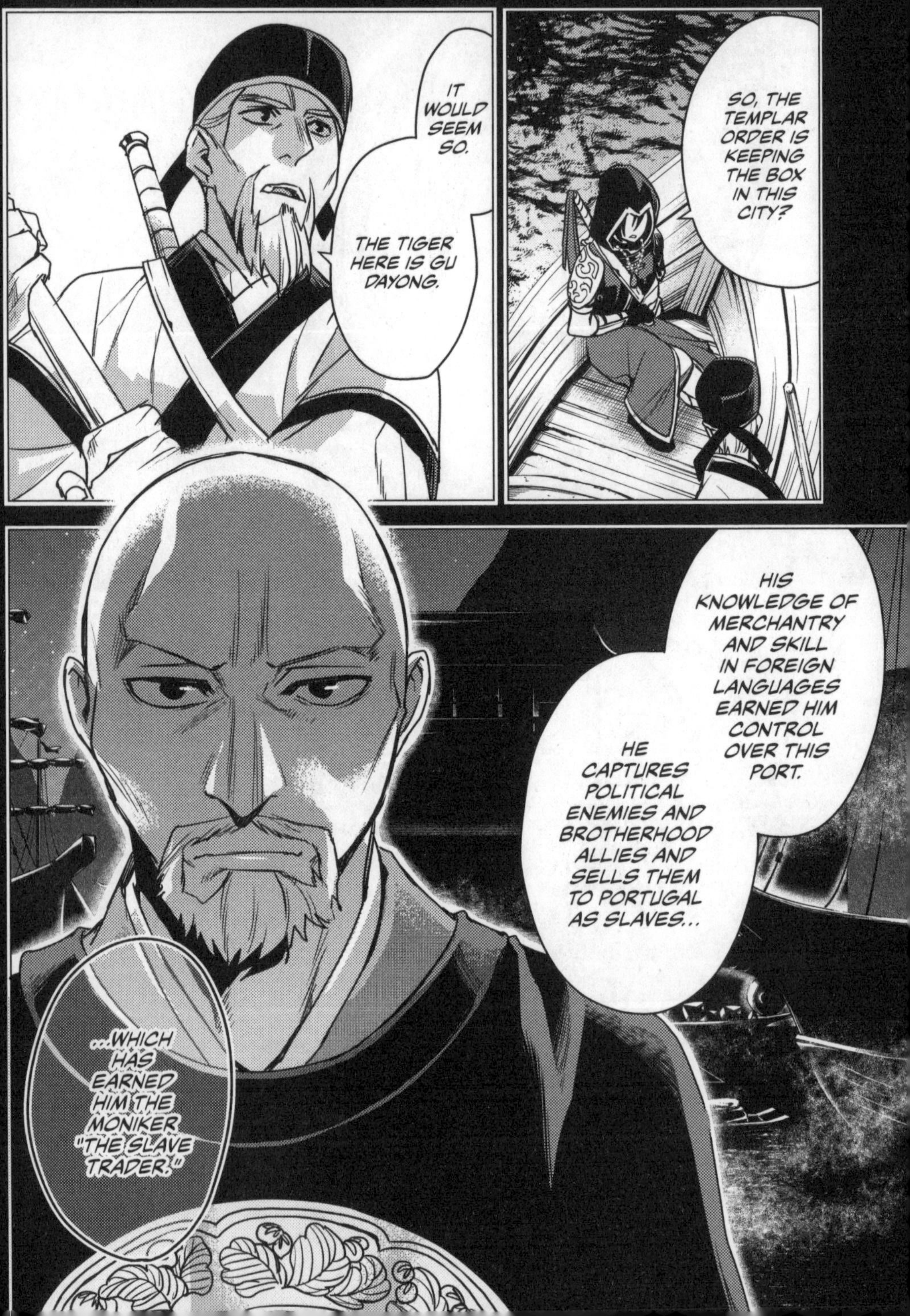
SO, THE TEMPLAR ORDER IS KEEPING THE BOX IN THIS CITY?
IT WOULD SEEM SO.
THE TIGER HERE IS GU DAYONG.
HIS KNOWLEDGE OF MERCHANTRY AND SKILL IN FOREIGN LANGUAGES EARNED HIM CONTROL OVER THIS PORT.
HE CAPTURES POLITICAL ENEMIES AND BROTHERHOOD ALLIES AND SELLS THEM TO PORTUGAL AS SLAVES...
...WHICH HAS EARNED HIM THE MONIKER "THE SLAVE TRADER."

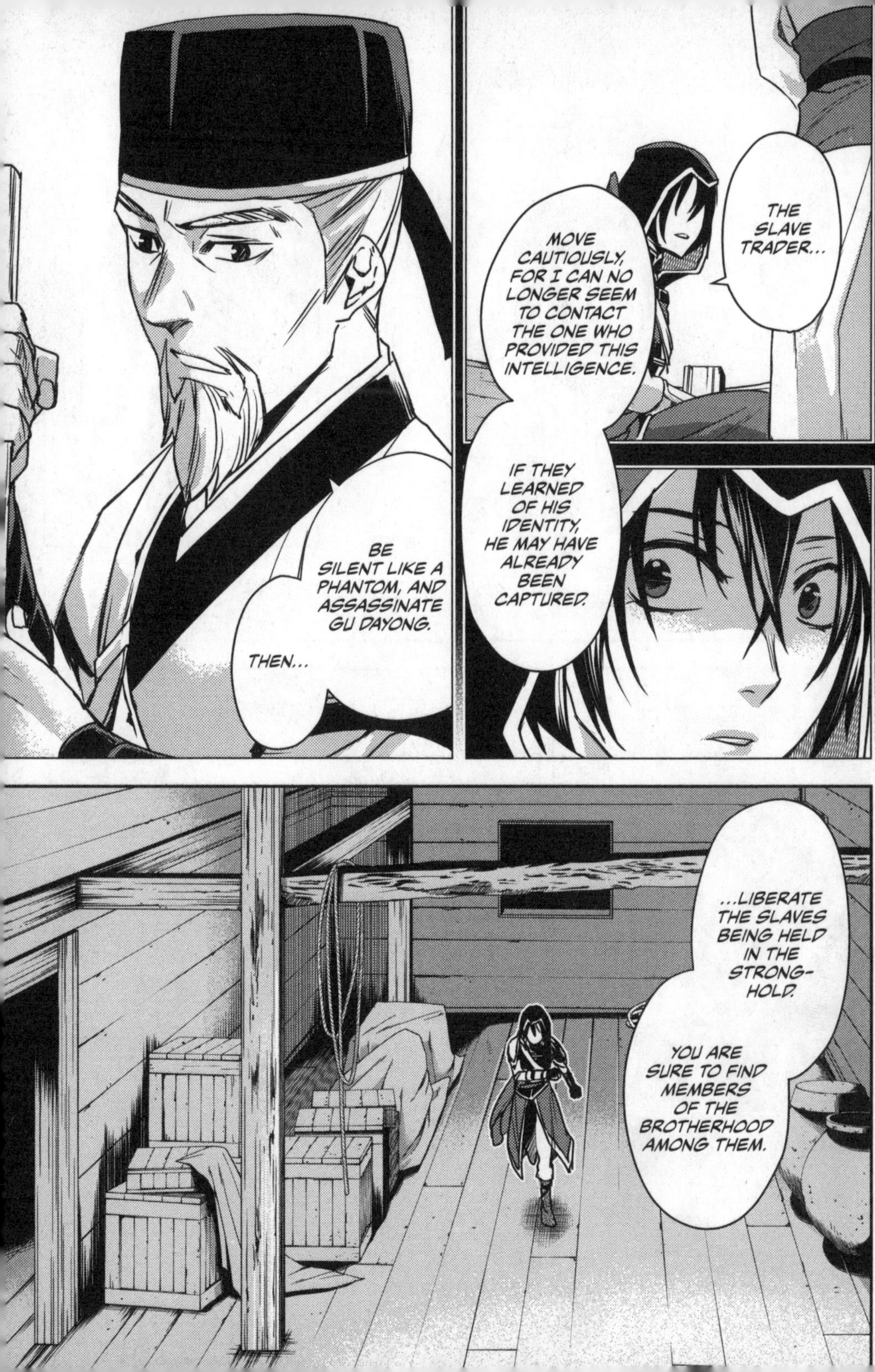
THE SLAVE TRADER...
MOVE CAUTIOUSLY, FOR I CAN NO LONGER SEEM TO CONTACT THE ONE WHO PROVIDED THIS INTELLIGENCE.
IF THEY LEARNED OF HIS IDENTITY, HE MAY HAVE ALREADY BEEN CAPTURED.
BE SILENT LIKE A PHANTOM, AND ASSASSINATE GU DAYONG.
THEN...
...LIBERATE THE SLAVES BEING HELD IN THE STRONGHOLD.
YOU ARE SURE TO FIND MEMBERS OF THE BROTHERHOOD AMONG THEM.

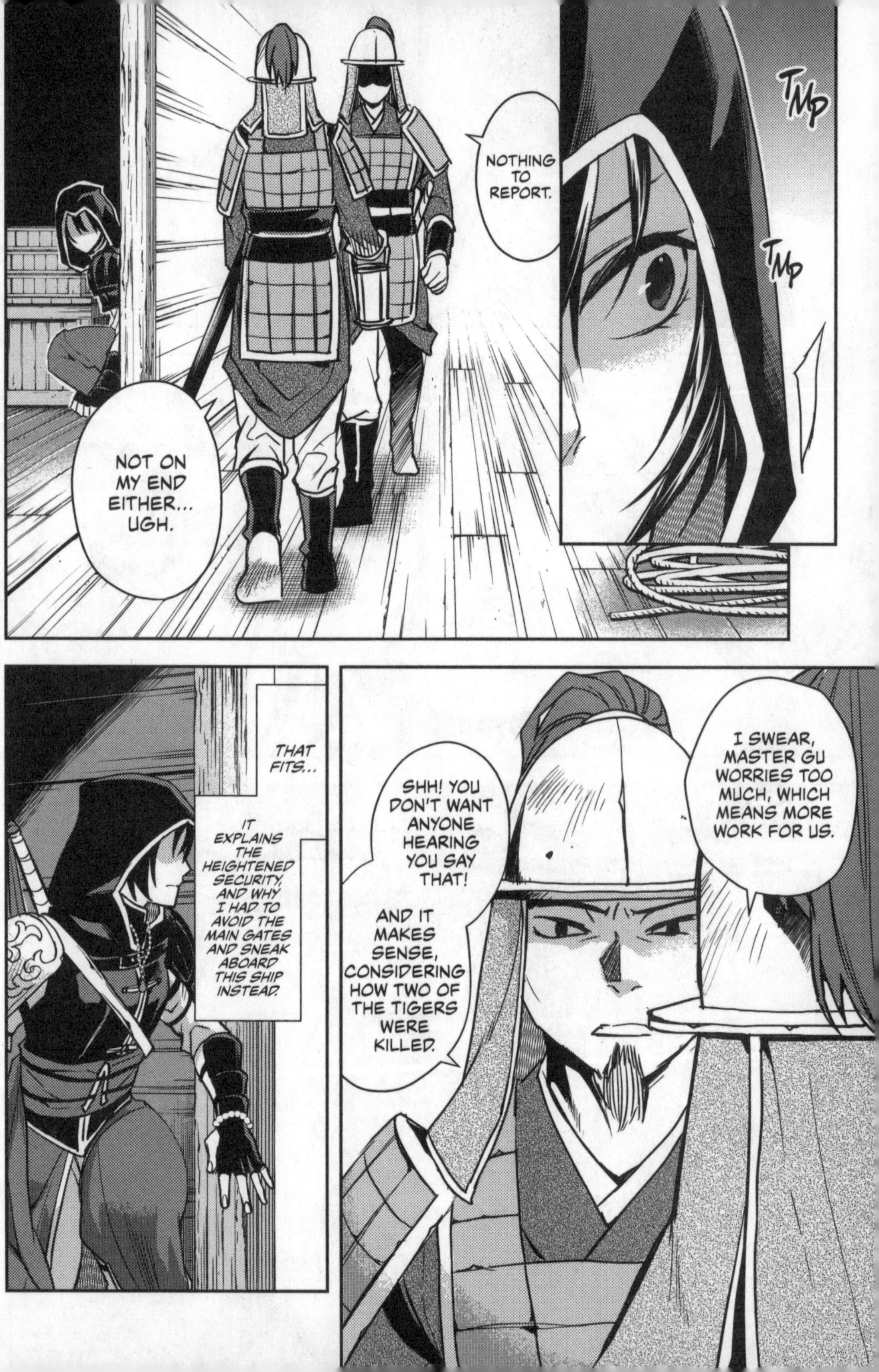
TMP
TMP
NOTHING TO REPORT.
NOT ON MY END EITHER... UGH.
I SWEAR, MASTER GU WORRIES TOO MUCH, WHICH MEANS MORE WORK FOR US.
SHH! YOU DON'T WANT ANYONE HEARING YOU SAY THAT!
AND IT MAKES SENSE, CONSIDERING HOW TWO OF THE TIGERS WERE KILLED.
THAT FITS...
IT EXPLAINS THE HEIGHTENED SECURITY, AND WHY I HAD TO AVOID THE MAIN GATES AND SNEAK ABOARD THIS SHIP INSTEAD.

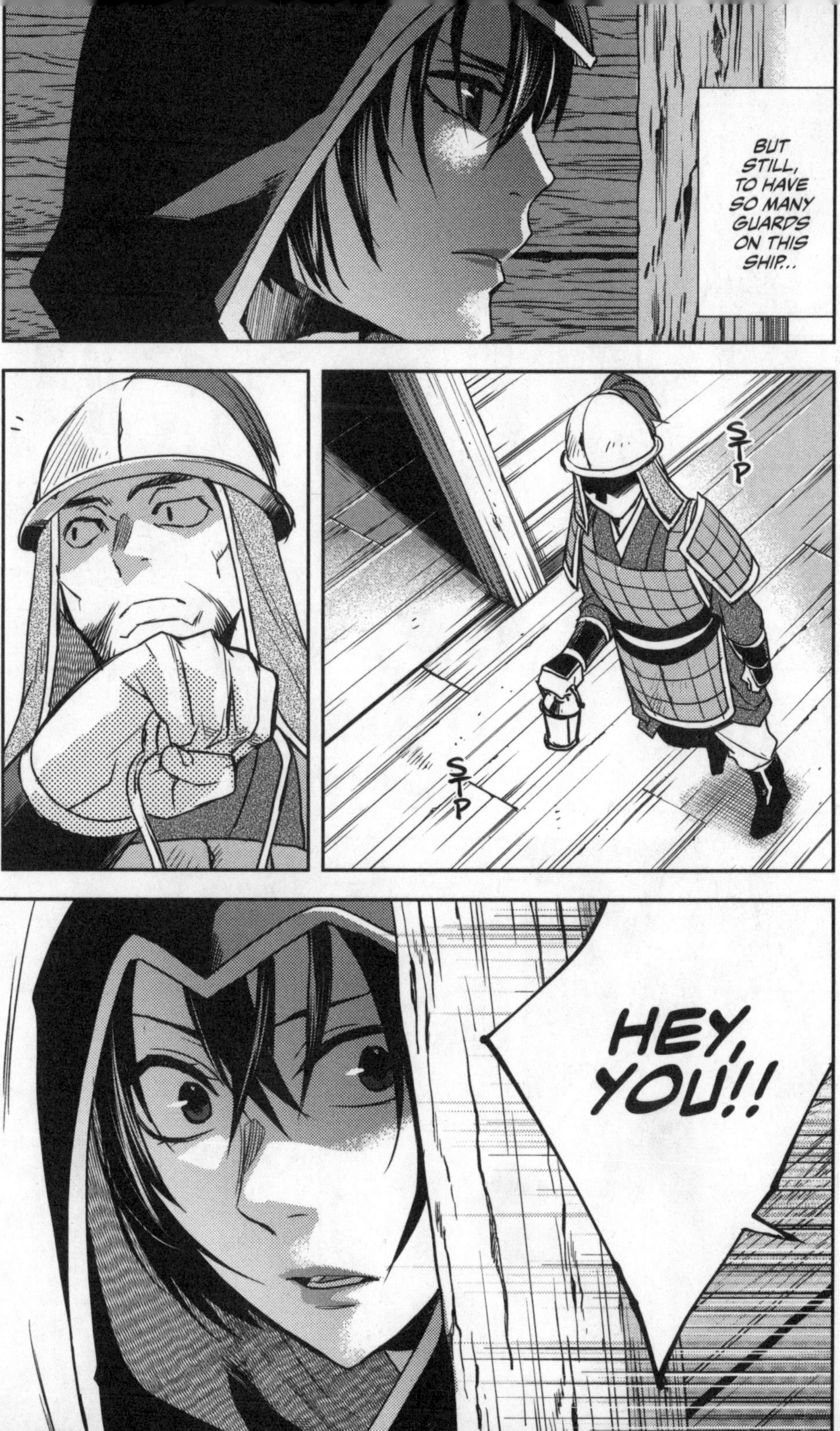
BUT STILL, TO HAVE SO MANY GUARDS ON THIS SHIP...
STP
STP
HEY, YOU!!

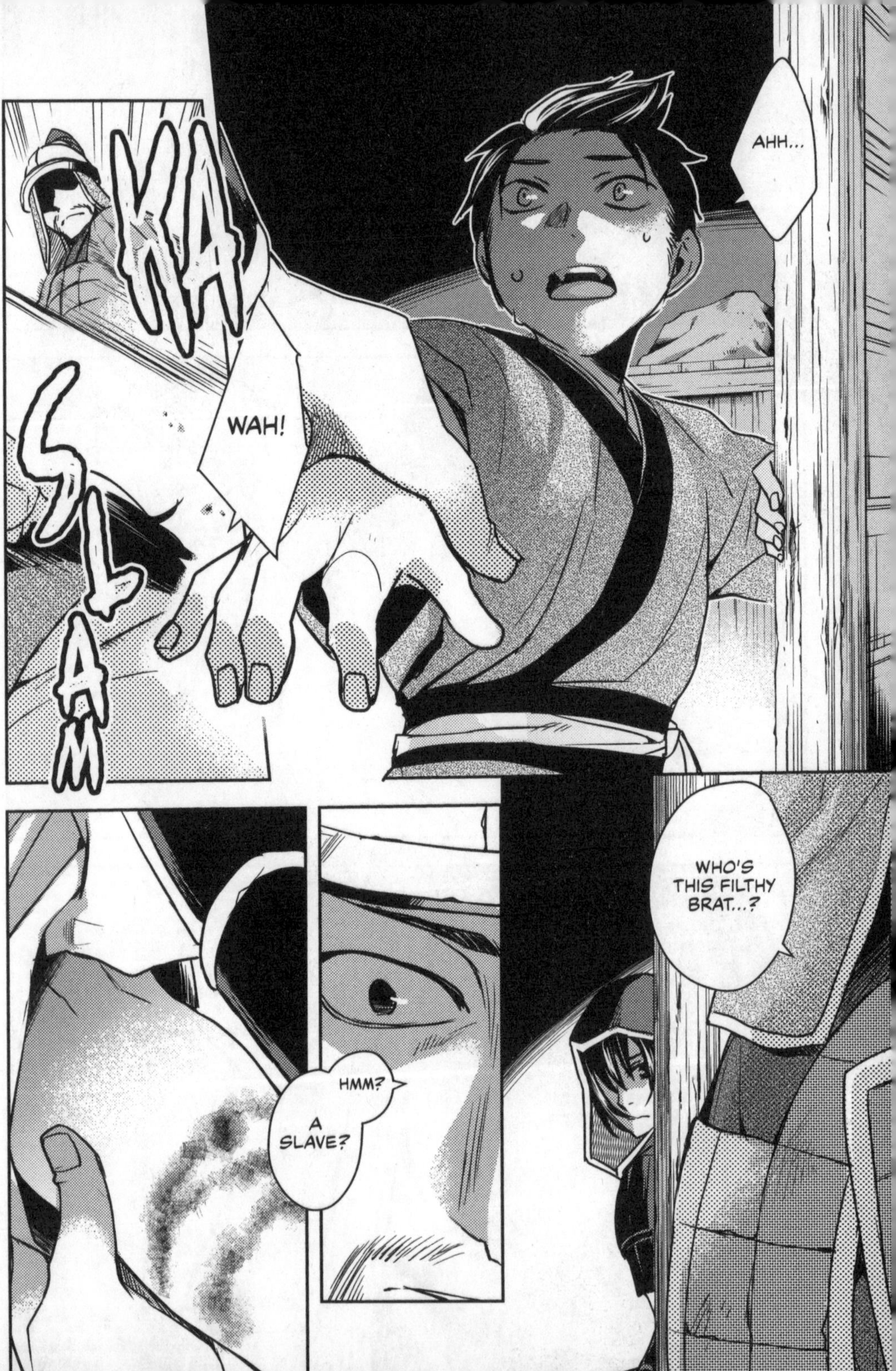
AHH...
WAH!
KA SLAM
WHO'S THIS FILTHY BRAT...?
HMM?
A SLAVE?

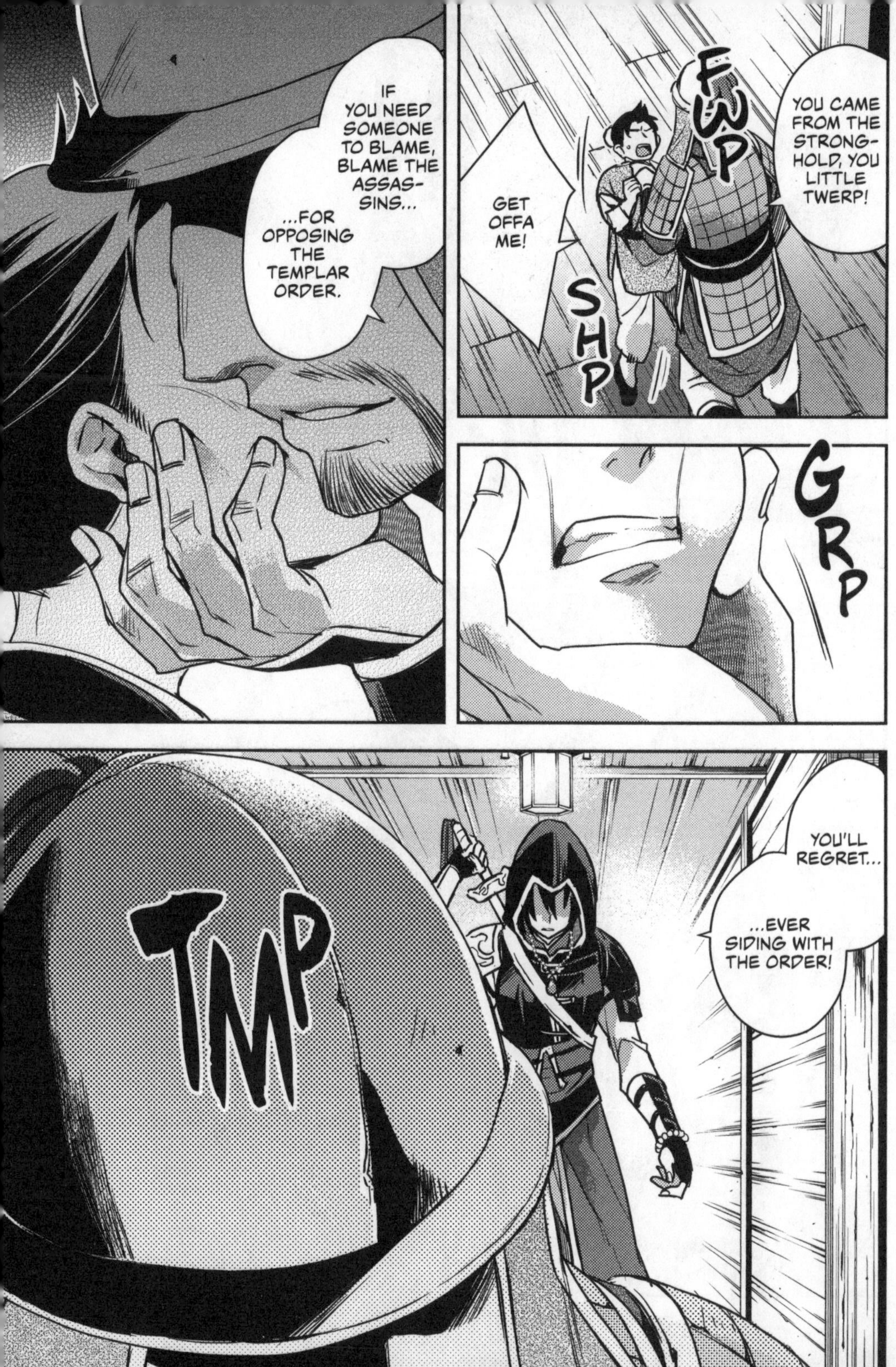
FWP
YOU CAME FROM THE STRONG-HOLD, YOU LITTLE TWERP!
GET OFFA ME!
SHP
SHP
GRP
IF YOU NEED SOMEONE TO BLAME, BLAME THE ASSAS-SINS...
...FOR OPPOSING THE TEMPLAR ORDER.
YOU'LL REGRET...
...EVER SIDING WITH THE ORDER!
TMP

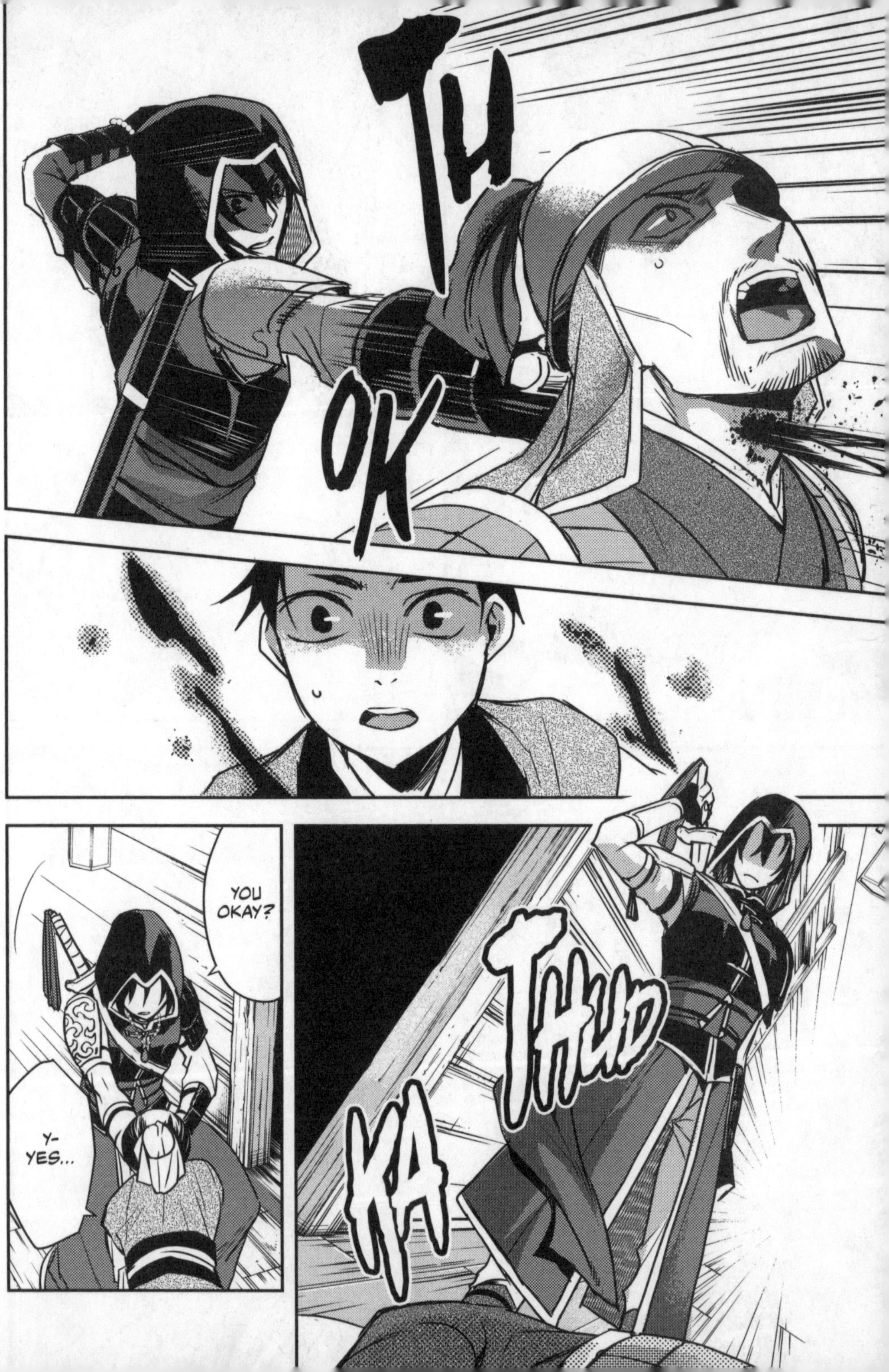
TH
OK
KA THUD
YOU OKAY?
Y- YES...

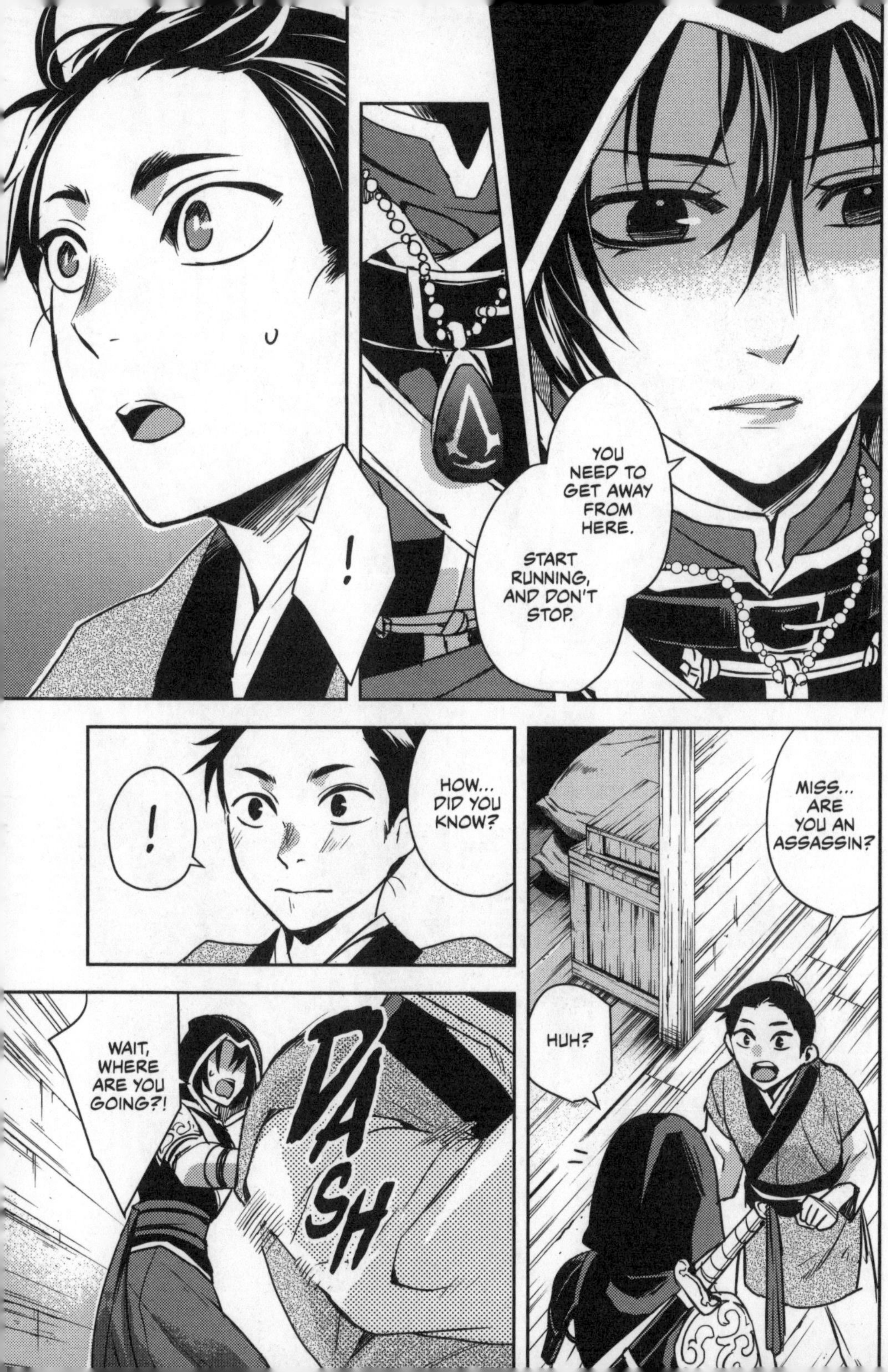
YOU NEED TO GET AWAY FROM HERE.
START RUNNING, AND DON'T STOP.
!
MISS... ARE YOU AN ASSASSIN?
HUH?
HOW... DID YOU KNOW?
!
DASH
WAIT, WHERE ARE YOU GOING?!

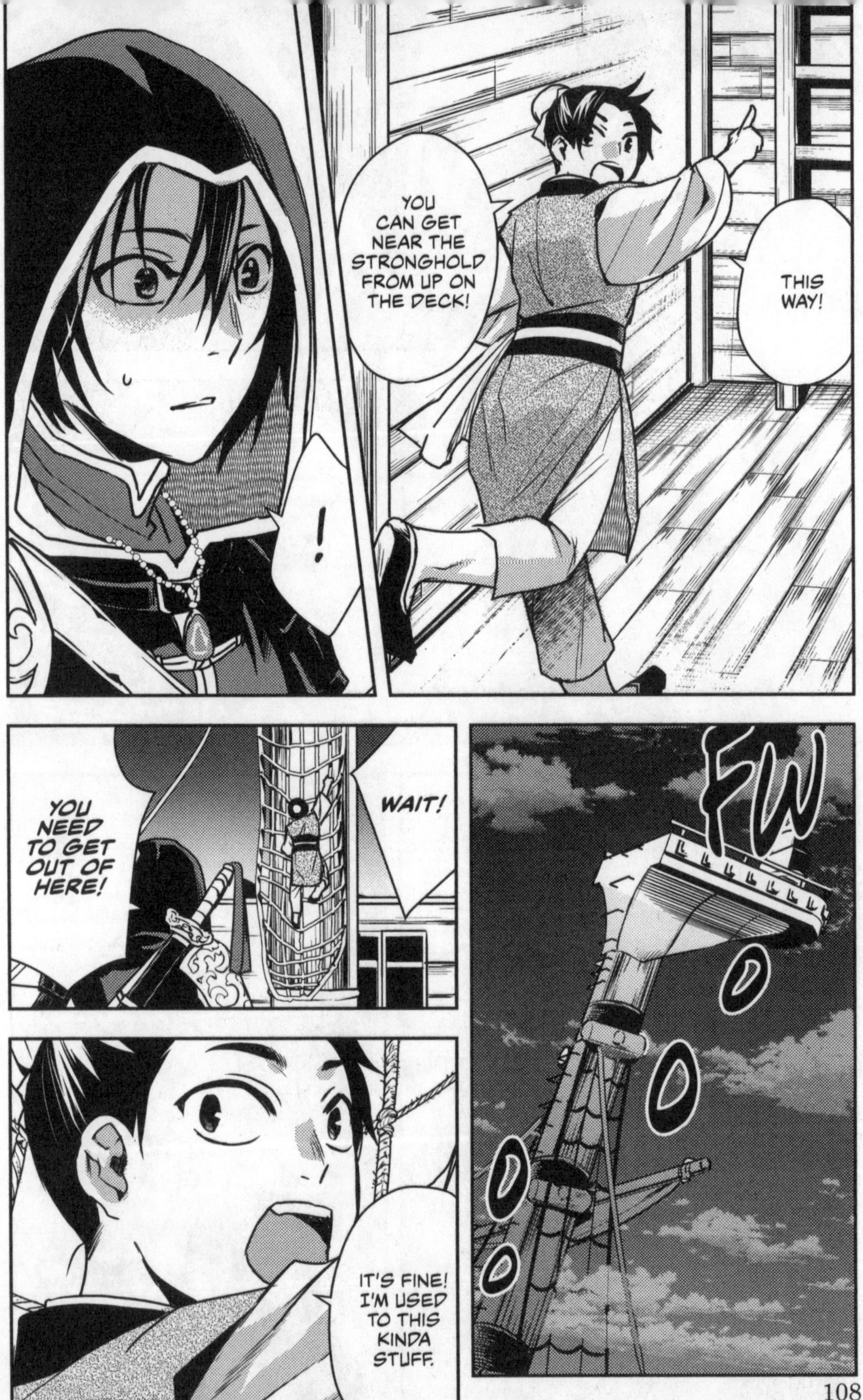
THIS WAY!
YOU CAN GET NEAR THE STRONGHOLD FROM UP ON THE DECK!
!
FW
WAIT!
YOU NEED TO GET OUT OF HERE!
IT'S FINE! I'M USED TO THIS KINDA STUFF.

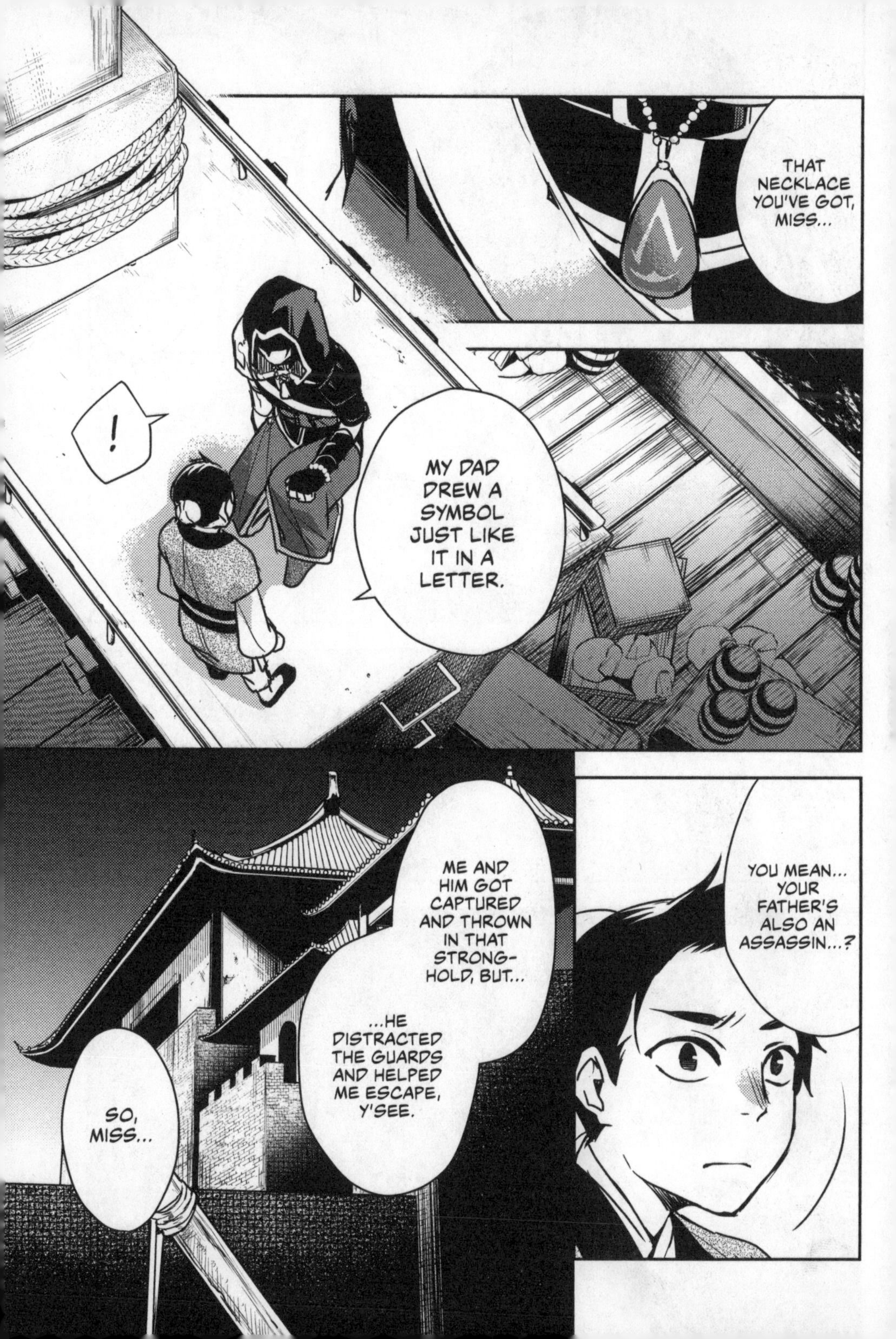
THAT NECKLACE YOU'VE GOT, MISS...
!
MY DAD DREW A SYMBOL JUST LIKE IT IN A LETTER.
YOU MEAN... YOUR FATHER'S ALSO AN ASSASSIN...?
ME AND HIM GOT CAPTURED AND THROWN IN THAT STRONG-HOLD, BUT...
...HE DISTRACTED THE GUARDS AND HELPED ME ESCAPE, Y'SEE.
SO, MISS...

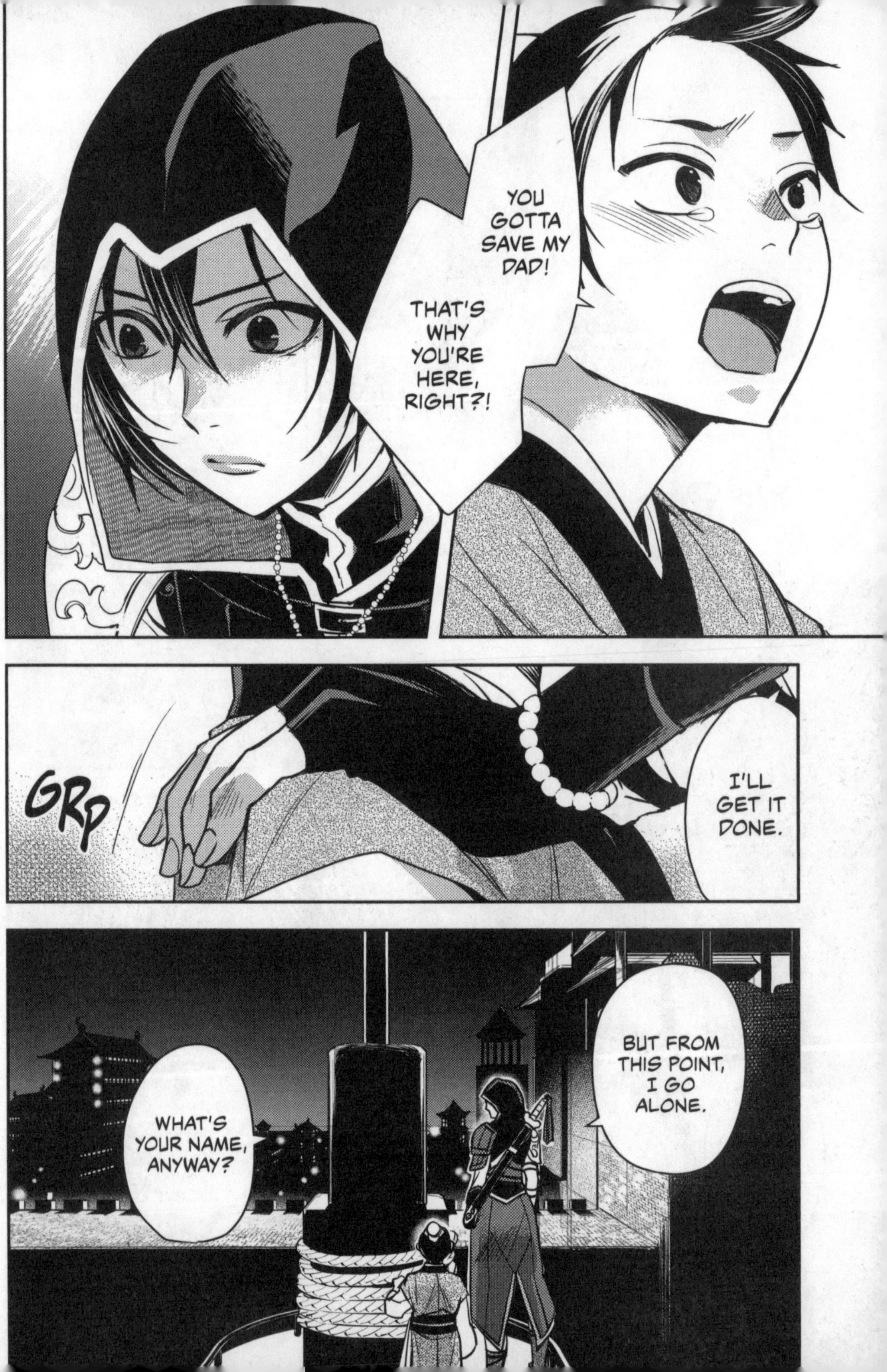
YOU GOTTA SAVE MY DAD!
THAT'S WHY YOU'RE HERE, RIGHT?!
I'LL GET IT DONE.
GRP
BUT FROM THIS POINT, I GO ALONE.
WHAT'S YOUR NAME, ANYWAY?

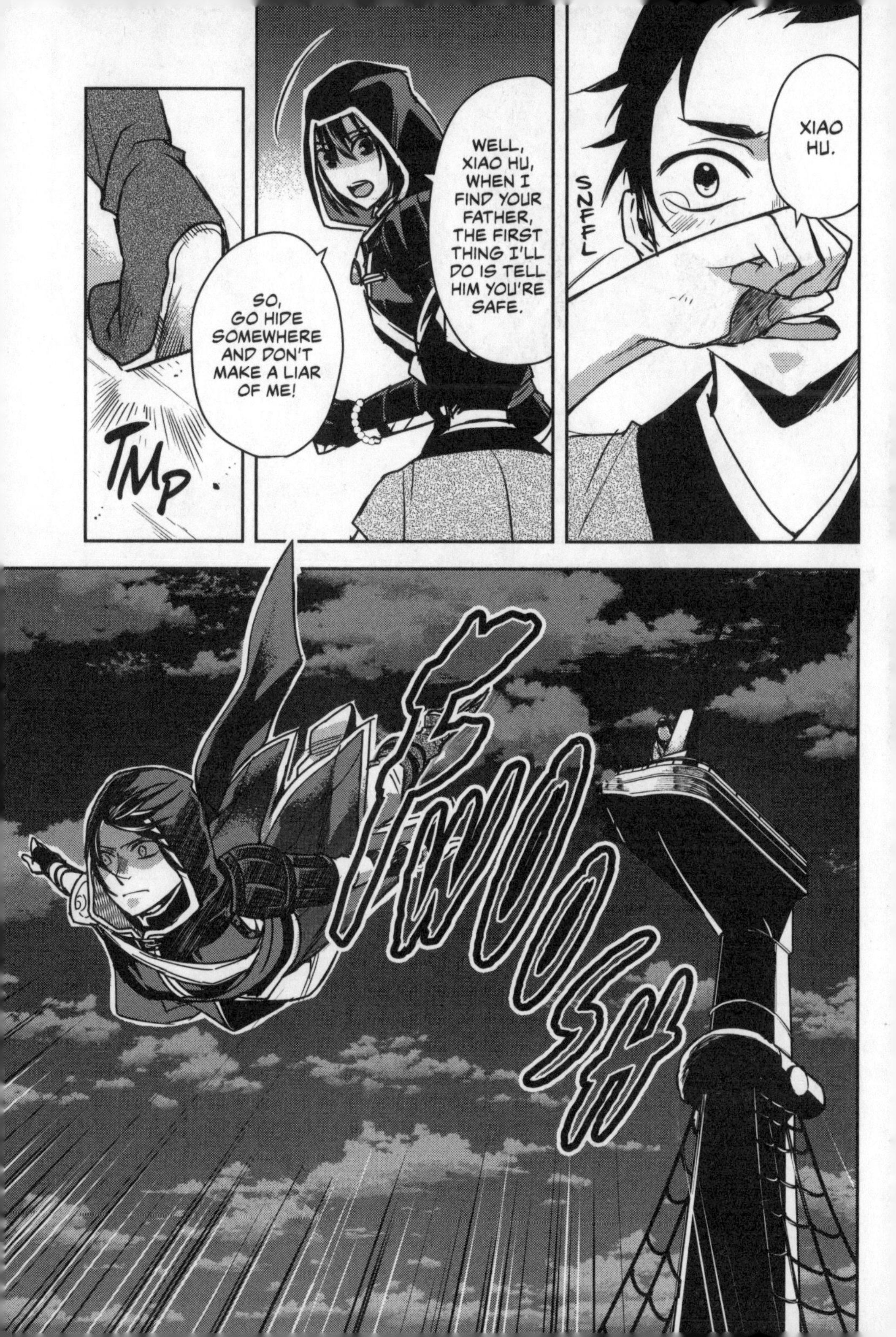
XIAO HU.
SNFFL
WELL, XIAO HU, WHEN I FIND YOUR FATHER, THE FIRST THING I'LL DO IS TELL HIM YOU'RE SAFE.
SO, GO HIDE SOMEWHERE AND DON'T MAKE A LIAR OF ME!
TMP
FWOOOSH

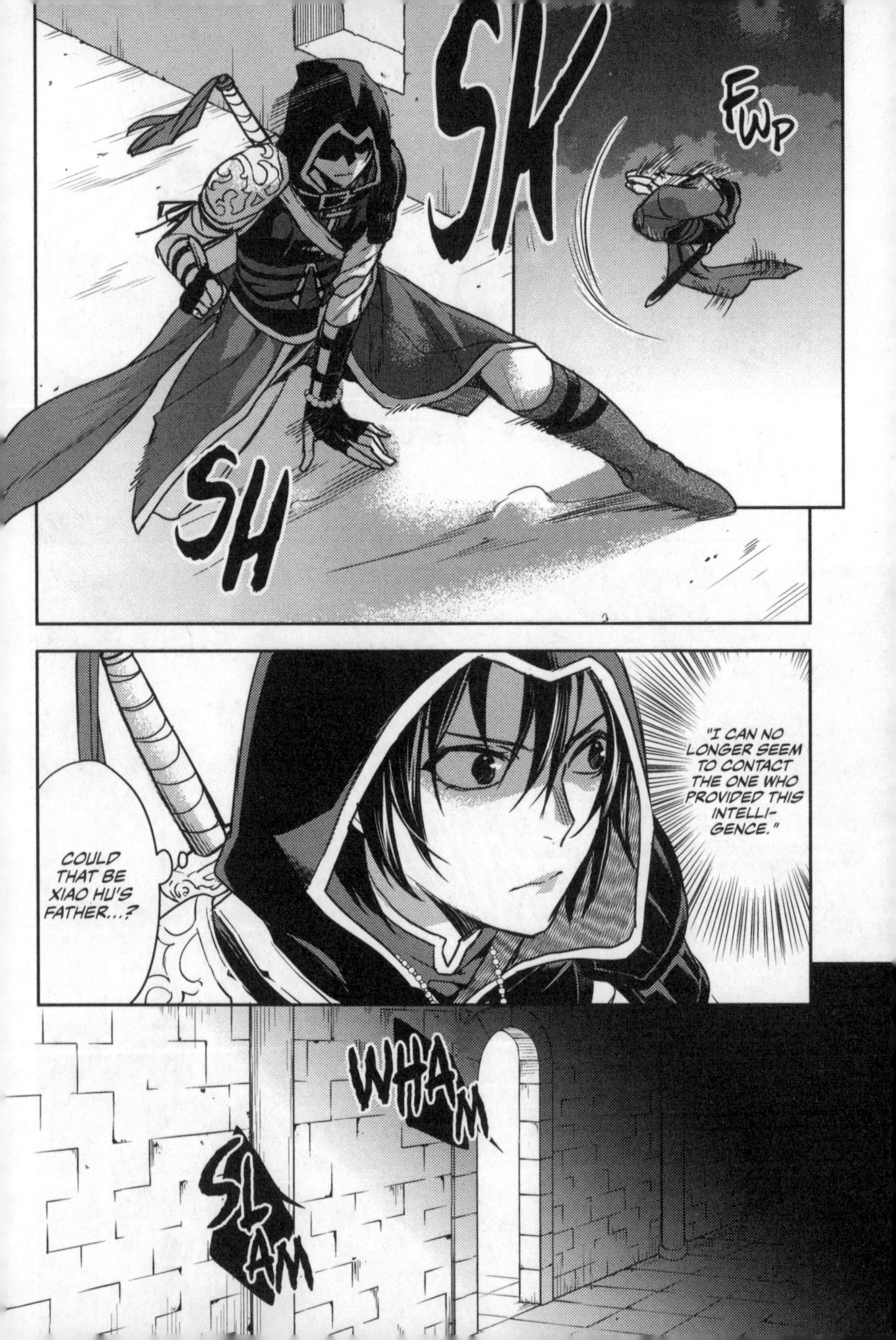
FWP
SK
SH
"I CAN NO LONGER SEEM TO CONTACT THE ONE WHO PROVIDED THIS INTELLI-GENCE."
COULD THAT BE XIAO HU'S FATHER...?
WHAM
SLAM

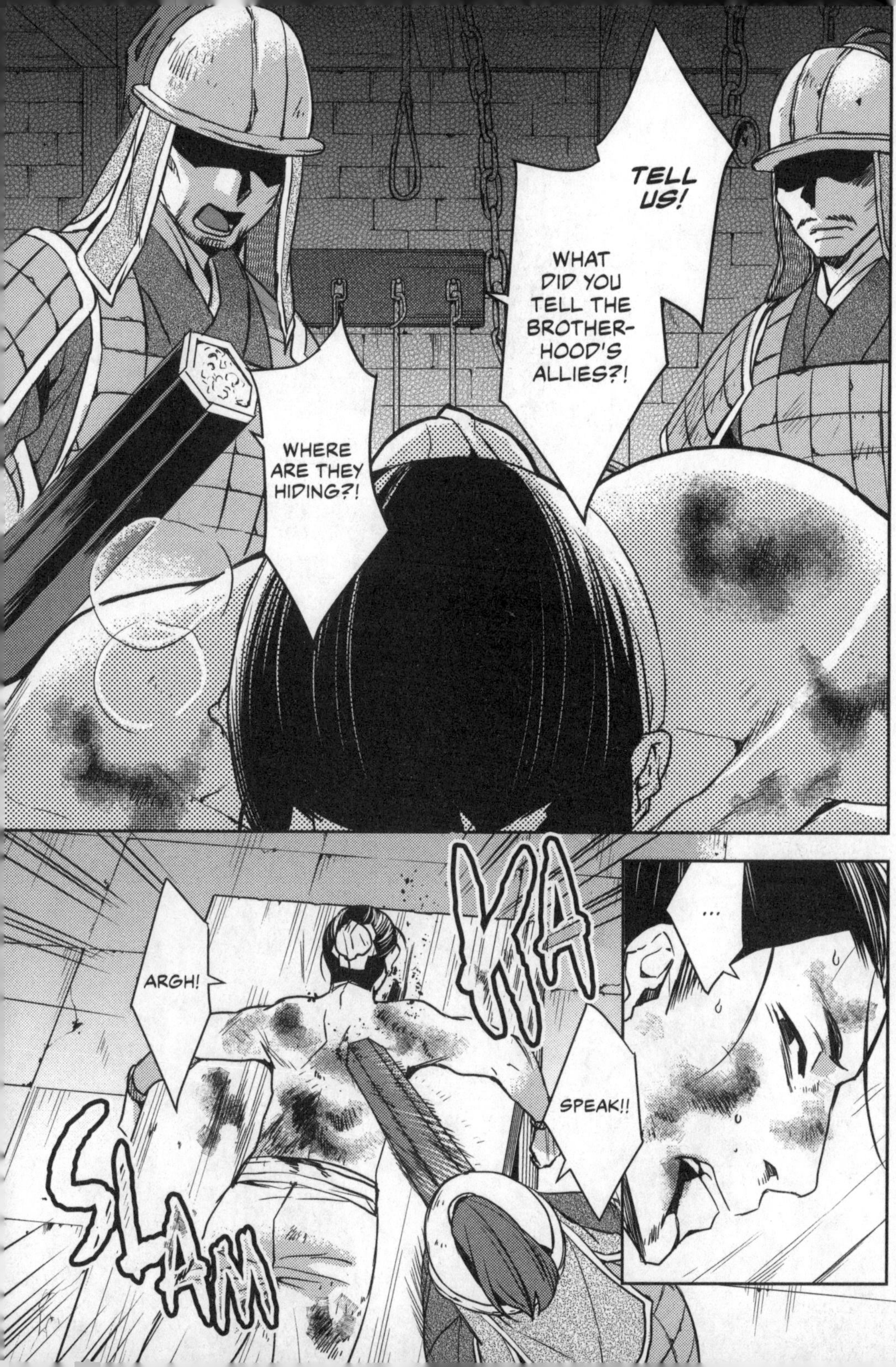
TELL US!
WHAT DID YOU TELL THE BROTHER-HOOD'S ALLIES?!
WHERE ARE THEY HIDING?!
...
SPEAK!!
KA
ARGH!
SLAM

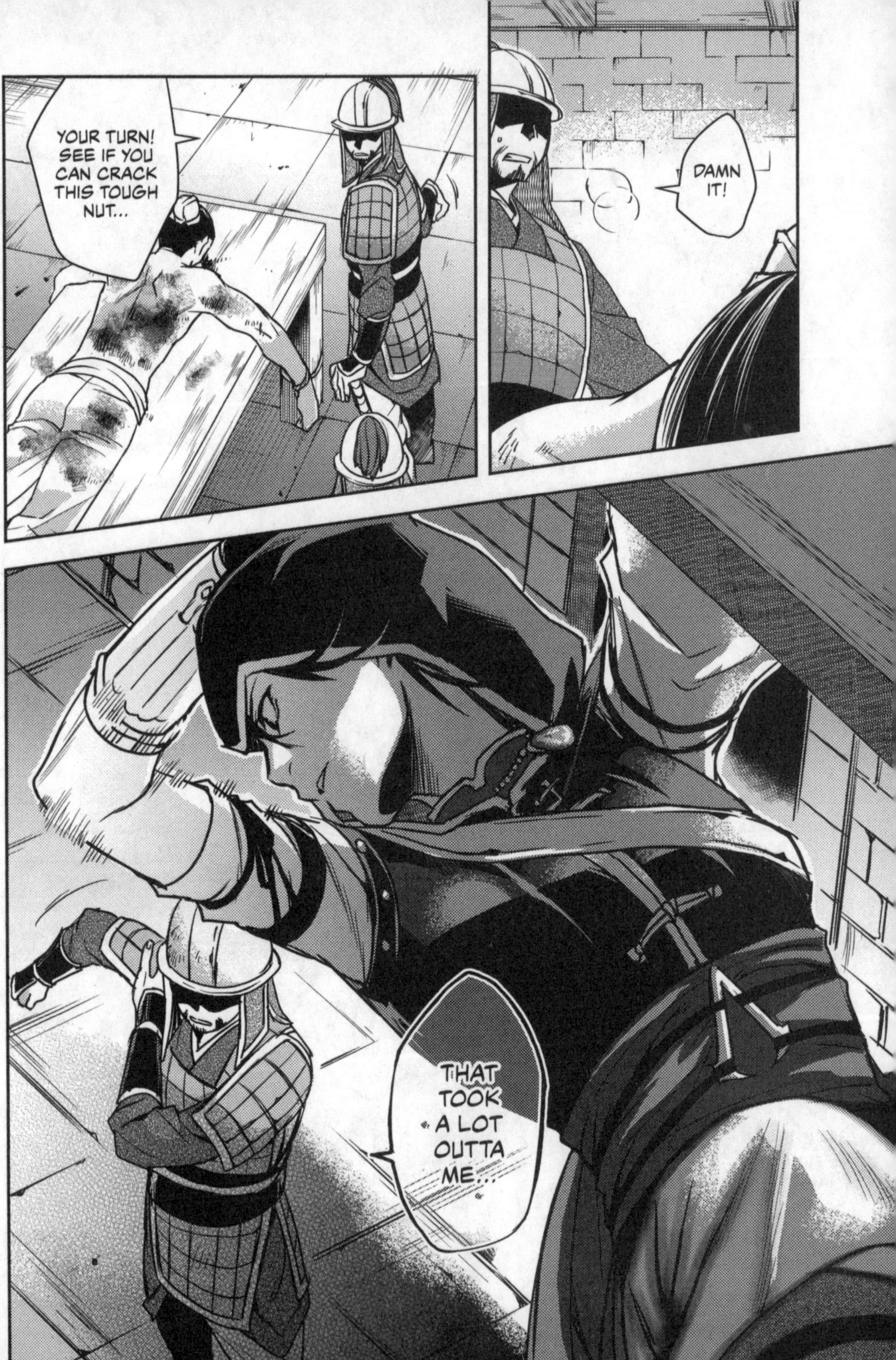
DAMN IT!
YOUR TURN! SEE IF YOU CAN CRACK THIS TOUGH NUT...
THAT TOOK A LOT OUTTA ME...

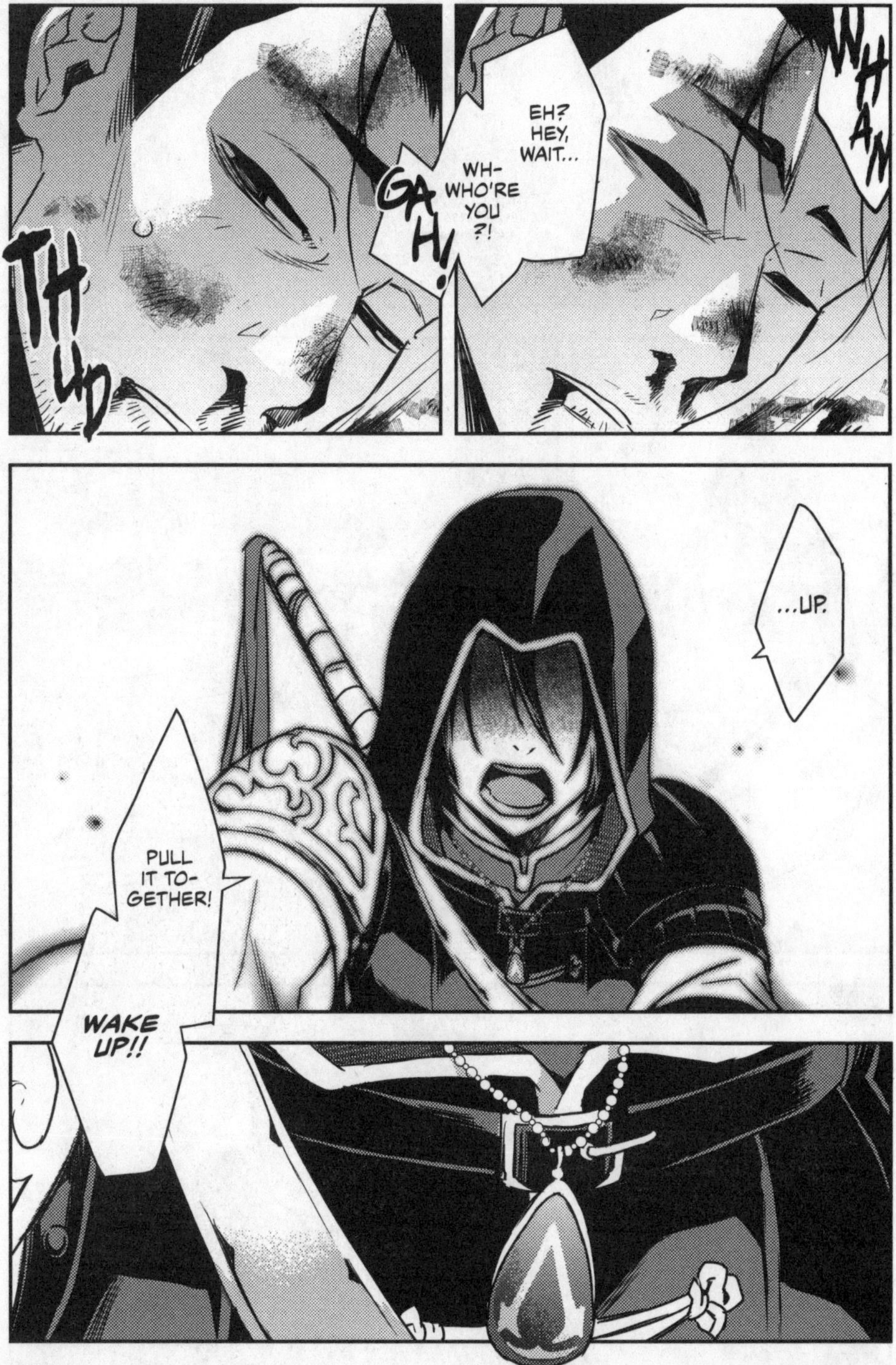
WHAM
EH? HEY, WAIT...
WH- WHO'RE YOU ?!
GAH!
THUD
...UP.
PULL IT TO-GETHER!
WAKE UP!!

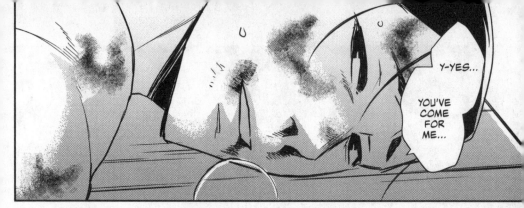

Y-YES...
YOU'VE COME FOR ME...
YOU'RE XIAO HU'S FATHER, RIGHT?
XIAO HU...
WHERE IS MY BOY?
HE'S SAFE AND WAITING FOR YOU OUTSIDE.
WE'RE GETTING OUT OF HERE NOW!
NO...I CAN'T.
MY FEET...

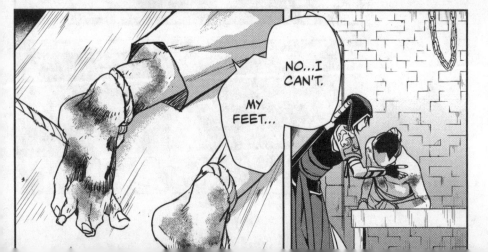

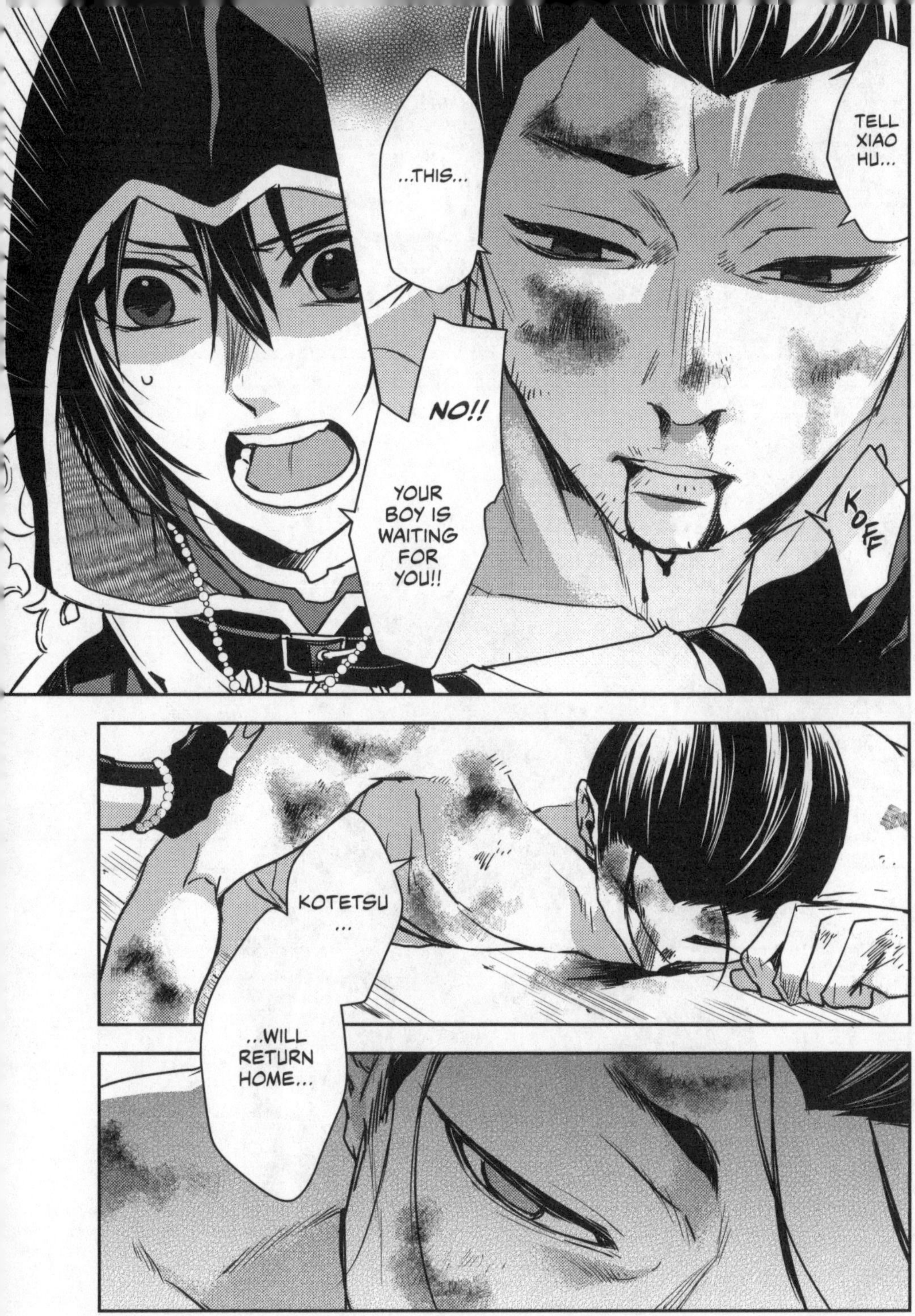
TELL XIAO HU...
...THIS...
KOFF
NO!!
YOUR BOY IS WAITING FOR YOU!!
KOTETSU ...
...WILL RETURN HOME...

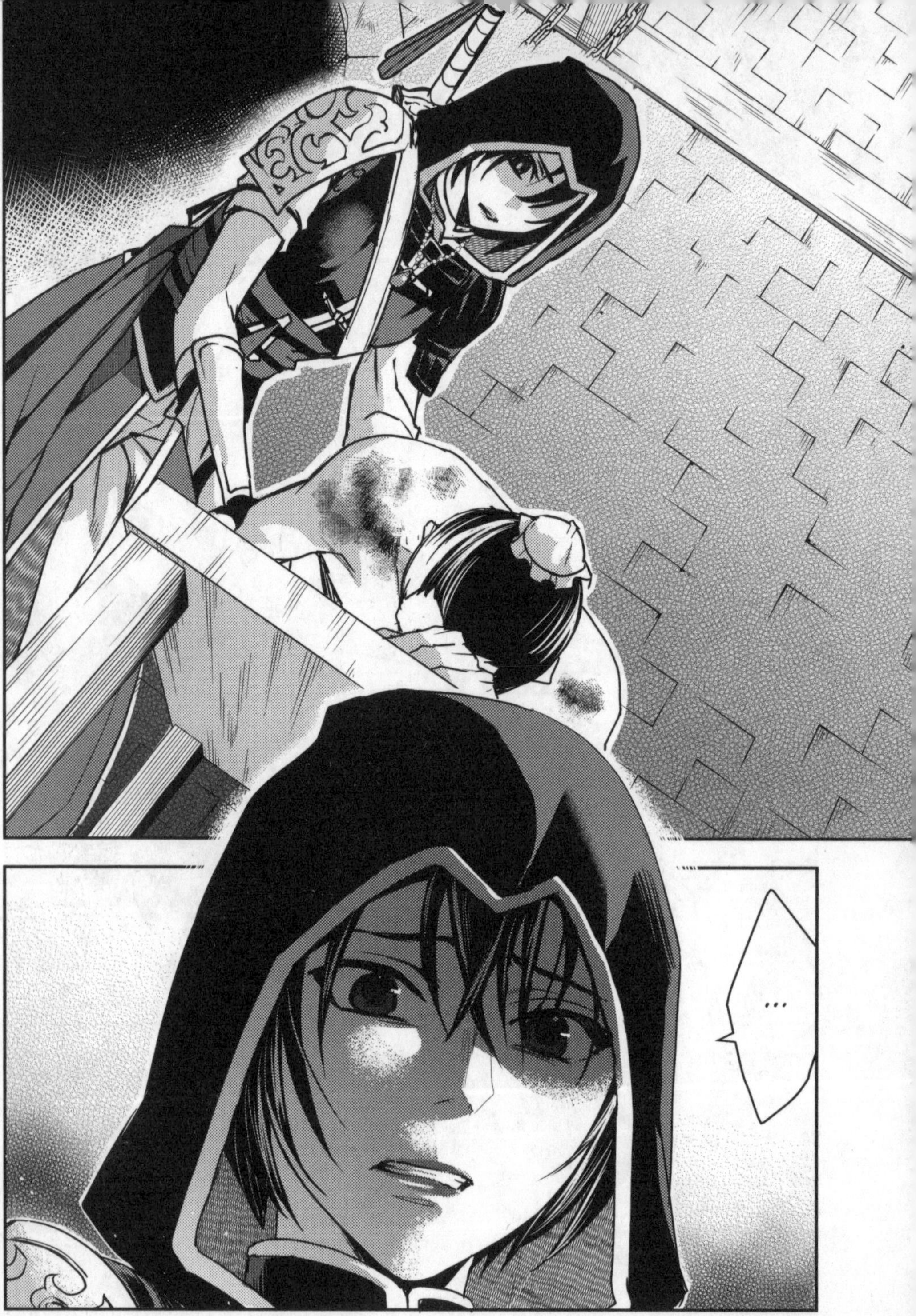
...

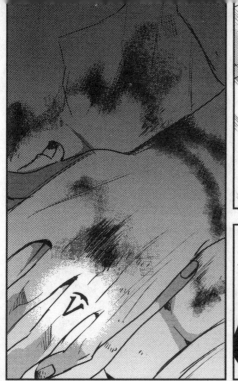

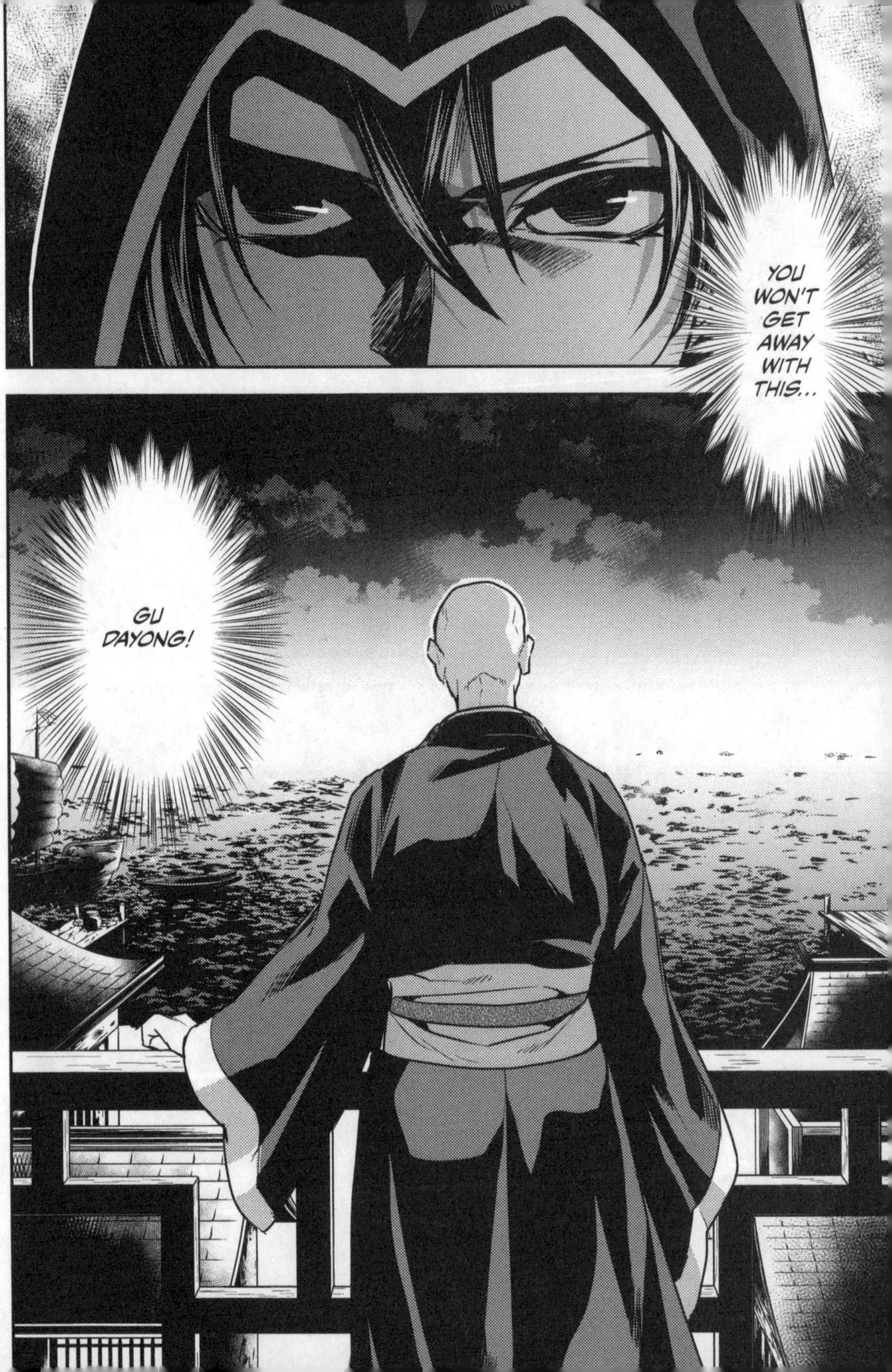
YOU WON'T GET AWAY WITH THIS...
GU DAYONG!

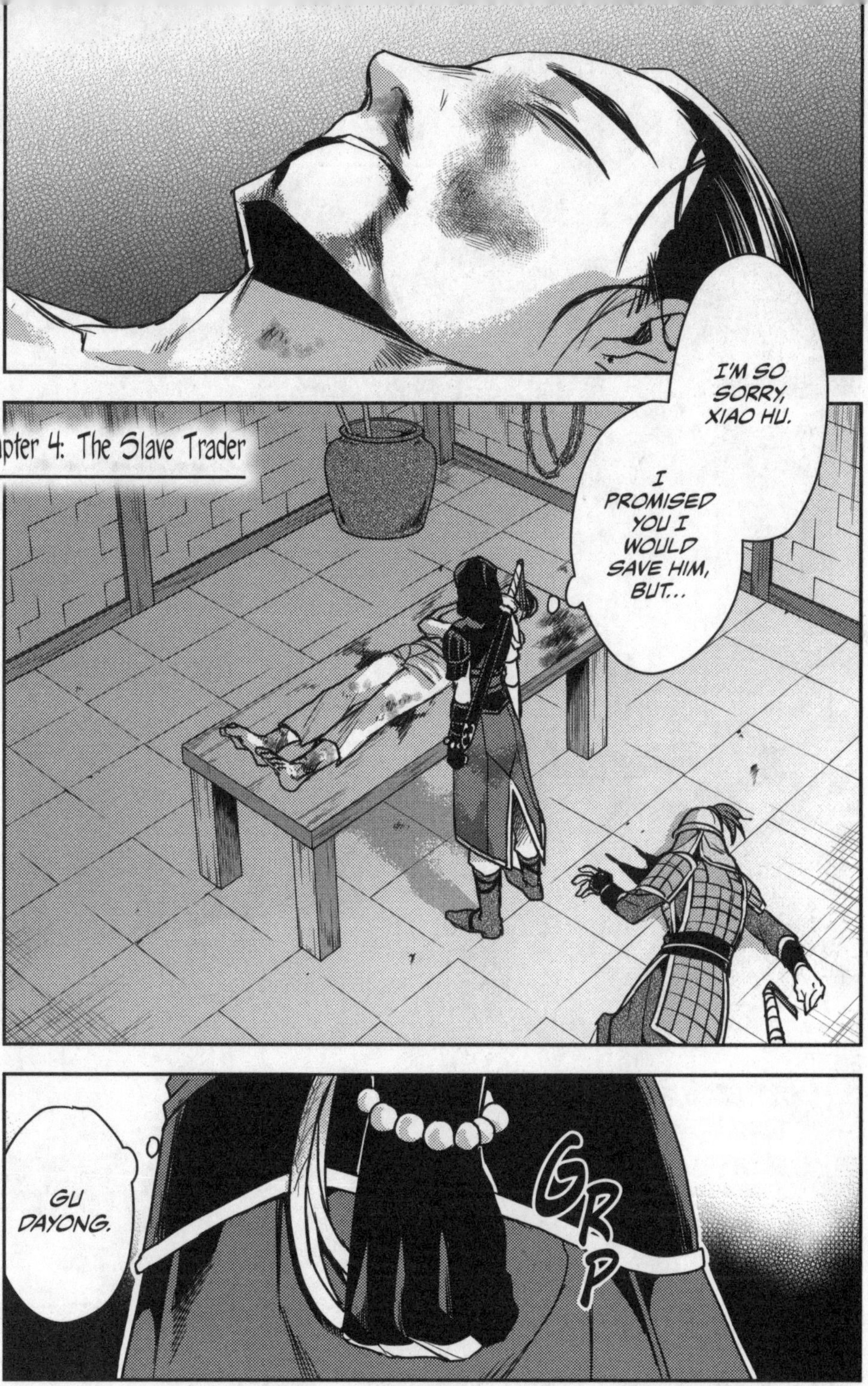
Chapter 4: The Slave Trader
I'M SO SORRY, XIAO HU.
I PROMISED YOU I WOULD SAVE HIM, BUT...
GRP
GU DAYONG.

Chapter 4: The Slave Trader

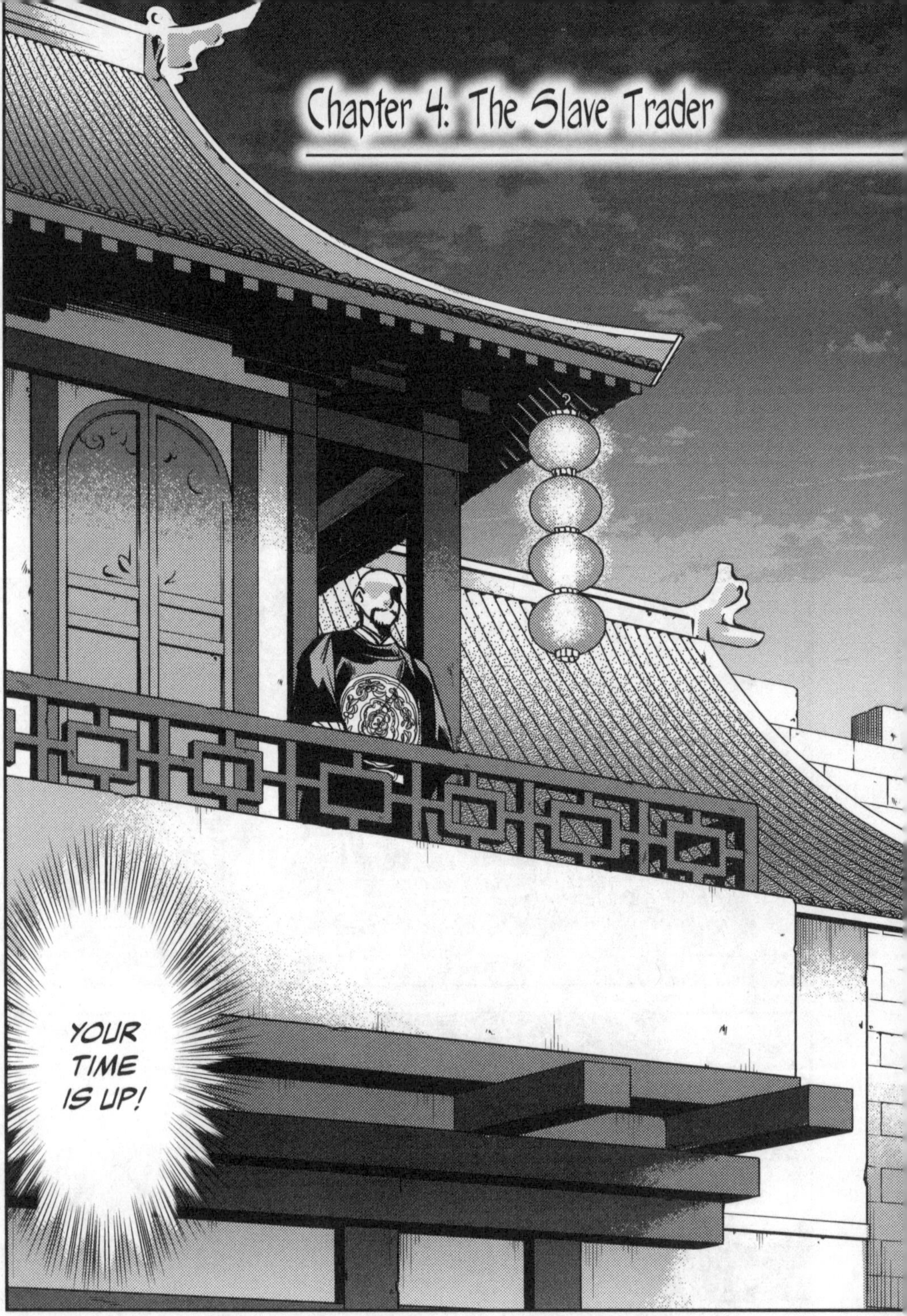
YOUR TIME IS UP!

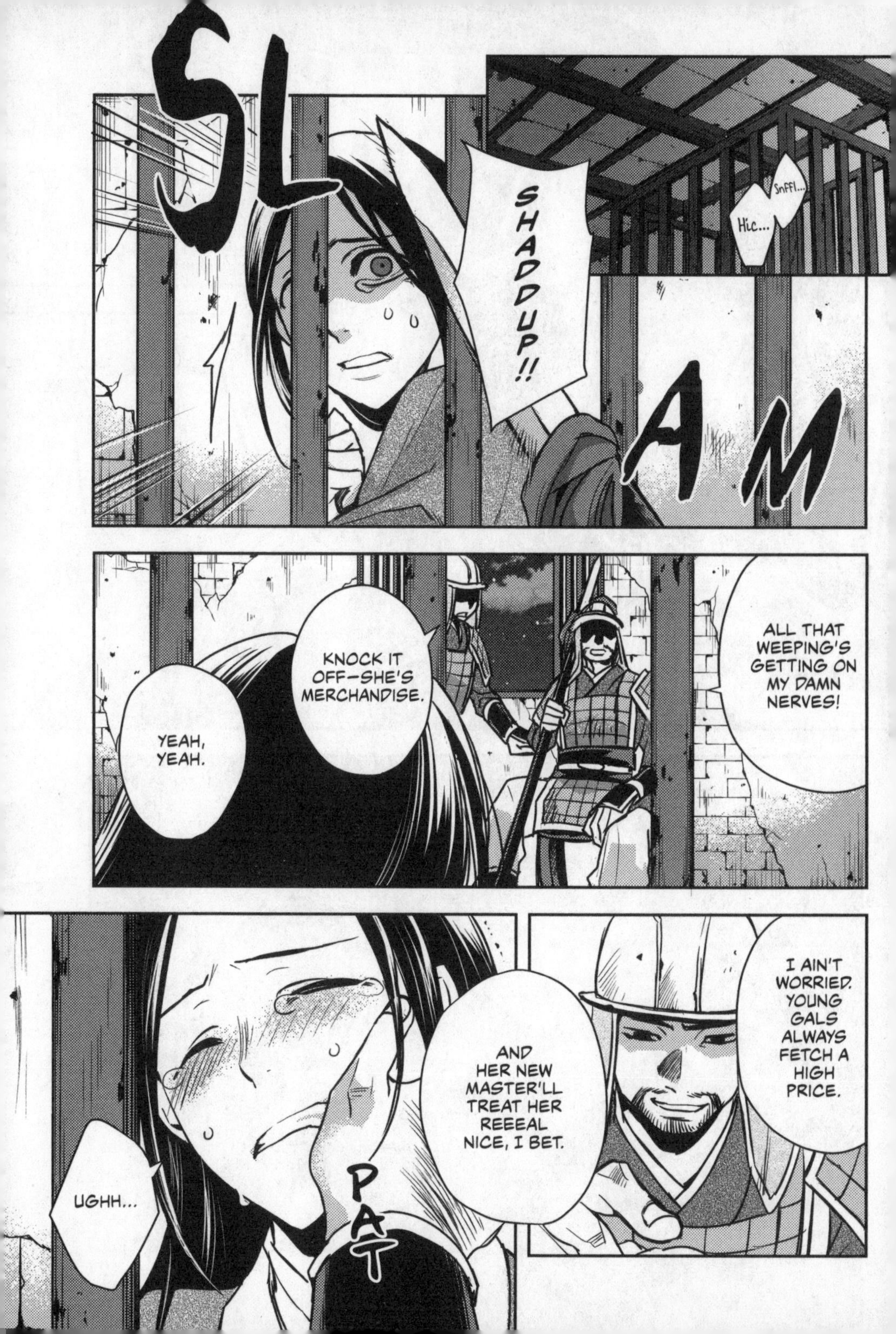
Snffl...
Hic...
SHADDUP!!
SLAM
ALL THAT WEEPING'S GETTING ON MY DAMN NERVES!
KNOCK IT OFF—SHE'S MERCHANDISE.
YEAH, YEAH.
I AIN'T WORRIED. YOUNG GALS ALWAYS FETCH A HIGH PRICE.
AND HER NEW MASTER'LL TREAT HER REEEAL NICE, I BET.
PAT
UGHH...

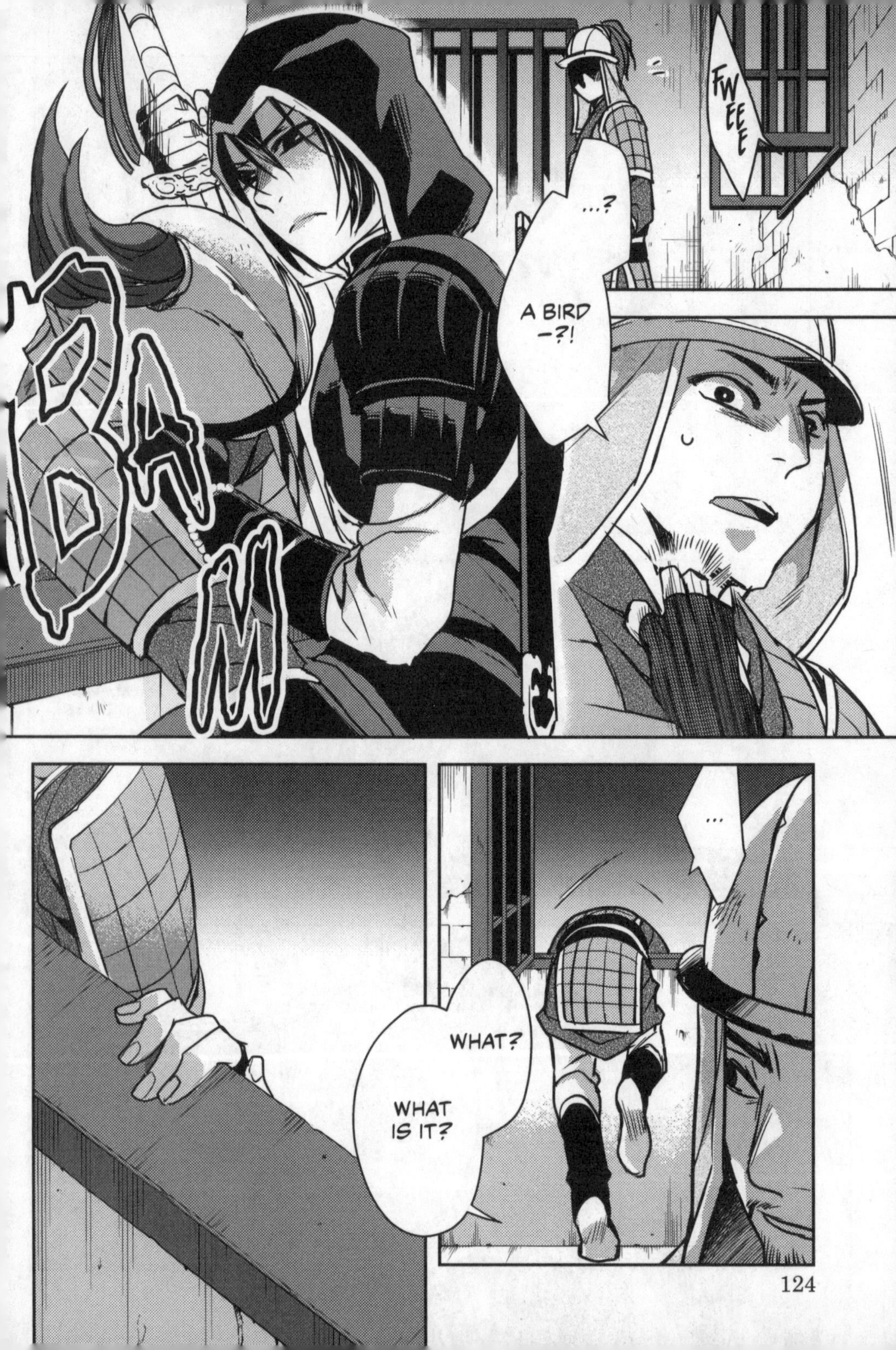
FWEEE
...?
A BIRD —?!
DAM
...
WHAT?
WHAT IS IT?

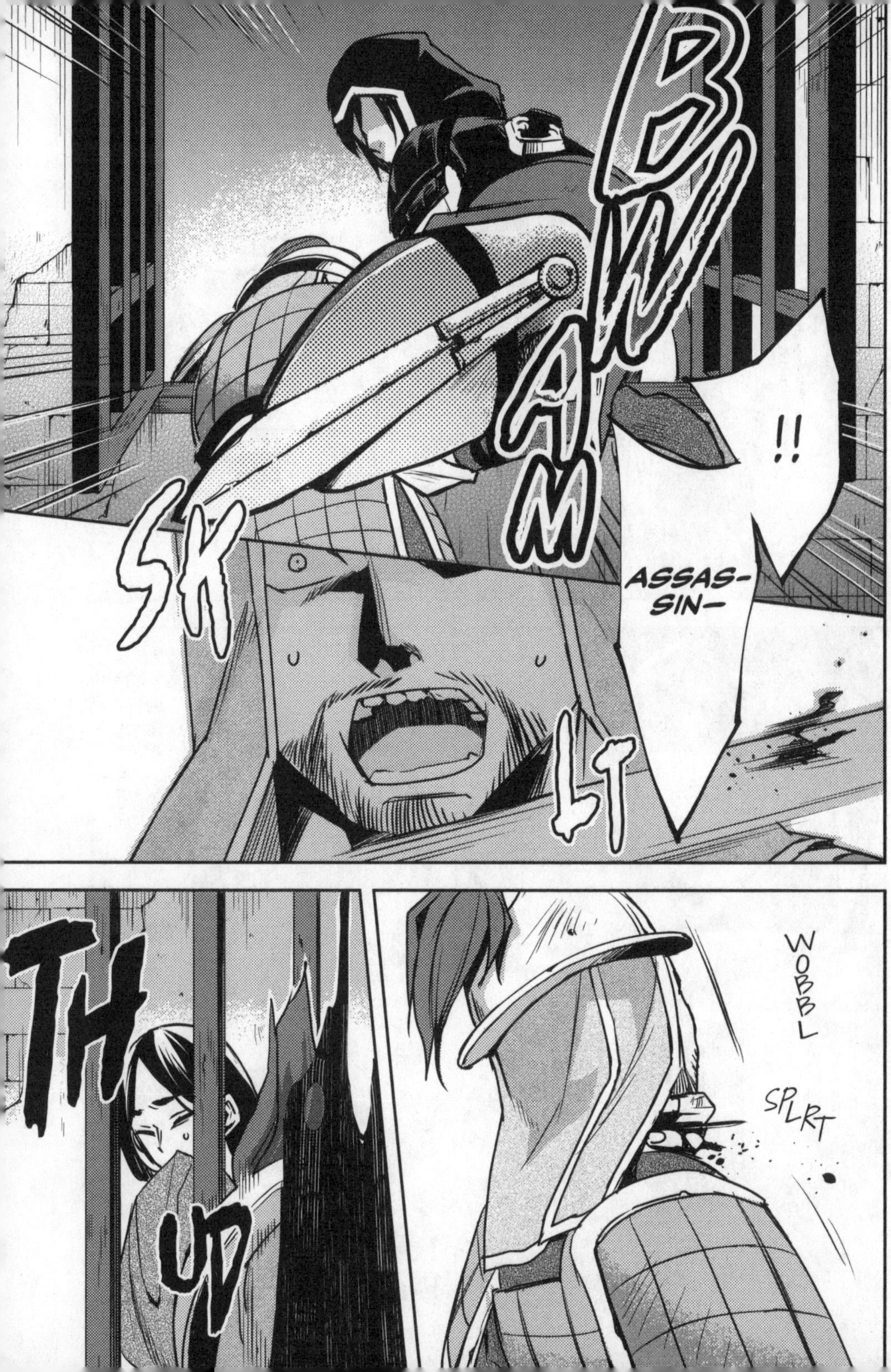
BWAM
!!
ASSAS-
SIN-
SKLT
WOBBL
SPLRT
THUD

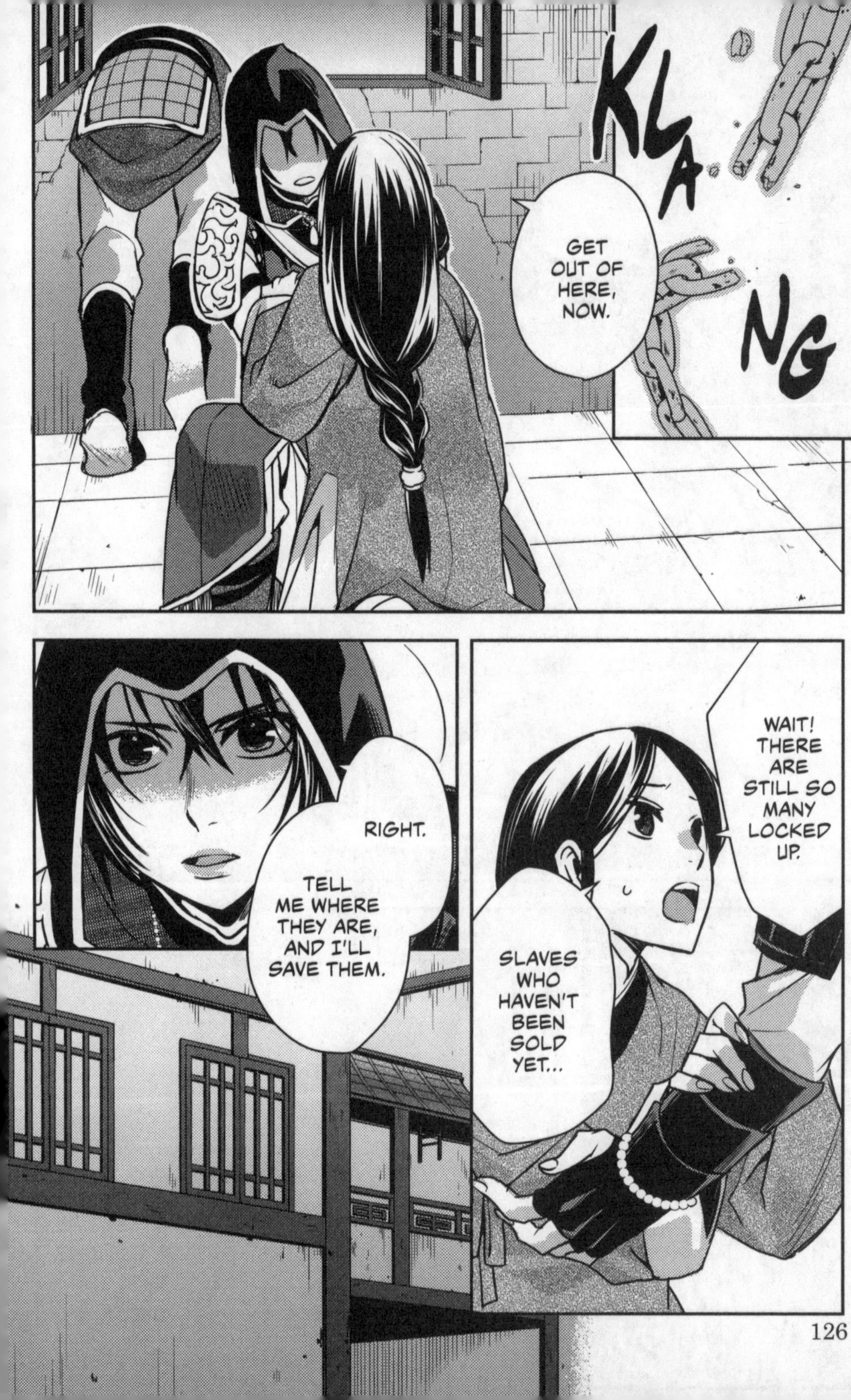
KLANG
GET OUT OF HERE, NOW.
WAIT! THERE ARE STILL SO MANY LOCKED UP.
SLAVES WHO HAVEN'T BEEN SOLD YET...
RIGHT.
TELL ME WHERE THEY ARE, AND I'LL SAVE THEM.

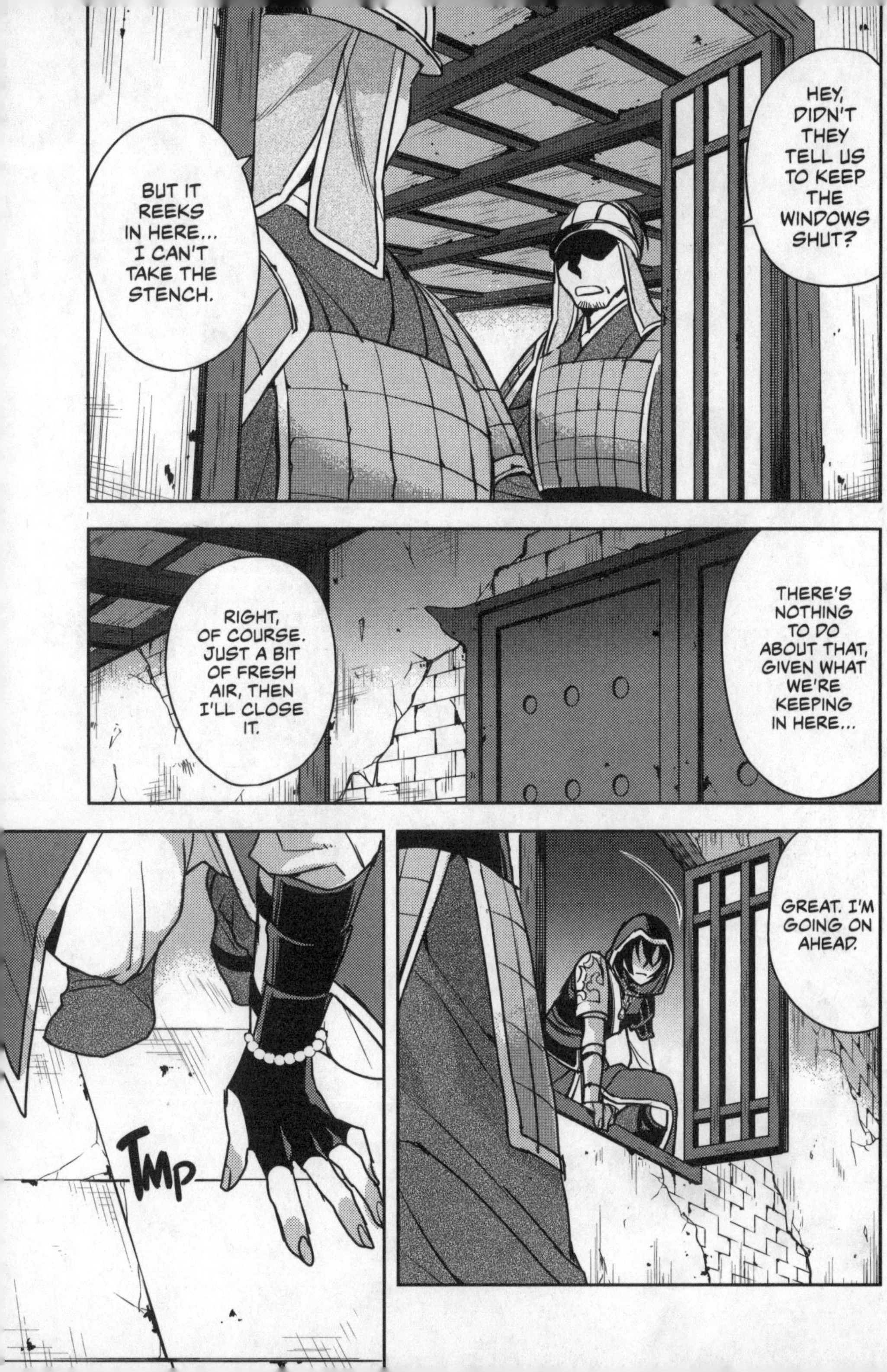
HEY, DIDN'T THEY TELL US TO KEEP THE WINDOWS SHUT?
BUT IT REEKS IN HERE... I CAN'T TAKE THE STENCH.
THERE'S NOTHING TO DO ABOUT THAT, GIVEN WHAT WE'RE KEEPING IN HERE...
RIGHT, OF COURSE. JUST A BIT OF FRESH AIR, THEN I'LL CLOSE IT.
GREAT. I'M GOING ON AHEAD.
TMP

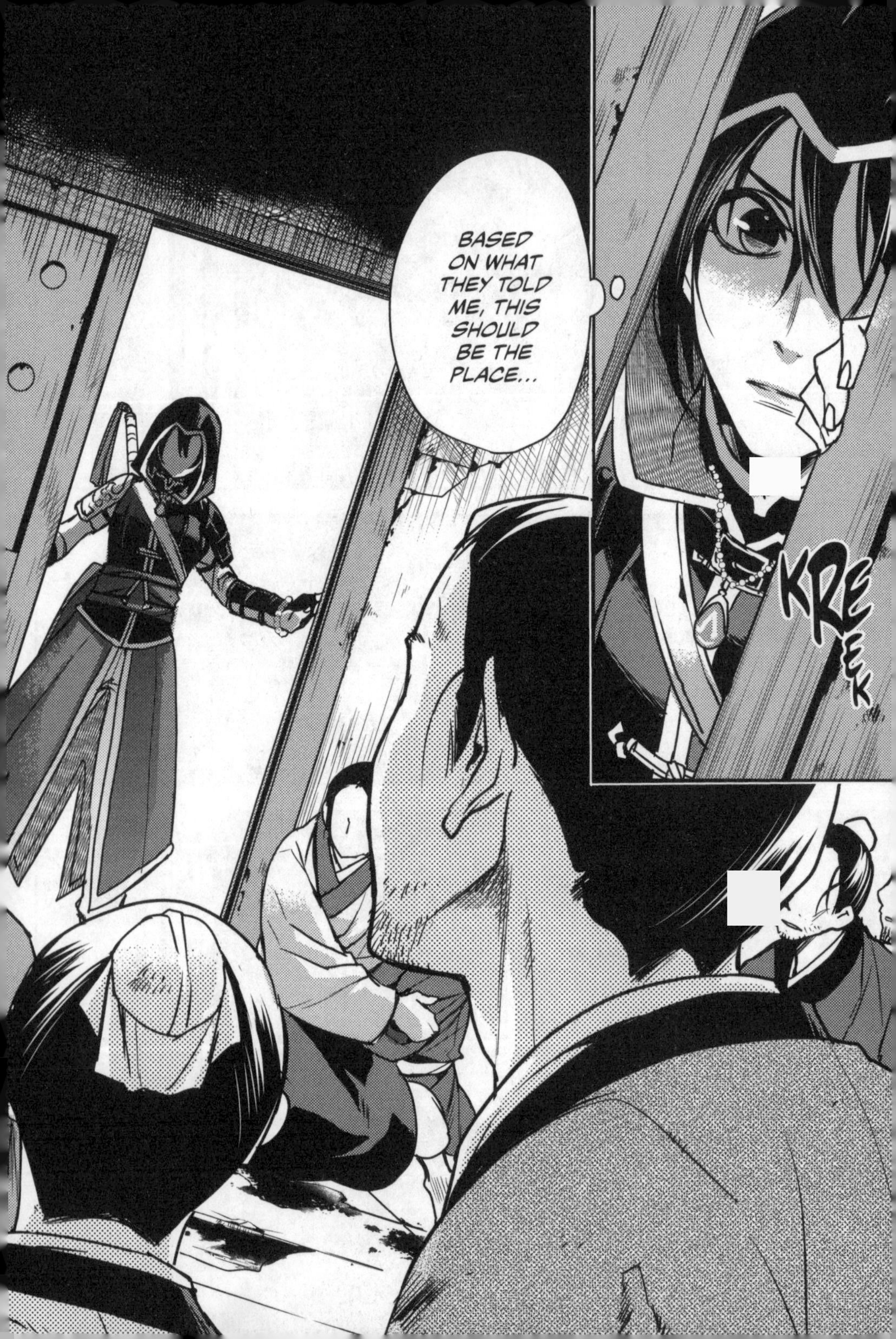
KREEK
BASED ON WHAT THEY TOLD ME, THIS SHOULD BE THE PLACE...

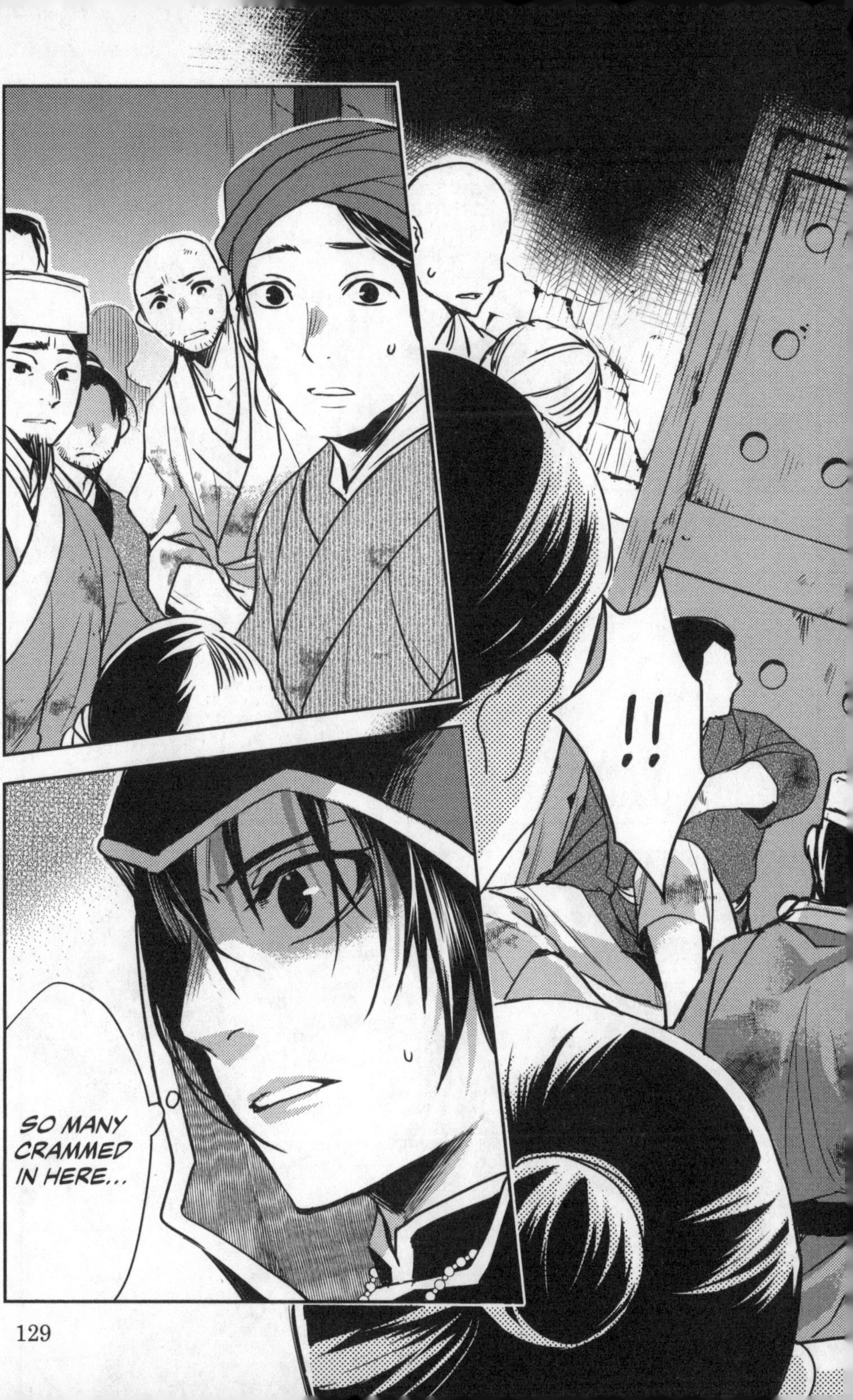
!!
SO MANY CRAMMED IN HERE...

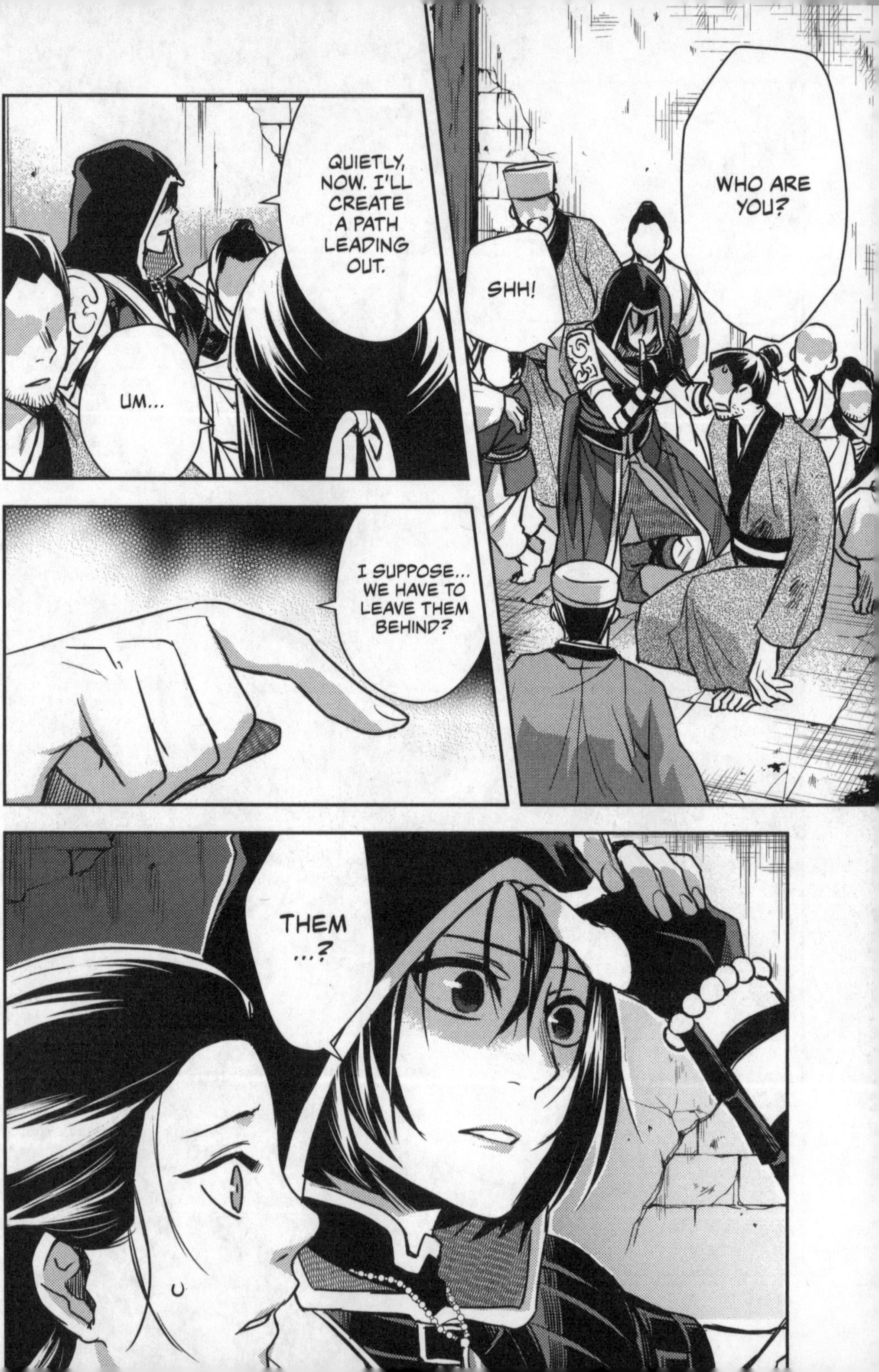
WHO ARE YOU?
SHH!
QUIETLY, NOW. I'LL CREATE A PATH LEADING OUT.
UM...
I SUPPOSE... WE HAVE TO LEAVE THEM BEHIND?
THEM ...?

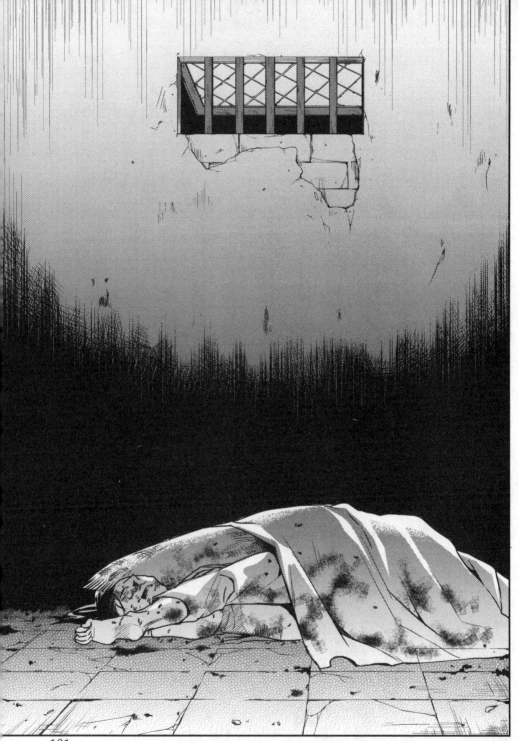

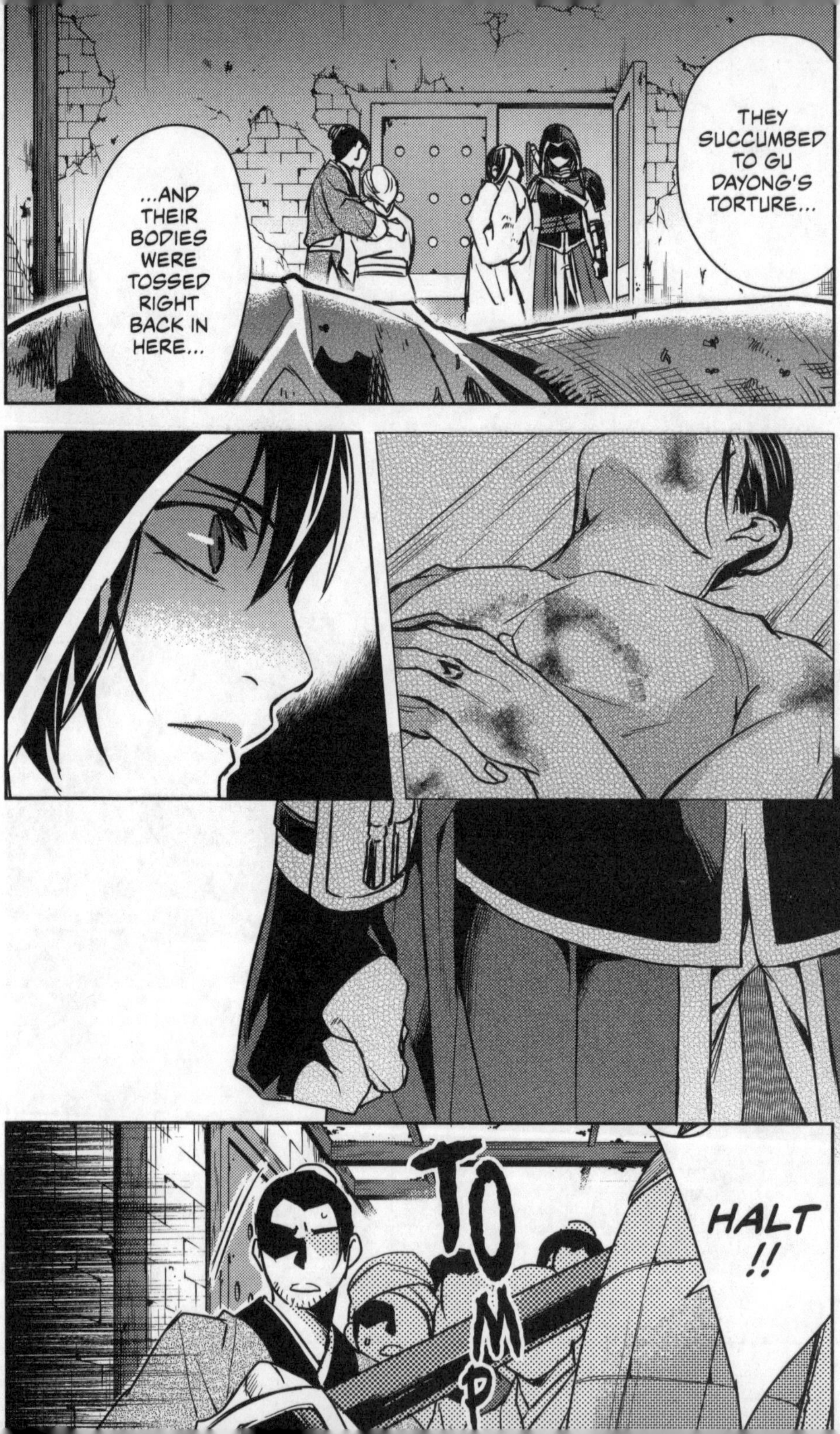
THEY SUCCUMBED TO GU DAYONG'S TORTURE...
...AND THEIR BODIES WERE TOSSED RIGHT BACK IN HERE...
HALT!!
TOMP

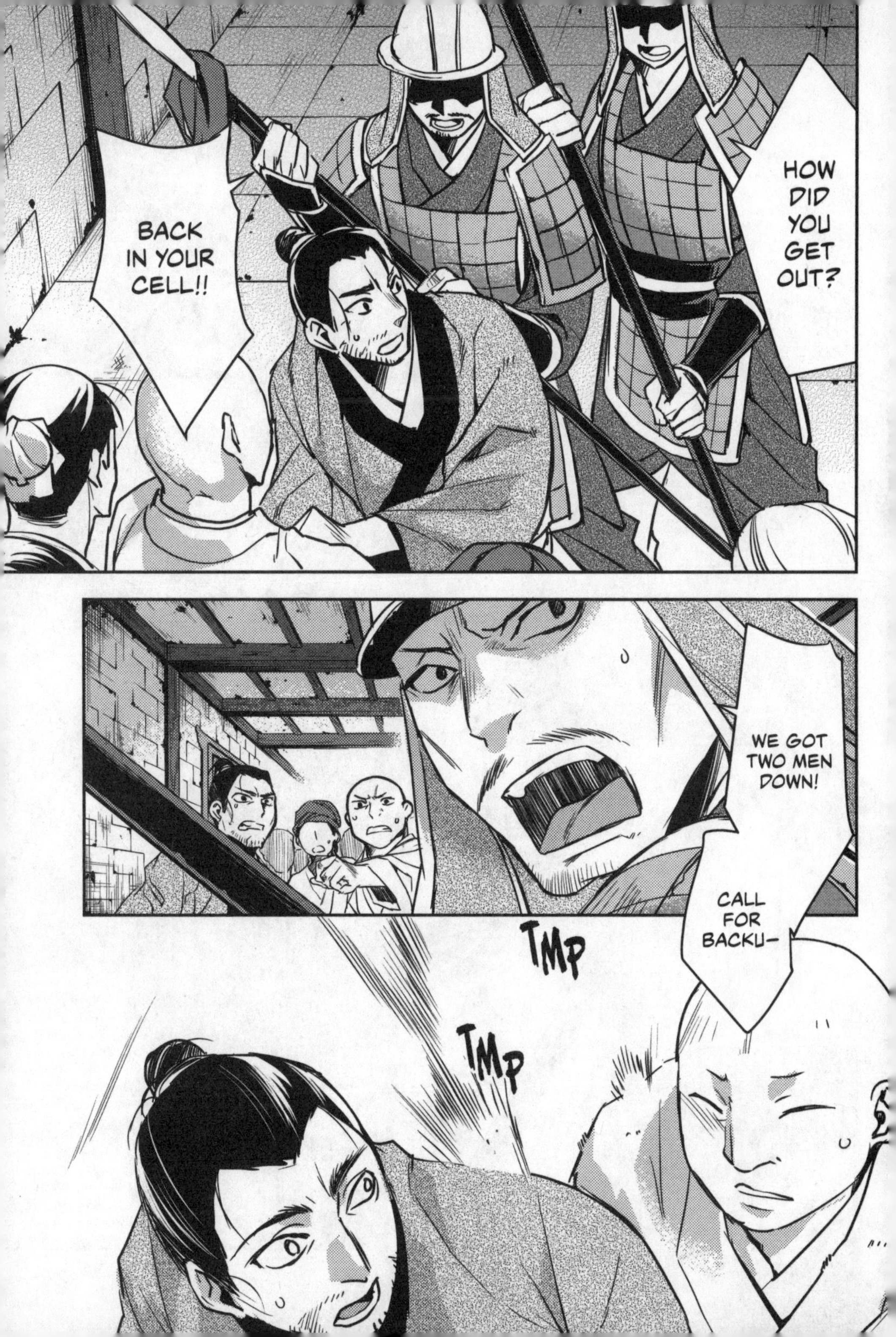
HOW DID YOU GET OUT?
BACK IN YOUR CELL!!
WE GOT TWO MEN DOWN!
CALL FOR BACKU-
TMP
TMP

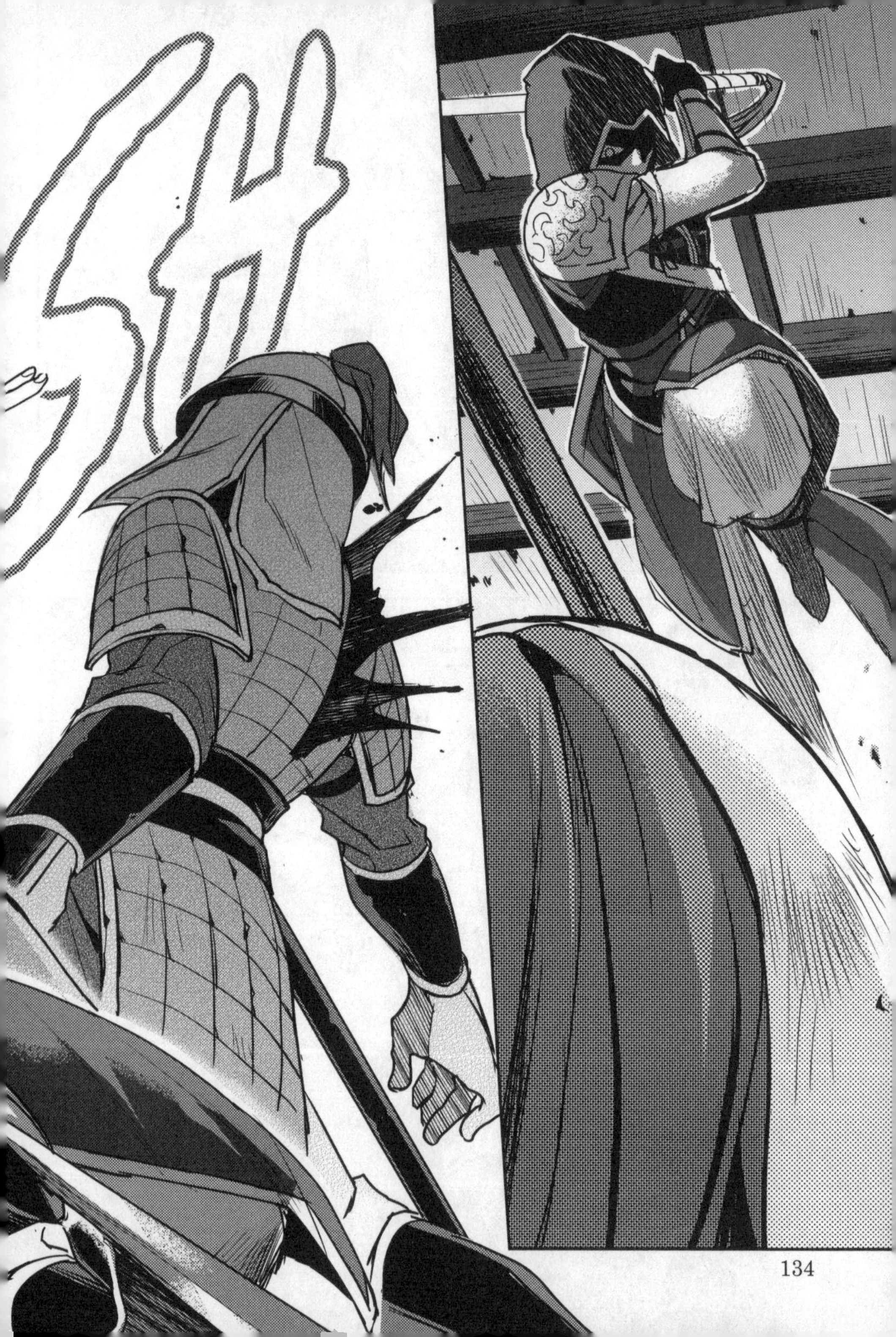
SH

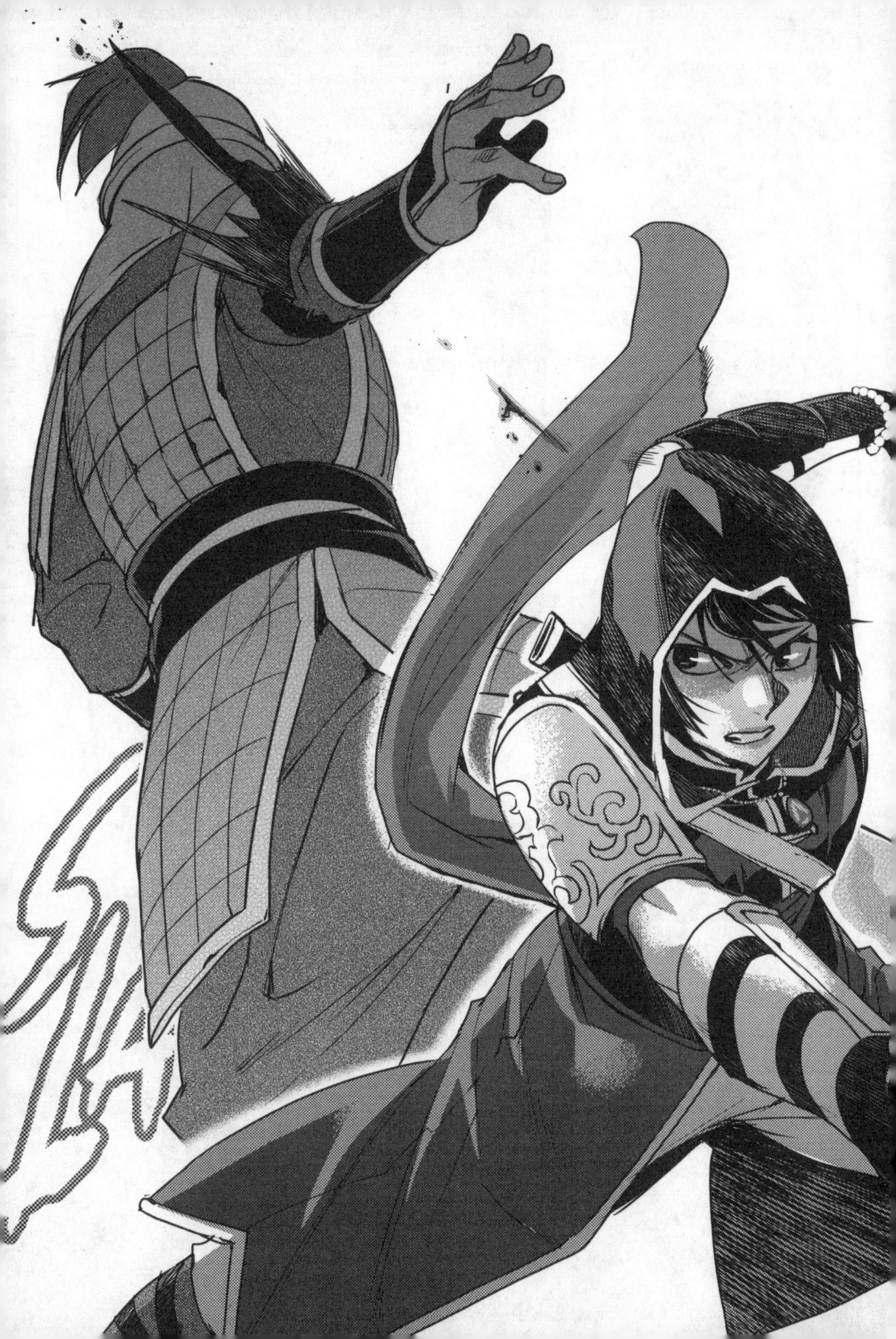

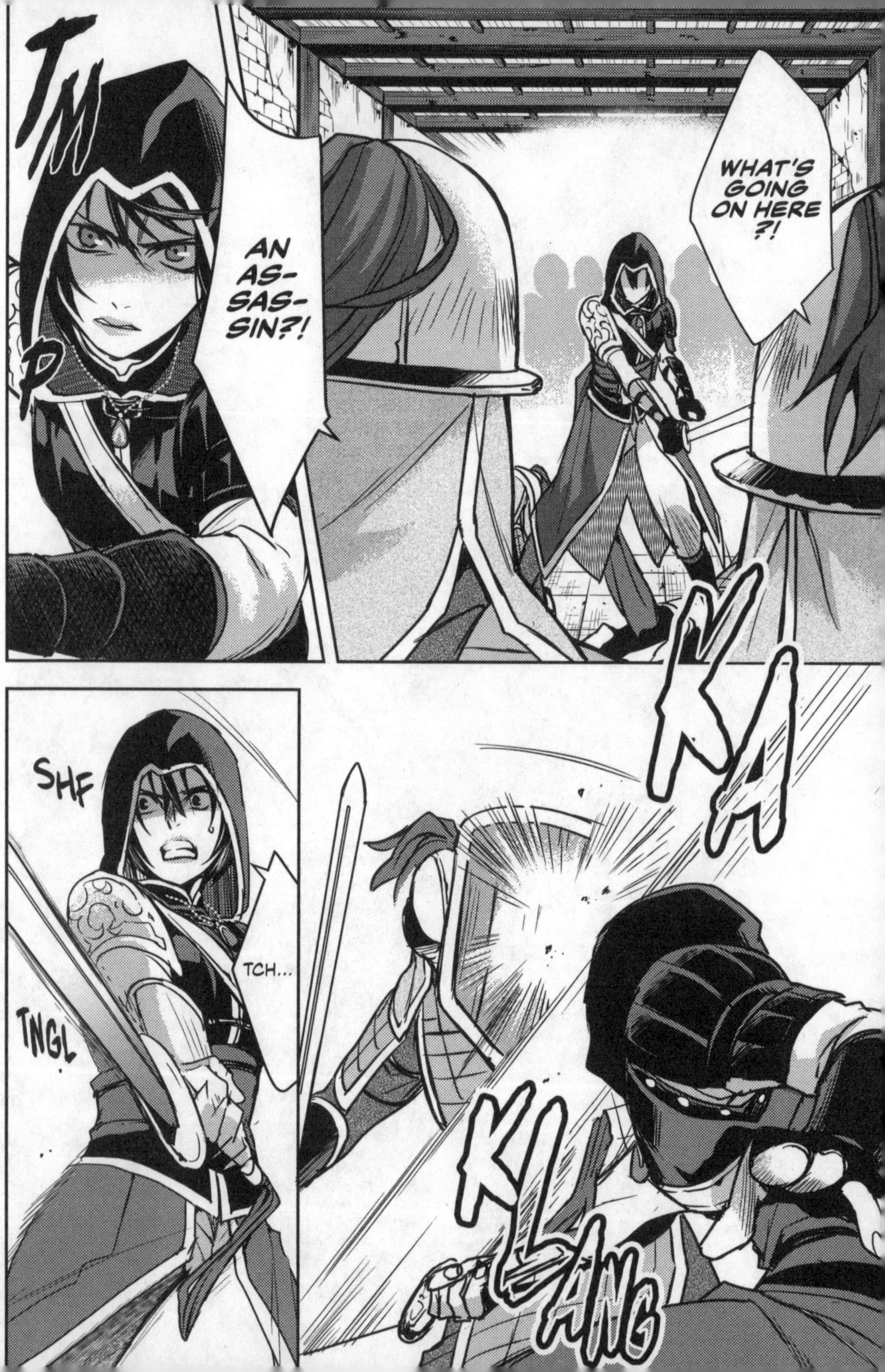

WHAT'S GOING ON HERE?!
AN AS-SAS-SIN?!
TMP
KA
KLANG
SHF
TCH...
TNGL

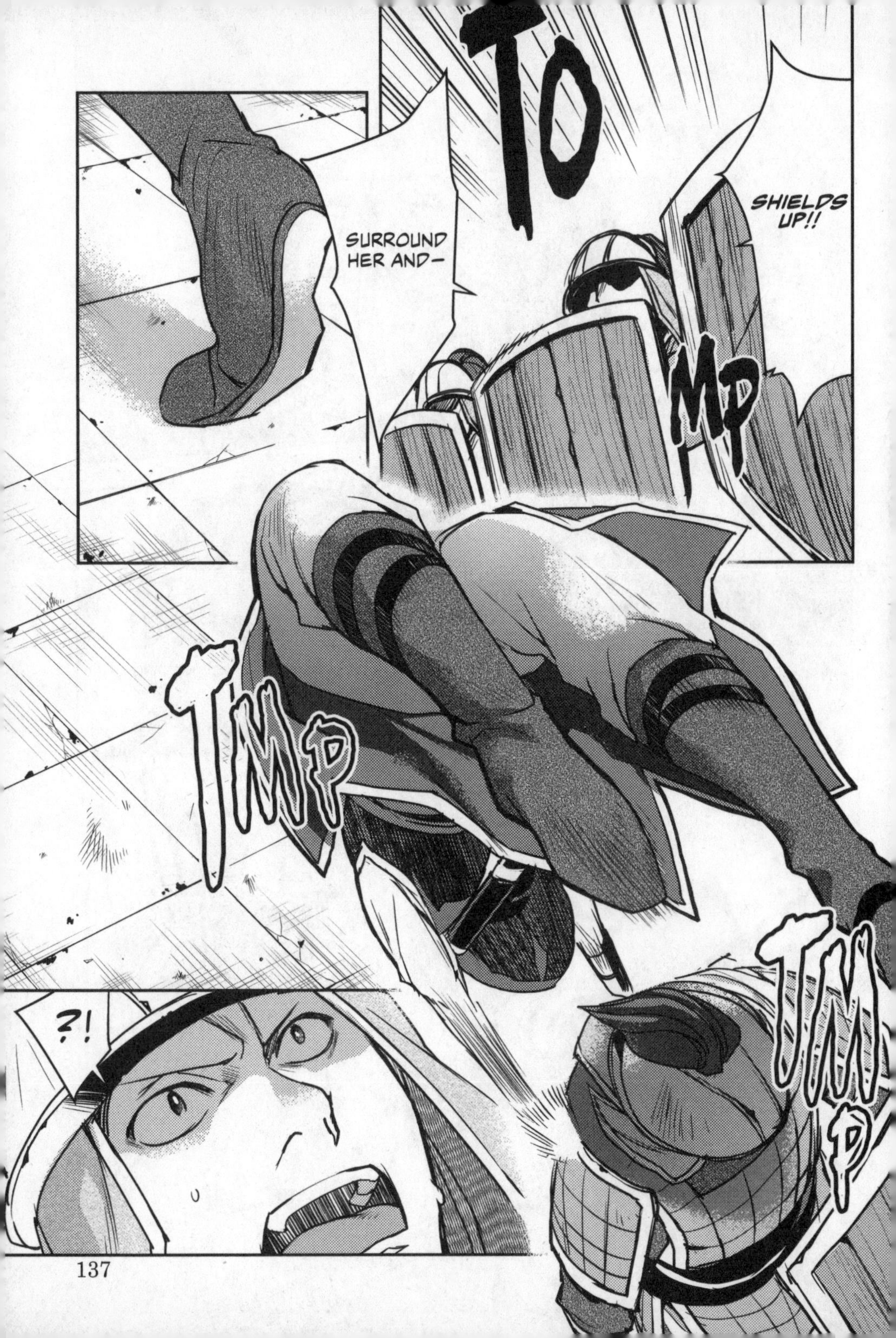

TO
SHIELDS UP!!
MP
SURROUND HER AND—
TMP
TMP
?!

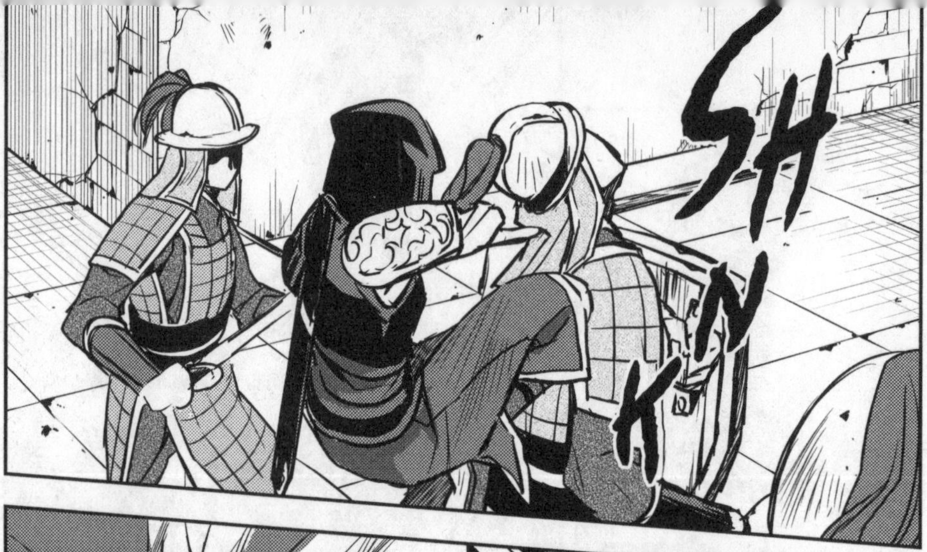
SHNK
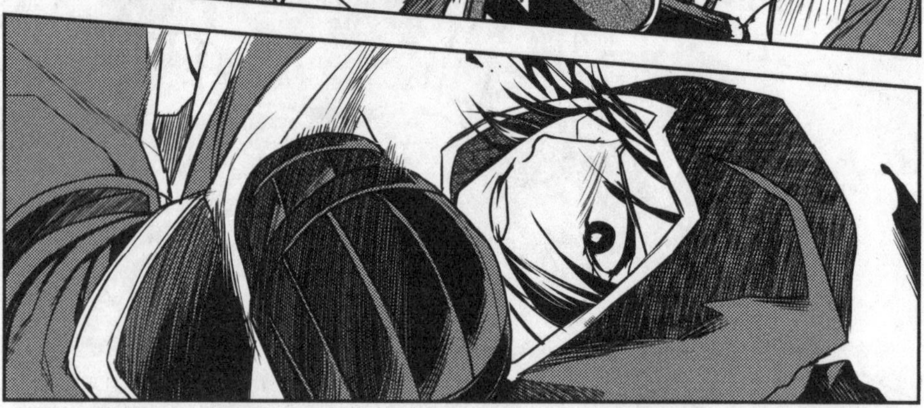
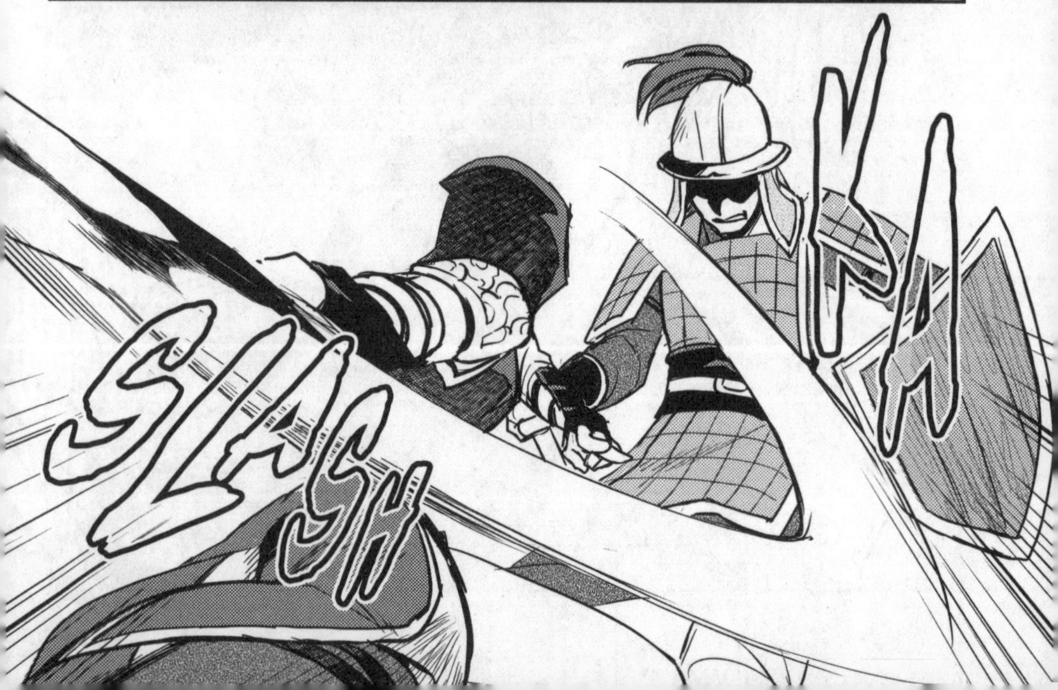
SLASH

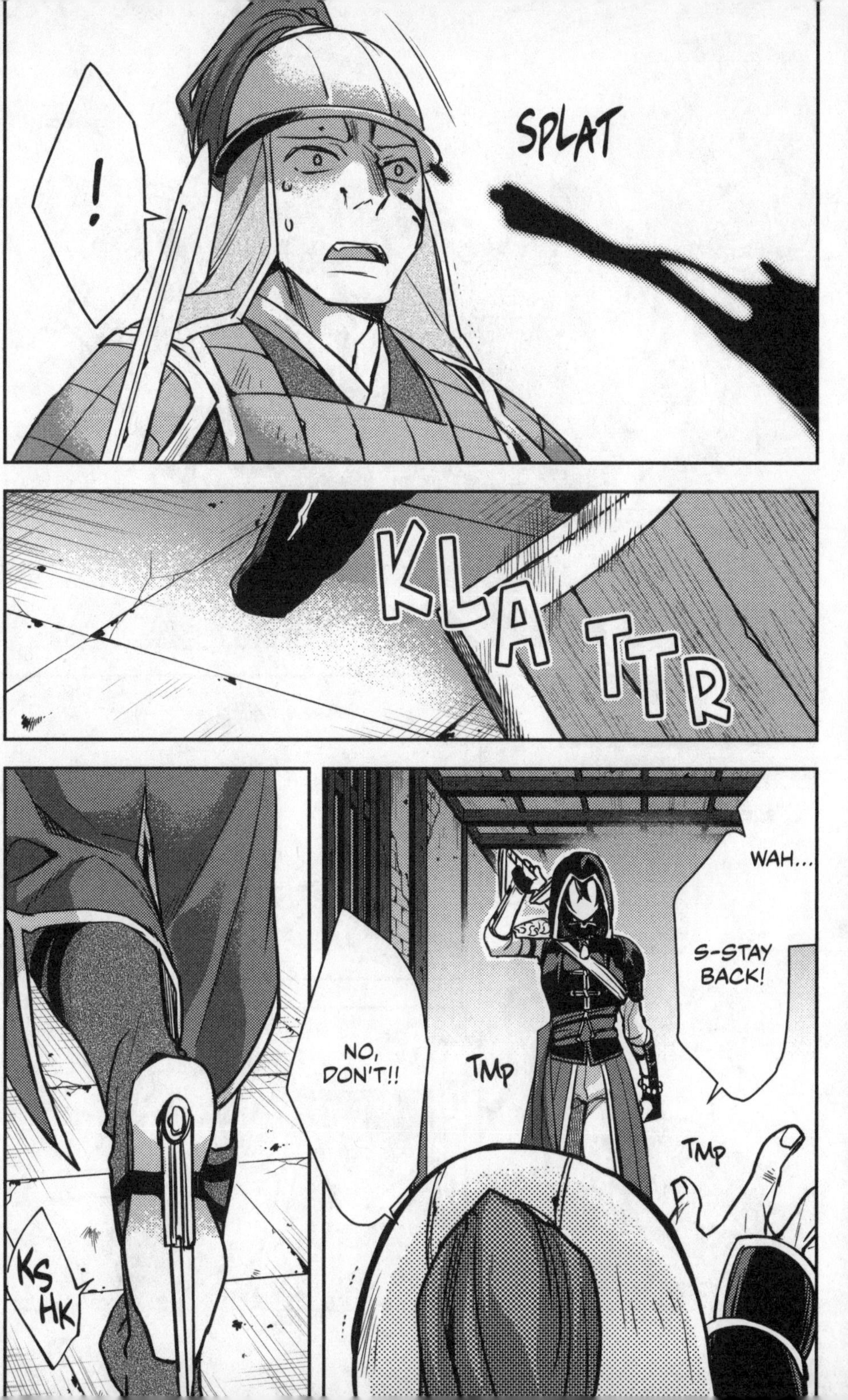
SPLAT
!
KLATTR
WAH...
S-STAY BACK!
TMP
NO, DON'T!!
TMP
KSHK

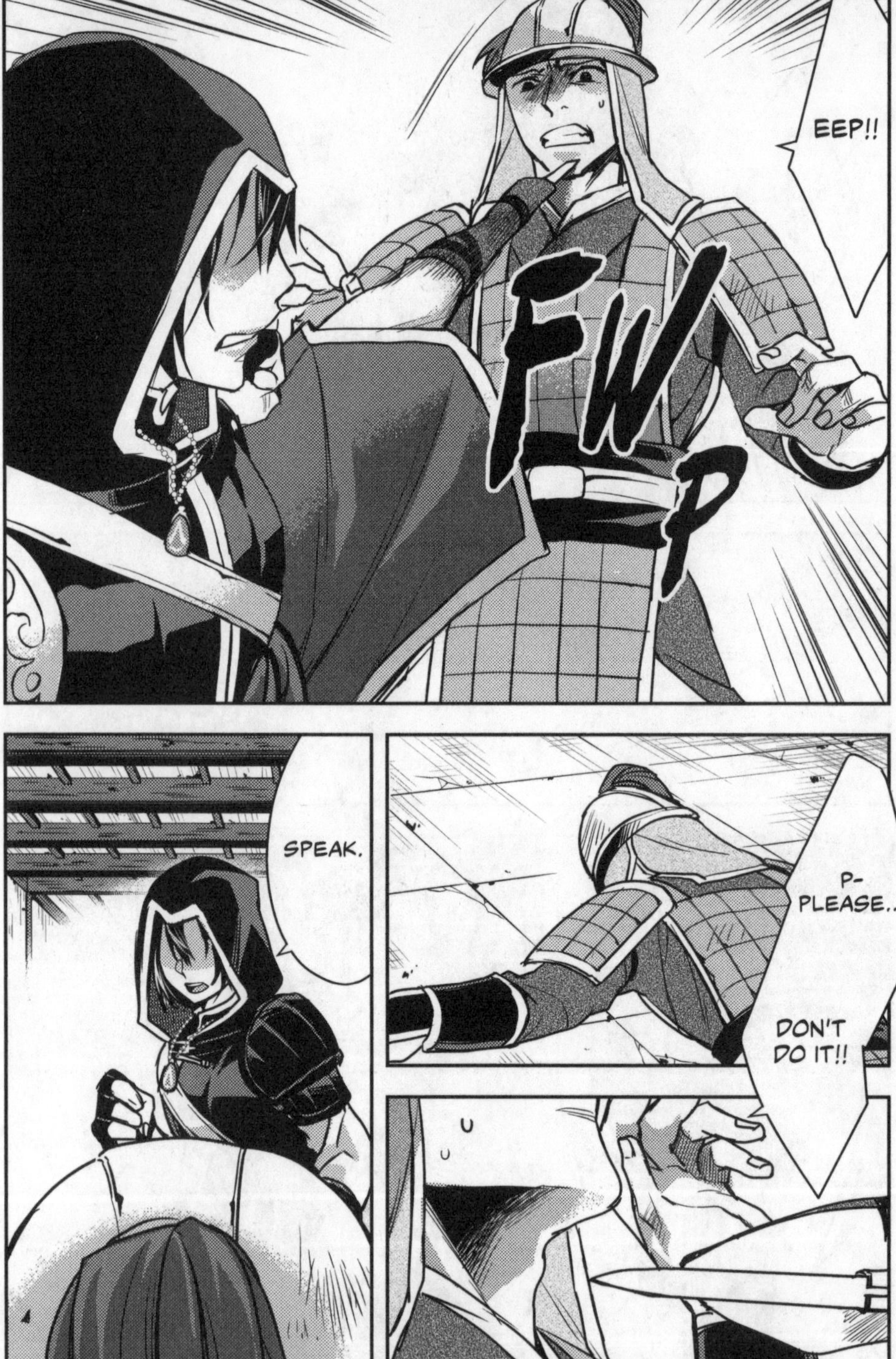
EEP!!
FWP
P-
PLEASE...
DON'T DO IT!!
U U
SPEAK.

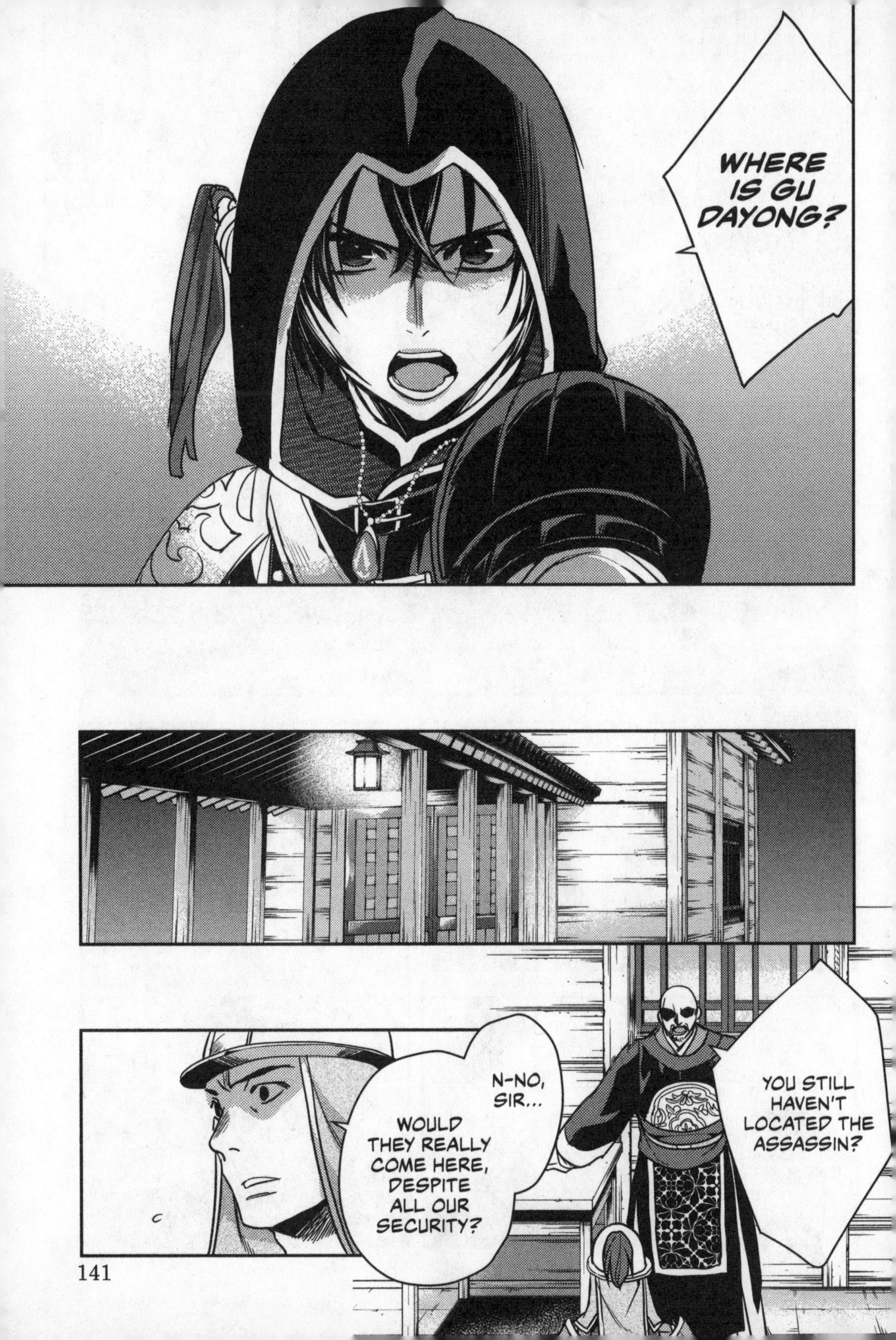
WHERE IS GU DAYONG?
YOU STILL HAVEN'T LOCATED THE ASSASSIN?
N-NO, SIR...
WOULD THEY REALLY COME HERE, DESPITE ALL OUR SECURITY?

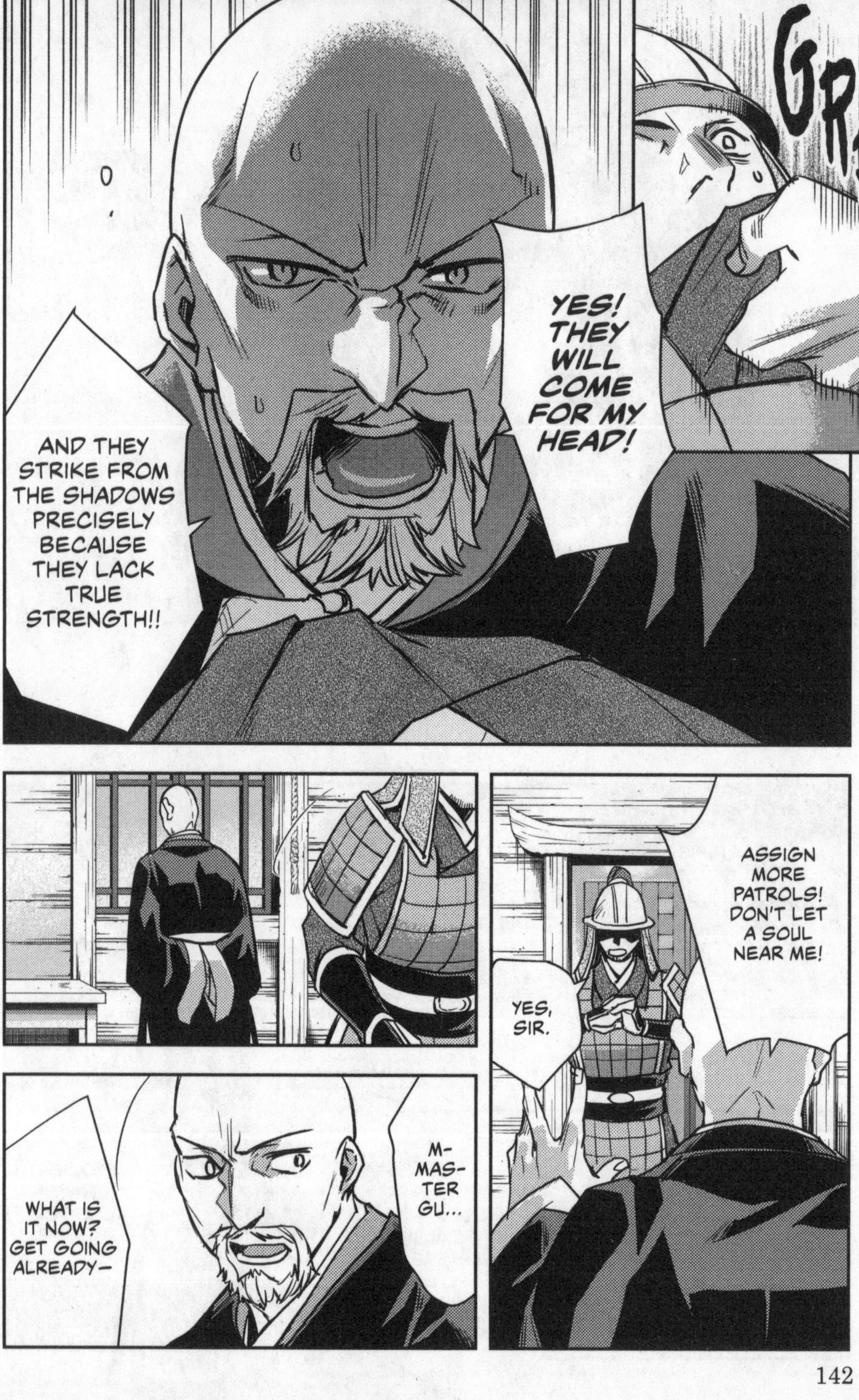
GRP
YES! THEY WILL COME FOR MY HEAD!
AND THEY STRIKE FROM THE SHADOWS PRECISELY BECAUSE THEY LACK TRUE STRENGTH!!
ASSIGN MORE PATROLS! DON'T LET A SOUL NEAR ME!
YES, SIR.
M-MASTER GU...
WHAT IS IT NOW? GET GOING ALREADY—

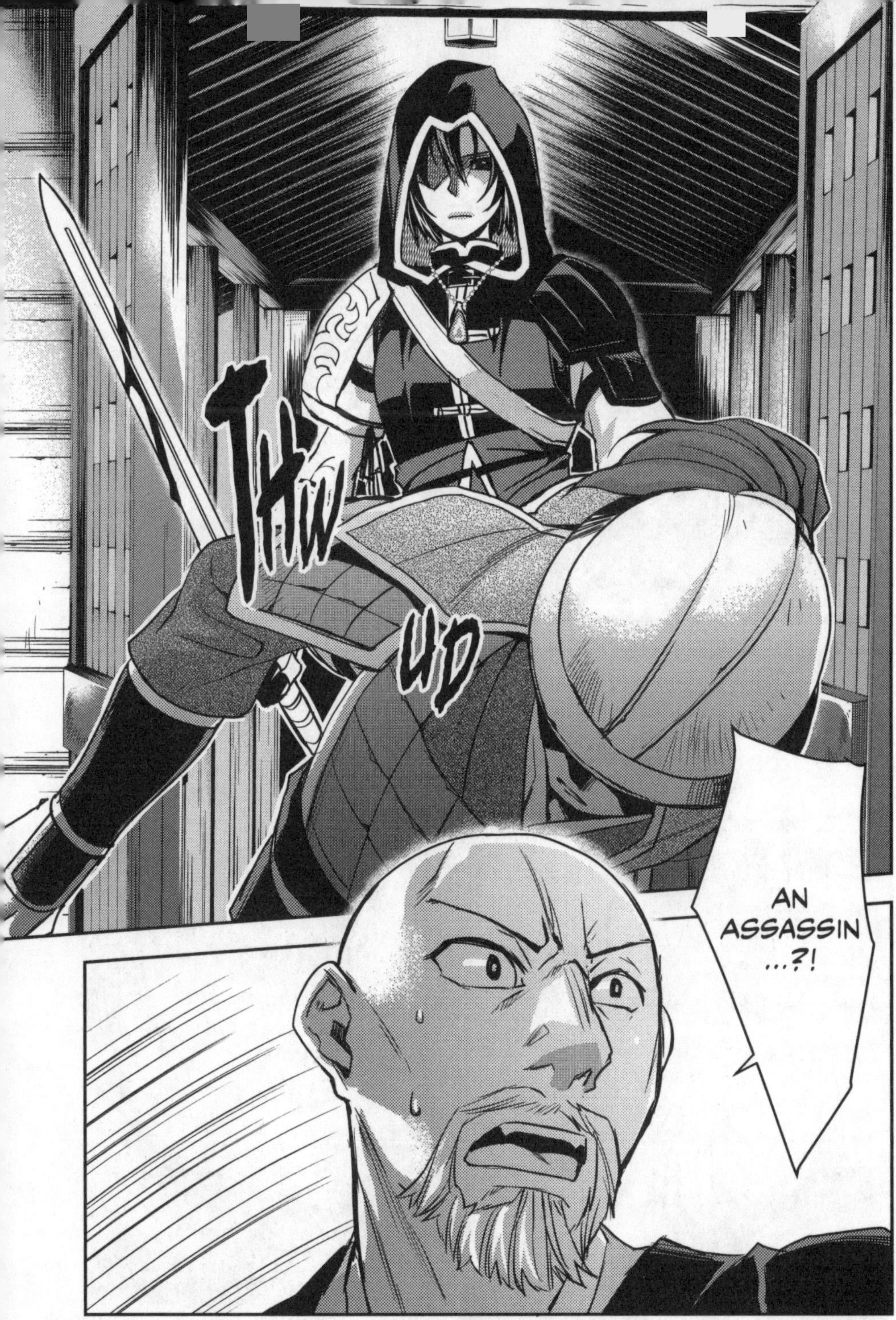
THUD
AN ASSASSIN ...?!

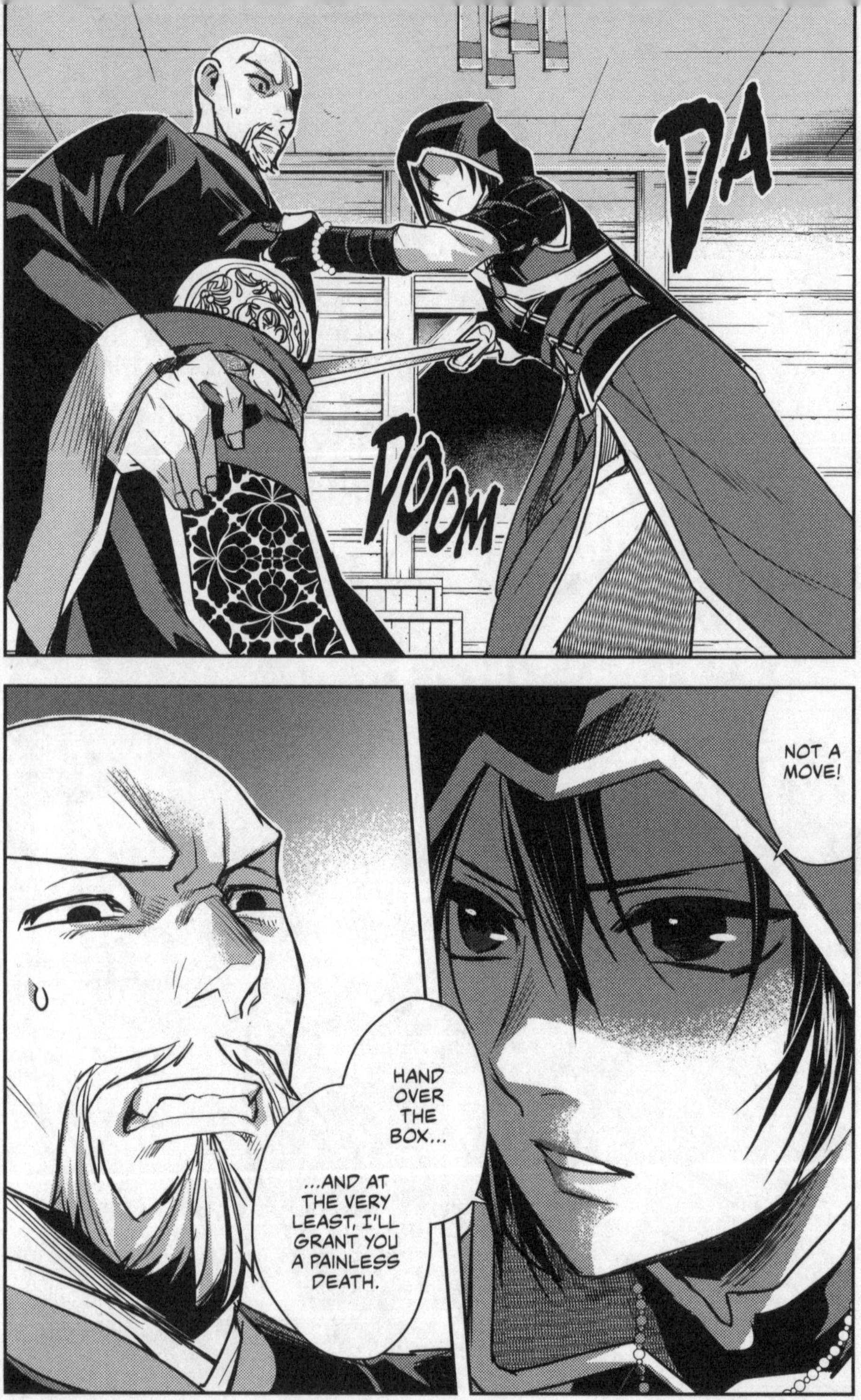
DA
DOOM
NOT A MOVE!
HAND OVER THE BOX...
...AND AT THE VERY LEAST, I'LL GRANT YOU A PAINLESS DEATH.

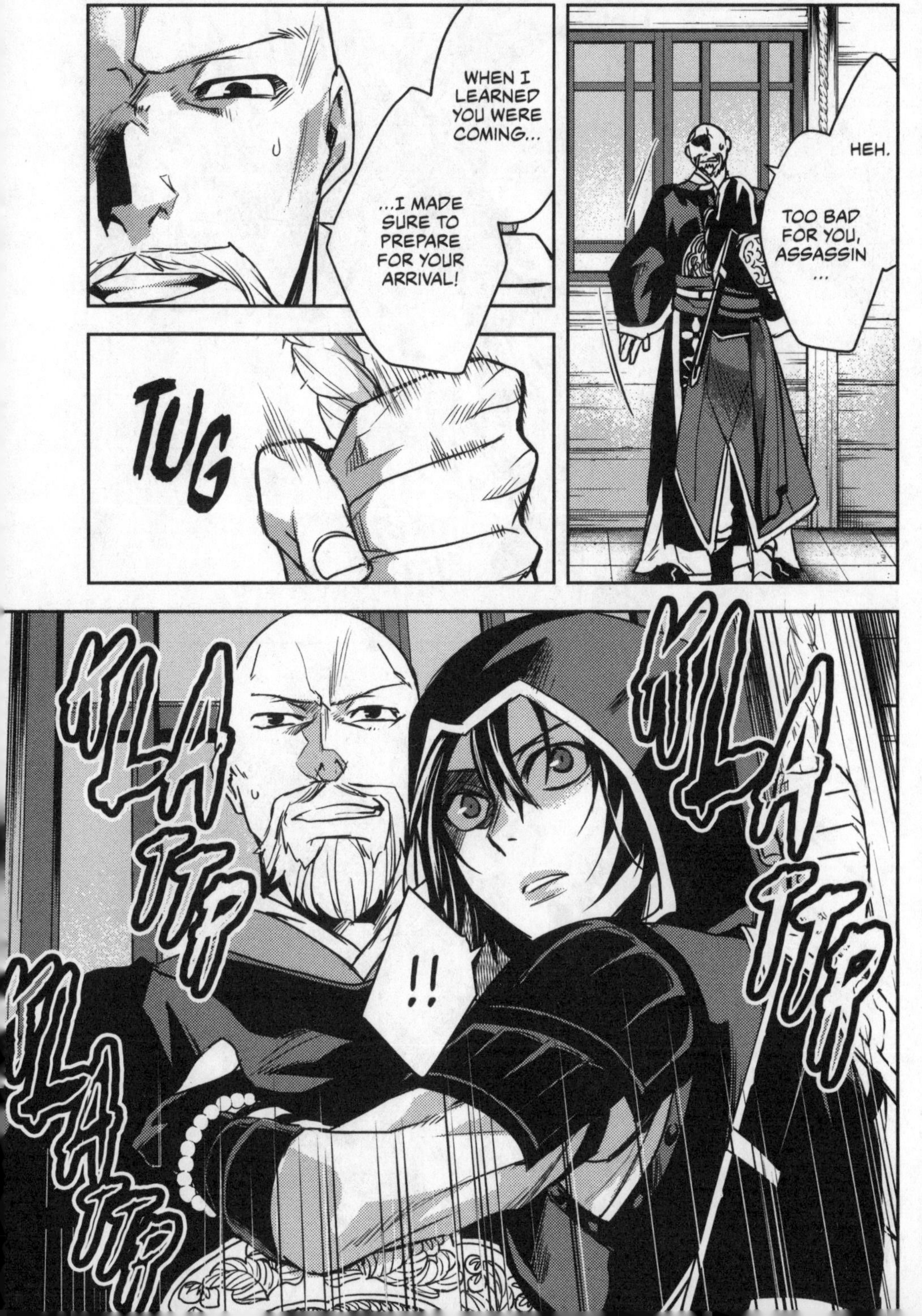
HEH.
TOO BAD FOR YOU, ASSASSIN ...
WHEN I LEARNED YOU WERE COMING...
...I MADE SURE TO PREPARE FOR YOUR ARRIVAL!
TUG
KLATTP
KLATTP
!!
KLATTP

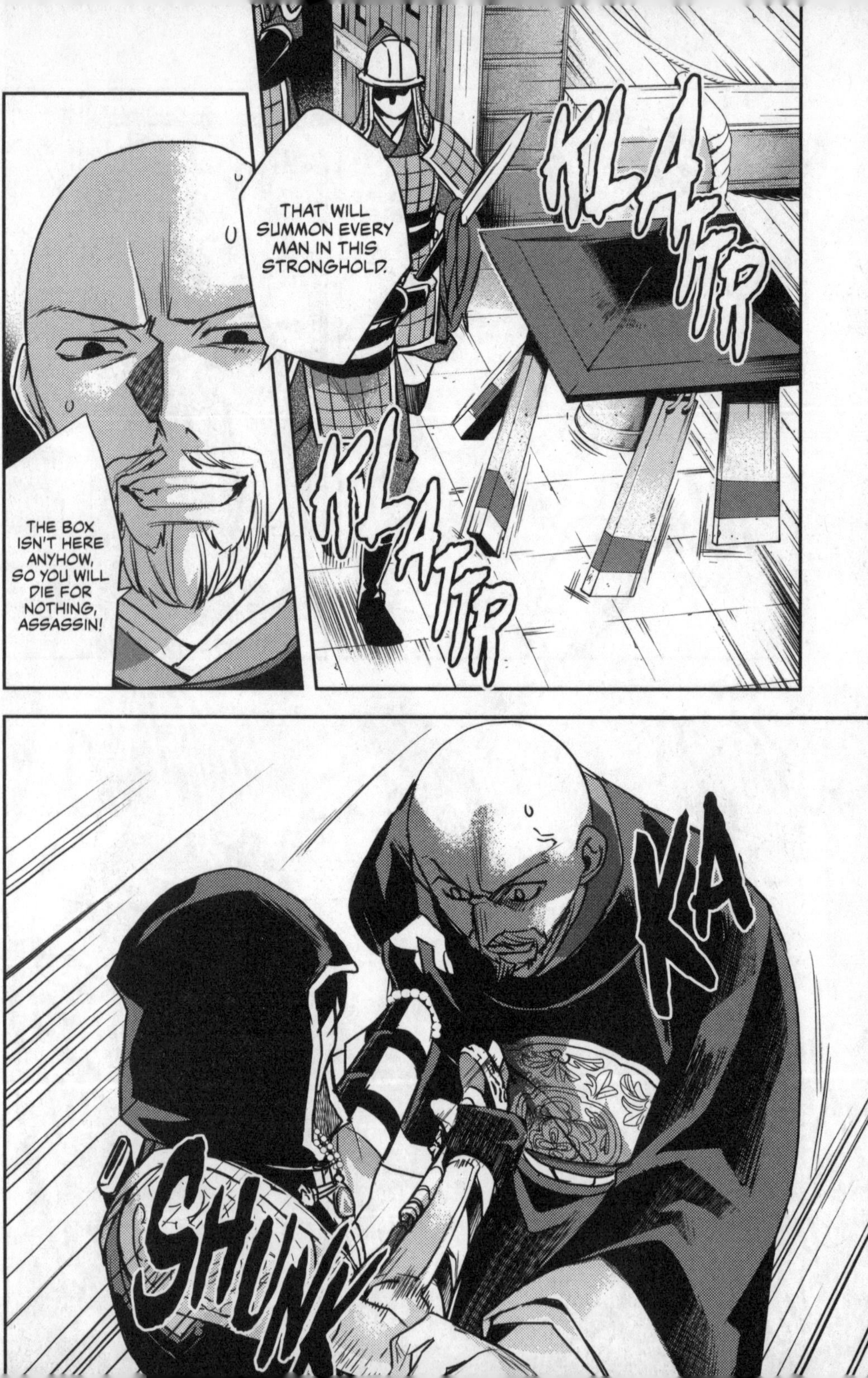
KLATTR
KLATTR
THAT WILL SUMMON EVERY MAN IN THIS STRONGHOLD.
THE BOX ISN'T HERE ANYHOW, SO YOU WILL DIE FOR NOTHING, ASSASSIN!
KA
SHUNK

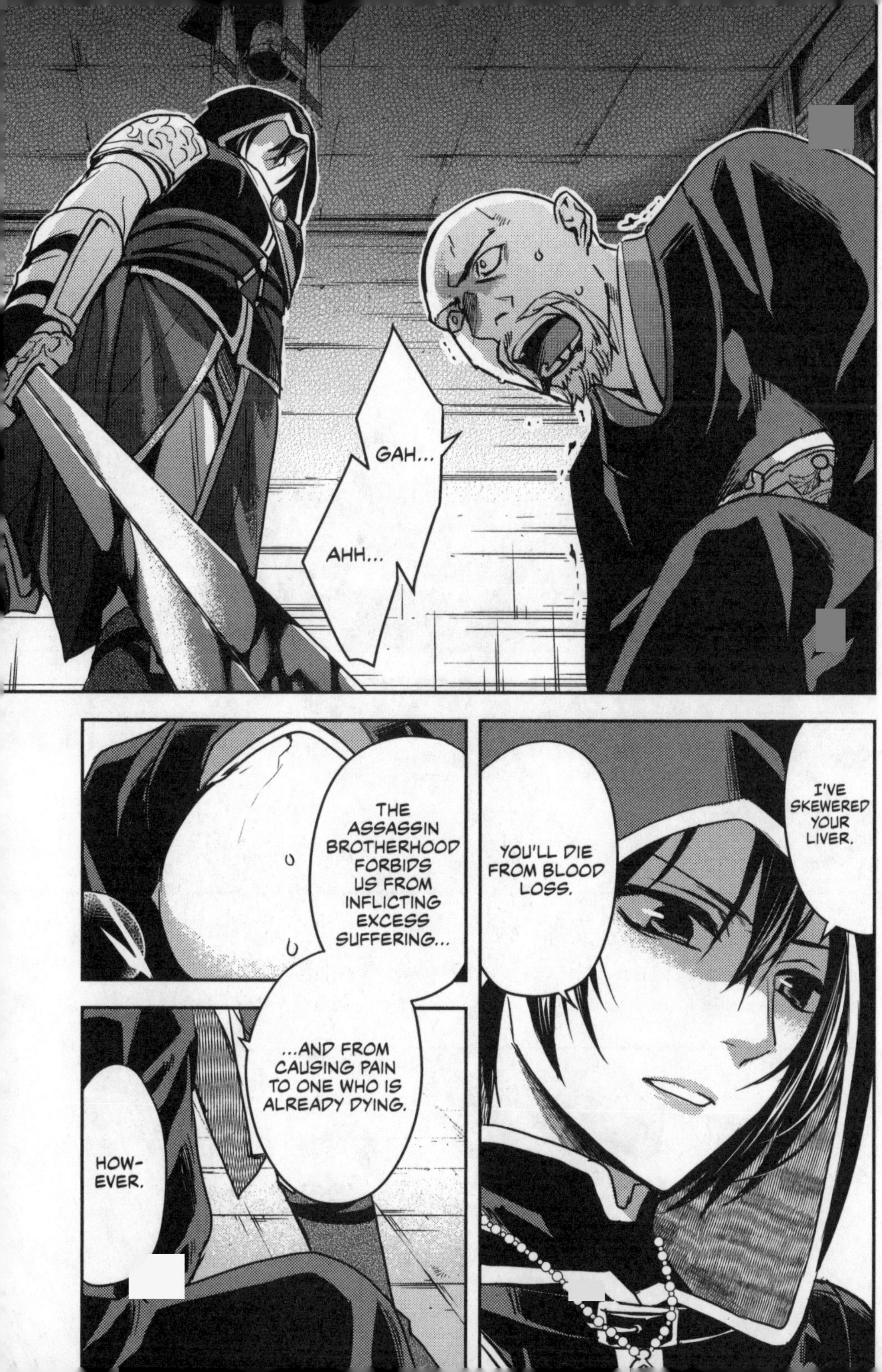
GAH...
AHH...
I'VE SKEWERED YOUR LIVER.
YOU'LL DIE FROM BLOOD LOSS.
THE ASSASSIN BROTHERHOOD FORBIDS US FROM INFLICTING EXCESS SUFFERING...
...AND FROM CAUSING PAIN TO ONE WHO IS ALREADY DYING.
HOW-EVER.

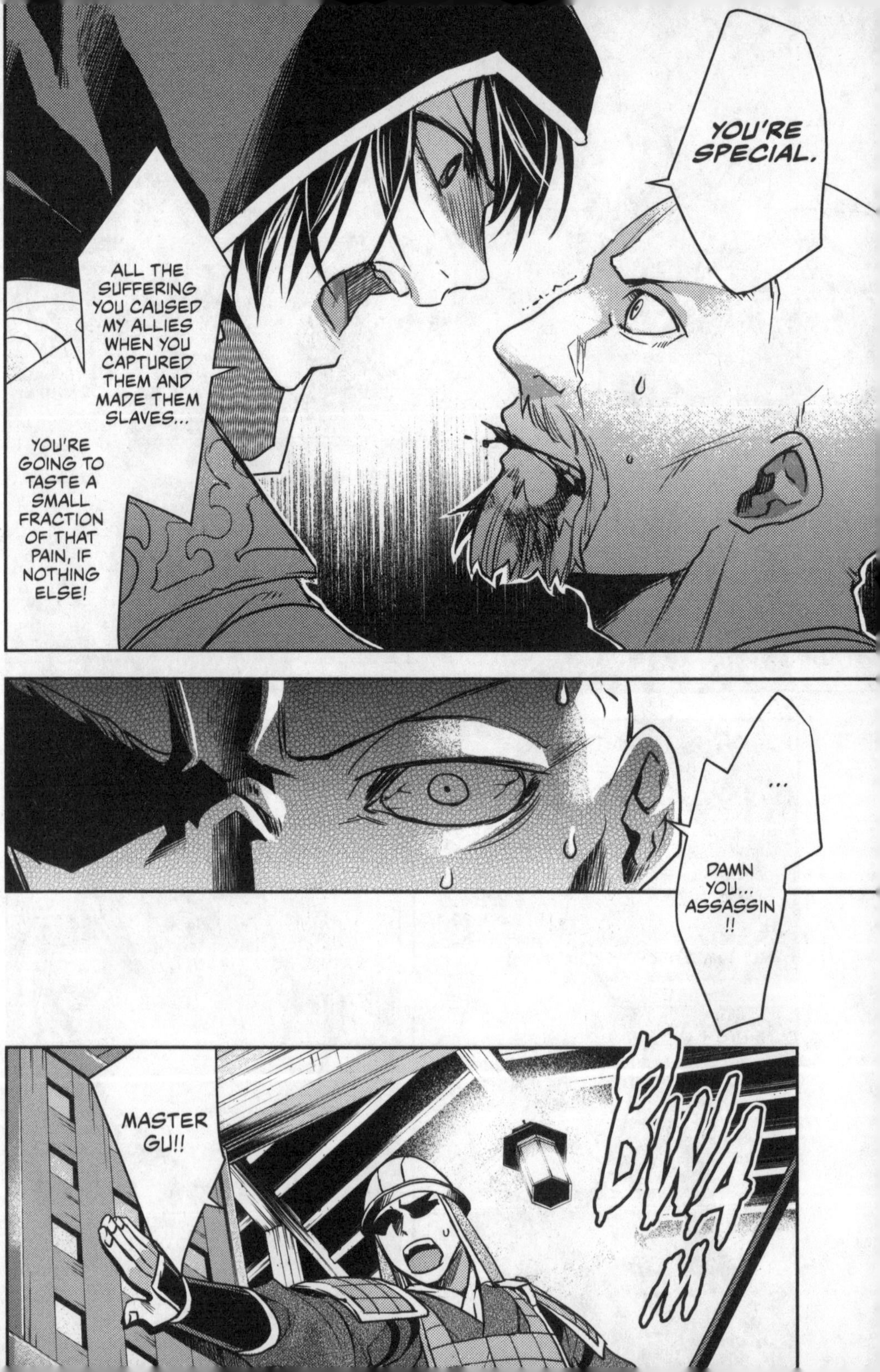
YOU'RE SPECIAL.
ALL THE SUFFERING YOU CAUSED MY ALLIES WHEN YOU CAPTURED THEM AND MADE THEM SLAVES...
YOU'RE GOING TO TASTE A SMALL FRACTION OF THAT PAIN, IF NOTHING ELSE!
...
DAMN YOU... ASSASSIN !!
BWAM
MASTER GU!!

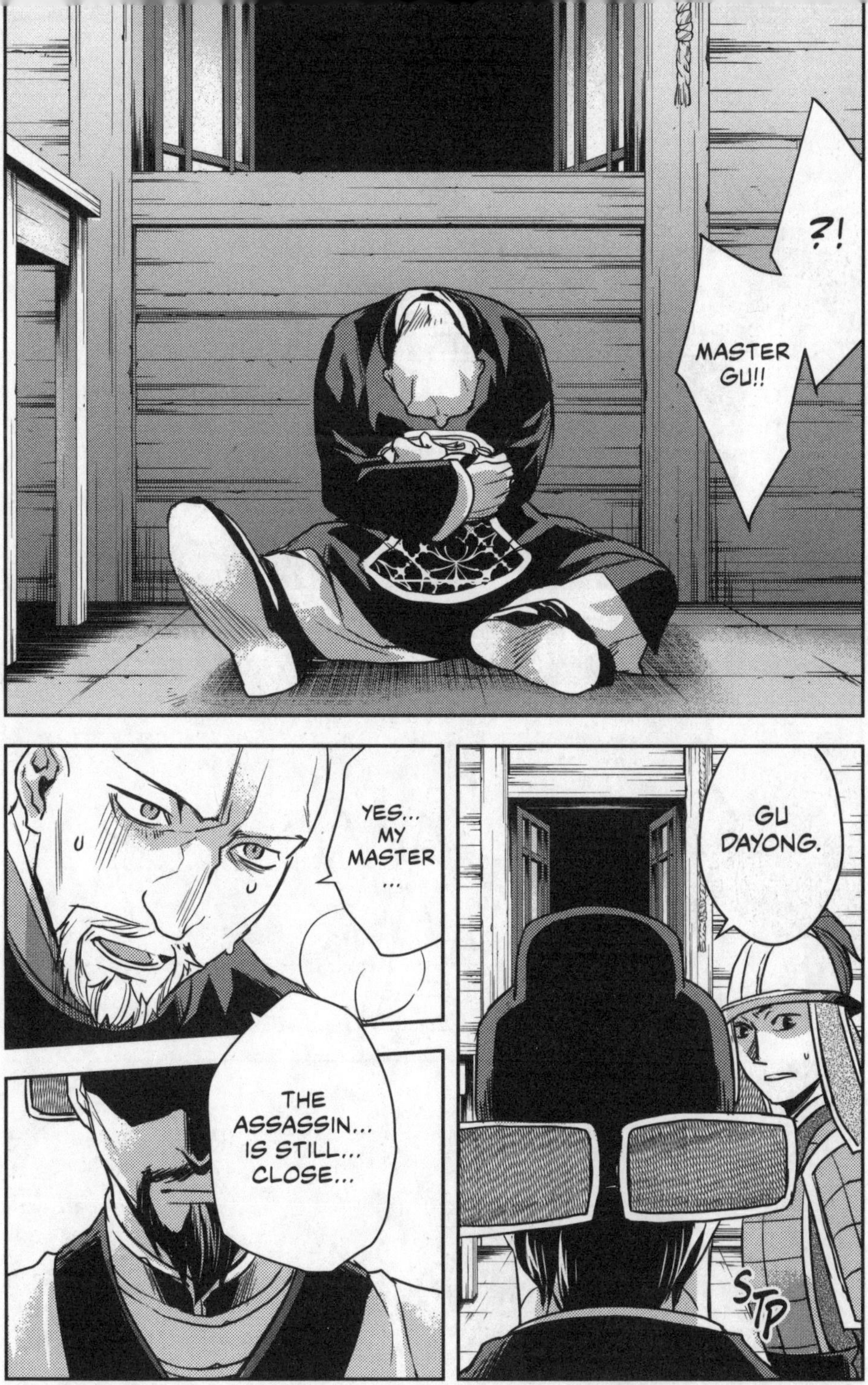
?!
MASTER GU!!
GU DAYONG.
STP
YES... MY MASTER ...
THE ASSASSIN... IS STILL... CLOSE...

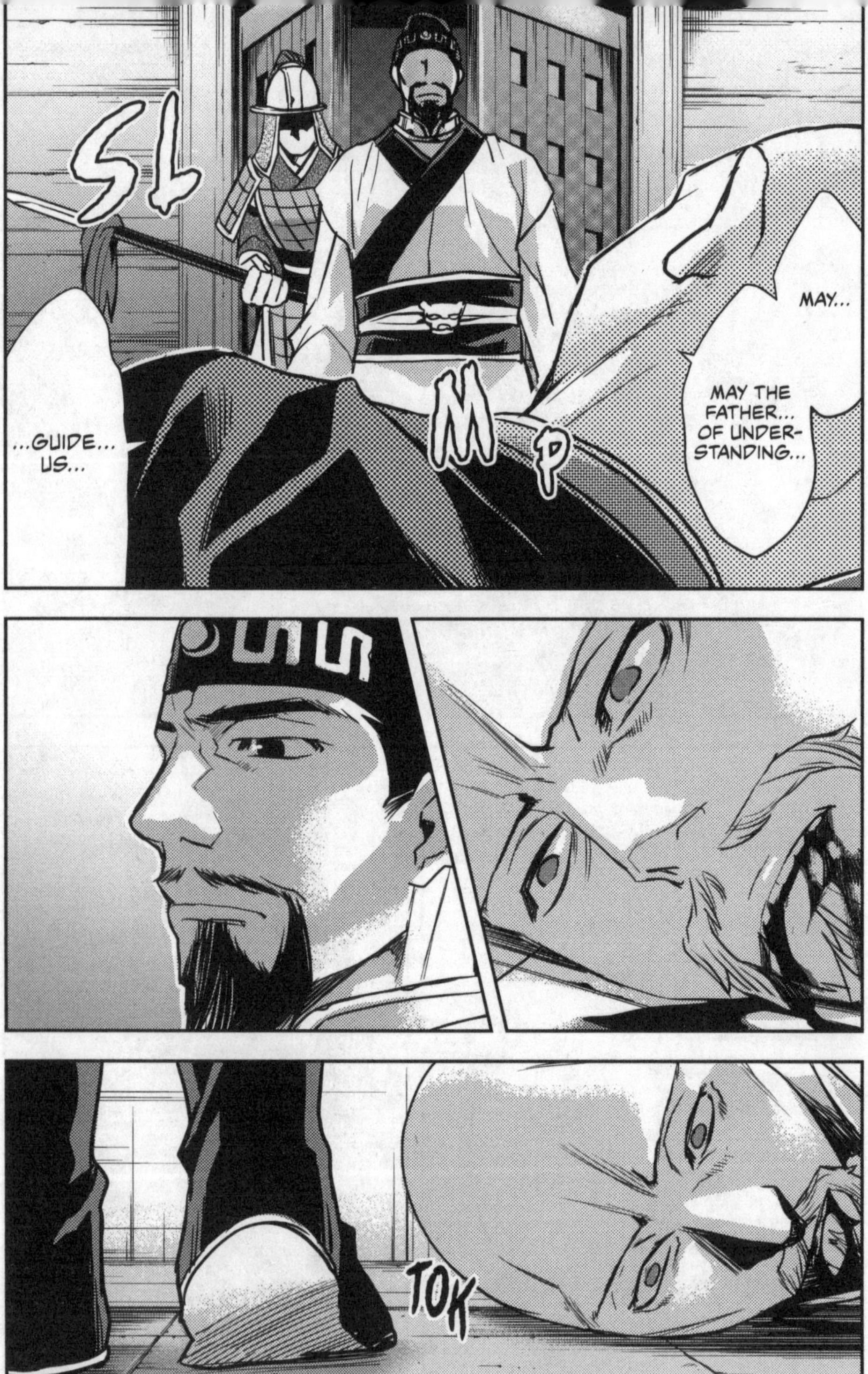
MAY...
MAY THE FATHER... OF UNDER-STANDING...
SL
MP
...GUIDE... US...
TOK

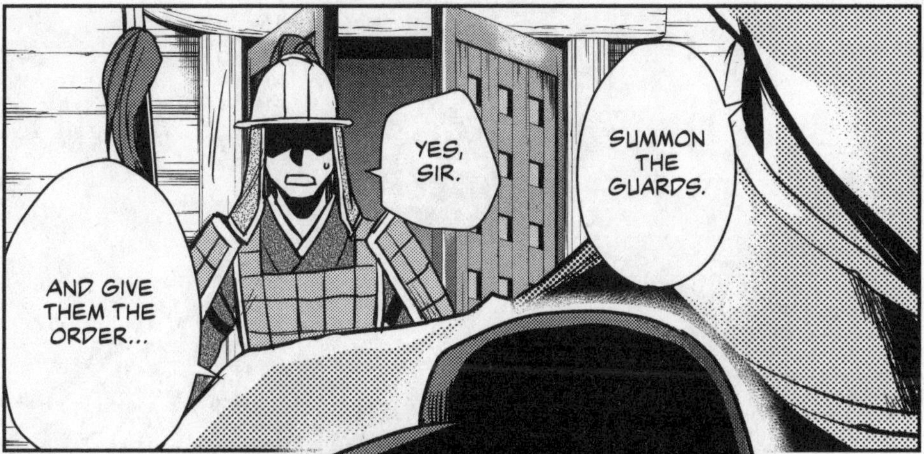
SUMMON THE GUARDS.
YES, SIR.
AND GIVE THEM THE ORDER...
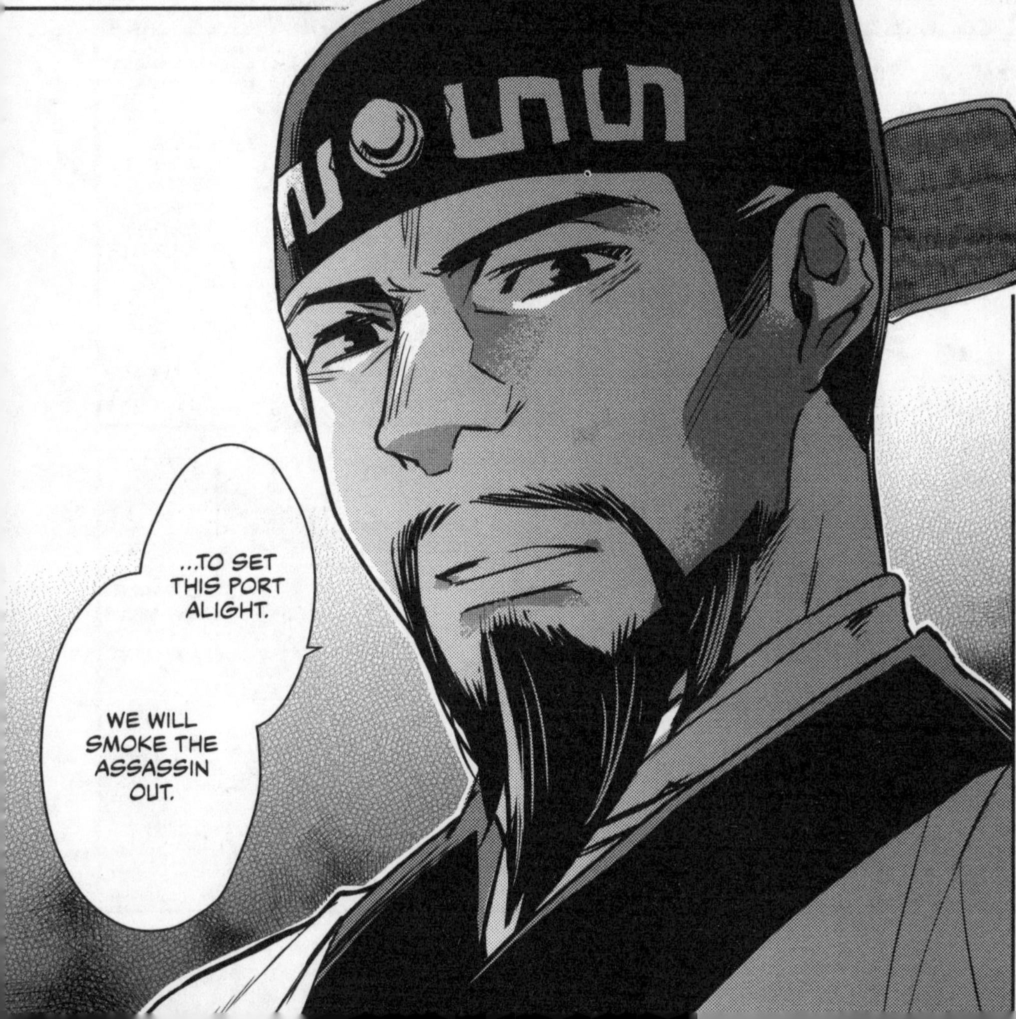
...TO SET THIS PORT ALIGHT.
WE WILL SMOKE THE ASSASSIN OUT.

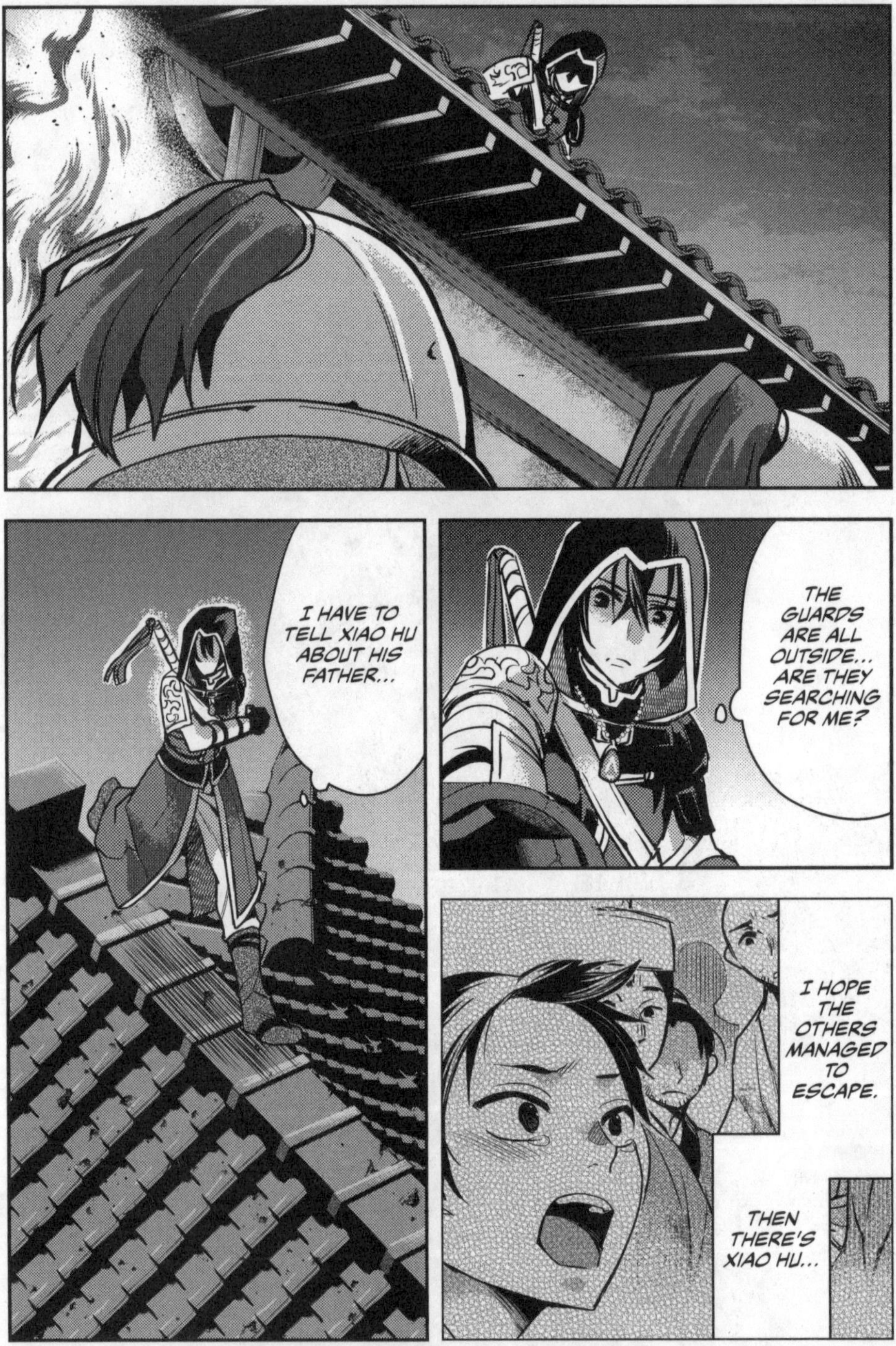
THE GUARDS ARE ALL OUTSIDE... ARE THEY SEARCHING FOR ME?
I HOPE THE OTHERS MANAGED TO ESCAPE.
THEN THERE'S XIAO HU...
I HAVE TO TELL XIAO HU ABOUT HIS FATHER...

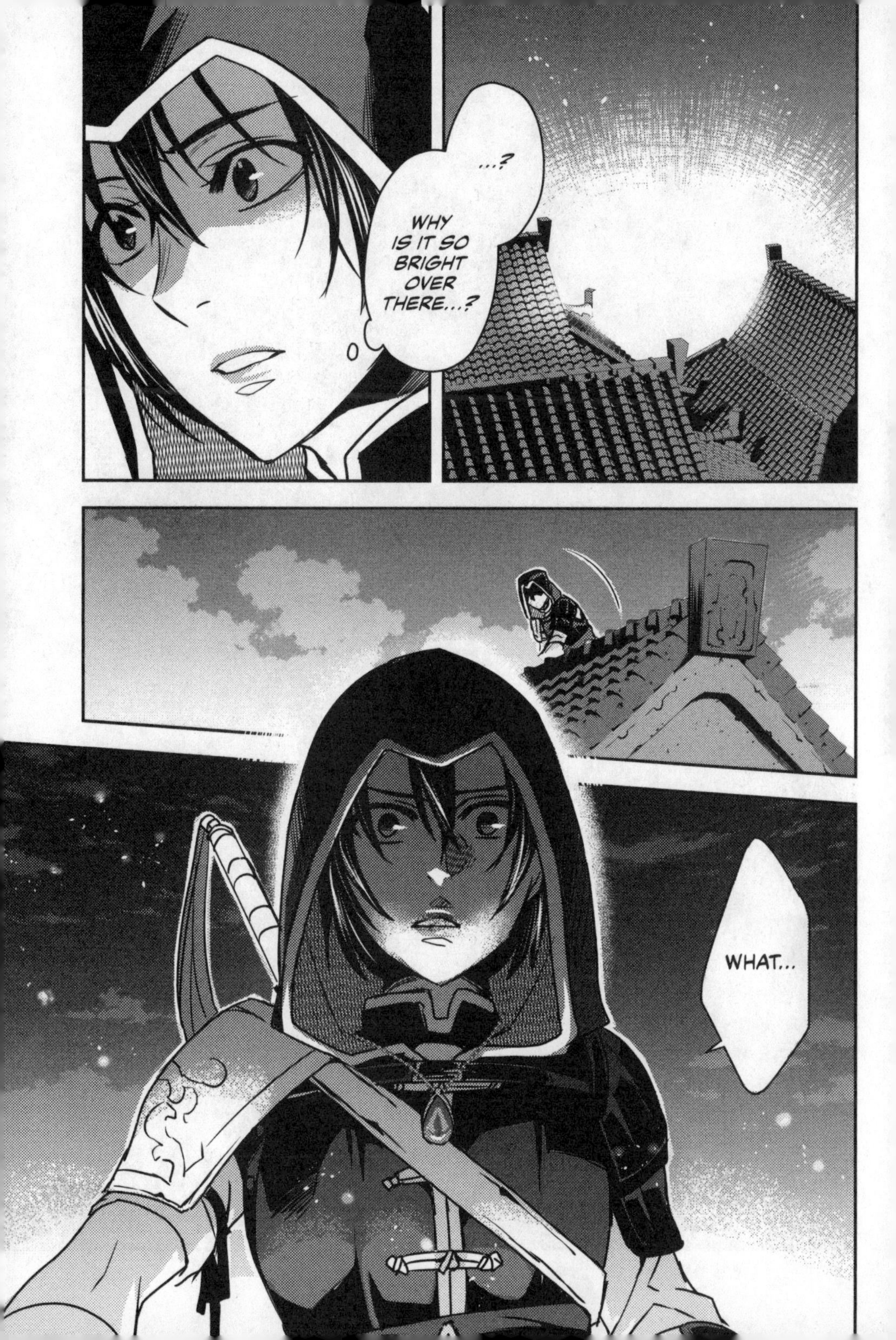
...?
WHY IS IT SO BRIGHT OVER THERE...?
WHAT...

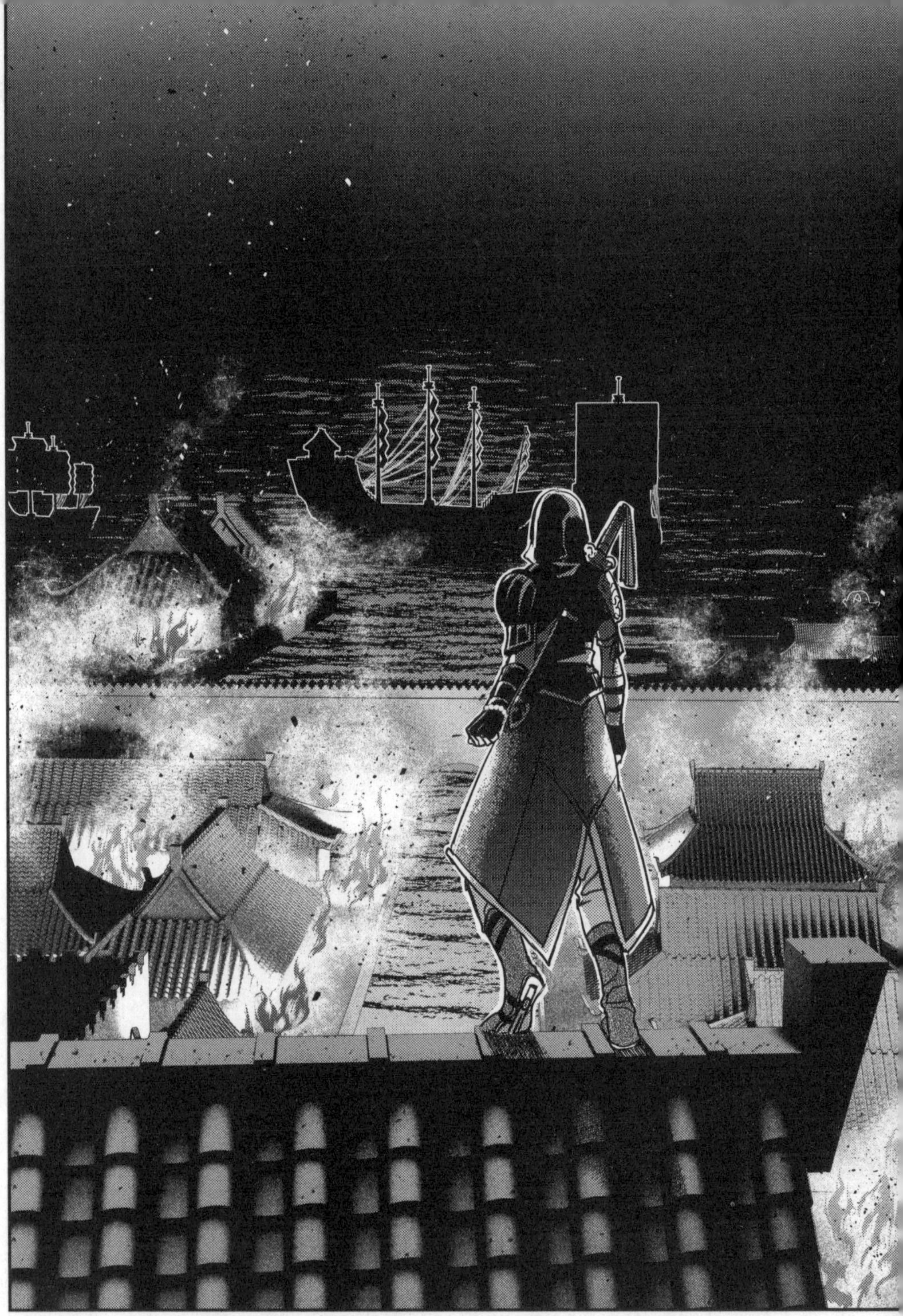

Assassin's Creed: Blade of Shao Jun/Volume 1-End

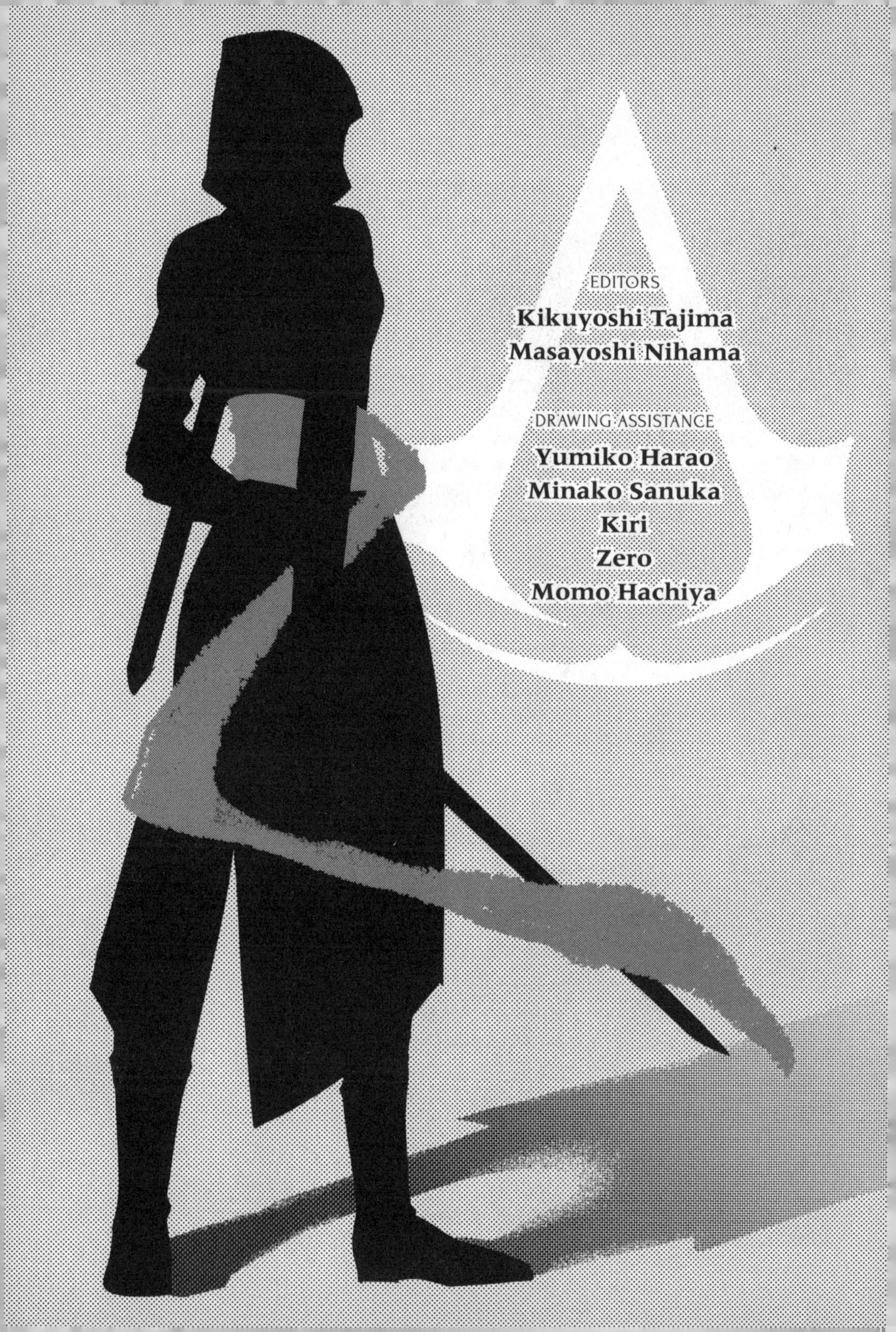

EDITORS

Kikuyoshi Tajima
Masayoshi Nihama

DRAWING ASSISTANCE

Yumiko Harao
Minako Sanuka
Kiri
Zero
Momo Hachiya

ASSASSIN'S CREED

BLADE OF SHAO JUN

VOLUME 1

VIZ SIGNATURE MANGA EDITION

ORIGINAL CONCEPT BY **Ubisoft**
STORY AND ART BY **Minoji Kurata**

TRANSLATION **Caleb Cook**
RETOUCH & LETTERING **Brandon Bovia**
DESIGN **Francesca Truman**
EDITOR **David Brothers**
COVER ILLUSTRATION **Minoji KURATA**
ORIGINAL COVER DESIGN **Junya ARAI + Bay Bridge Studio**

Original Japanese edition published by SHOGAKUKAN. English translation
rights in the United States of America, Canada, the United Kingdom,
Ireland, Australia, South Africa and India arranged with SHOGAKUKAN.

The stories, characters and incidents mentioned
in this publication are entirely fictional.

Printed in Canada

Published by VIZ Media, LLC
P.O. Box 77010 | San Francisco, CA 94107

10 9 8 7 6 5 4 3 2 1
First printing, February 2021

viz.com

vizsignature.com

UBISOFT

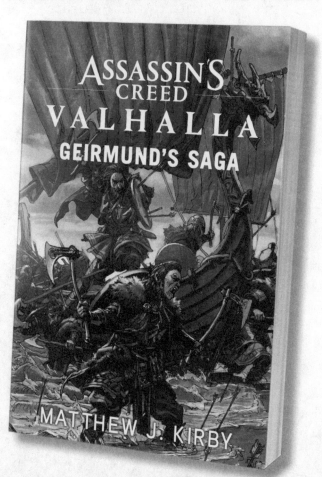

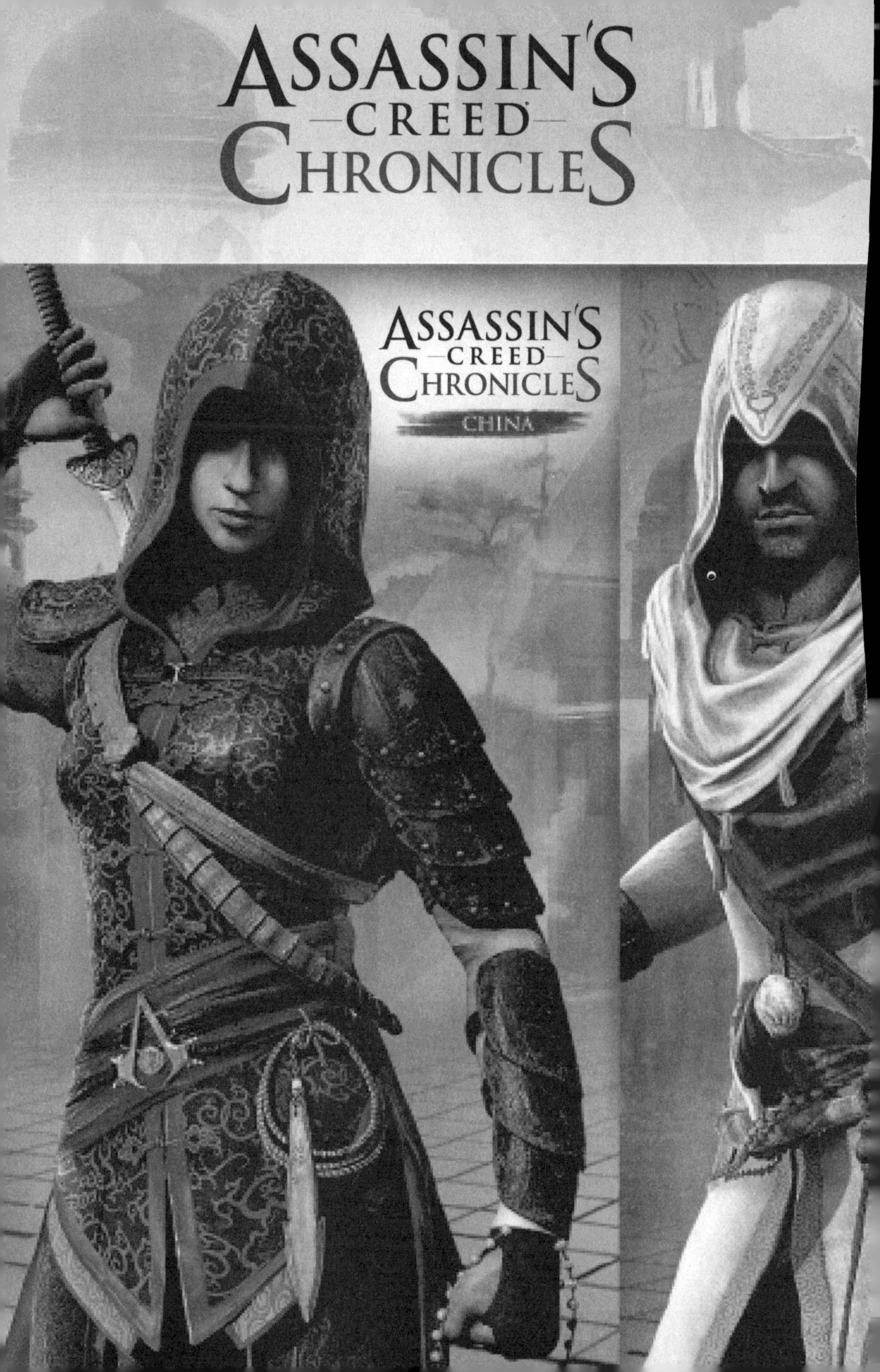
ASSASSIN'S CREED CHRONICLES
ASSASSIN'S CREED CHRONICLES
CHINA

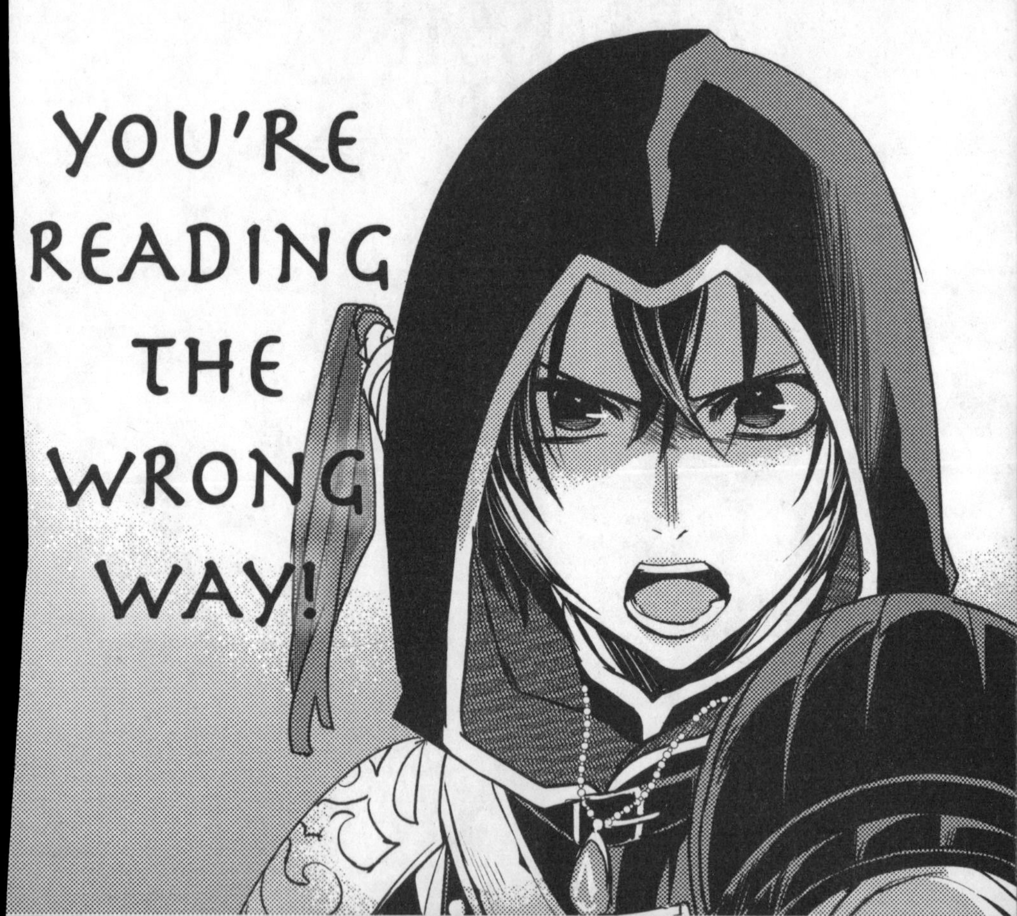
YOU'RE READING THE WRONG WAY!

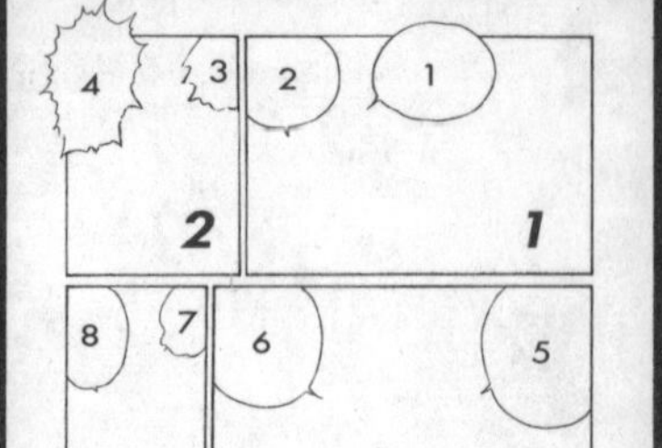
1
2
3
4
5
6
7
8
9
1
2
3
4
5

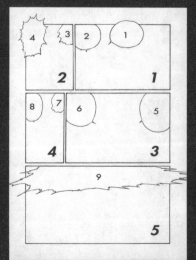

Assassin's Creed: Blade of Shao Jun reads from right to left, starting in the upper-right corner. Japanese is read from right to left, meaning that action, sound effects, assassinations, and word balloon reading order are completely reversed from English order.